MINORITY REPORT

MINORITY REPORT
Confessions of an unrepentant non-conformist

Andrew Herron

THE SAINT ANDREW PRESS
EDINBURGH ·

First published in 1990 by
THE SAINT ANDREW PRESS
121 George Street, Edinburgh EH2 4YN
Copyright © Andrew Herron 1990

ISBN 0 7152 0638 9 (cased)
ISBN 0 7152 0641 9 (limp)

British Library Cataloguing in Publication Data
Herron, Andrew, 1909 -
     Minority report: confessions of an unrepentant
     non-conformist.
     1. Church of Scotland. Ministry
     I. Title
     262.1452411

ISBN 0-7152-0638-9 cased
ISBN 0-7152-0641-9 limp

This book has been set in 11/12 pt Times.

Printed and bound in Great Britain by
Collins, Glasgow

Contents

Prologue: By Way of Explanation i

1   Alma Mater   1
2   Minister Most Ordinary   24
3   'Wi' Champit Tatties . . . '   50
4   The Clerk's Tale   68
5   The Cost of Conservation   95
6   Ecumenical Extravaganza   126
7   Let's Have the Ladies Join Us   152
8   Going Global   171
9   Keeping the Nation On Course   190
10   Scottish Nationalism   208
11   Dabbling in the Law   229
12   In Pursuit of Evangelism   252
13   The Minister and the Media   270
14   A Tale of Three Parishes   292

Epilogue: By Way of Apology   323

By Way of Explanation

I HAVE CHOSEN to entitle this book *Minority Report*, and in doing so I have not been forgetful of the fact that Minority Reports are not looked upon with favour by the law of the Kirk—indeed an Assembly resolution of 1939 goes so far as contemptuously to dismiss them as incompetent. Should a group within a reporting committee feel dissatisfied with the decision reached by the majority, their only method of presenting their point of view is to put forward an appropriate opposing motion when the matter comes to be presented to the court concerned.

In 1962, the Assembly relented to the extent of making provision whereby a committee might—if it were so minded—incorporate in its report a statement of the position of any dissentient members. This can be seen as a Minority Report of sorts, but it is available only as an act of grace conceded by the majority, and at best it represents the position of the minority as seen through the eyes of their adversaries.

Some, including myself, would take the view that a minority within a committee should have an opportunity for presenting their own case in their own terms, and should enjoy this as a matter of right. It would seem, though, that in my attitude to Minority Reports I am myself a minority! This I find neither distressing nor disturbing. Nor is it for me a new experience. What I hope to do in the following pages (where I will be in no way inhibited by the Standing Orders of the General Assembly) is to set forth the case for some of the minorities on which, over the years, I have found myself, and of which, in some cases, I may even have been the sole member. For I earnestly believe the minority has a right—it may even have a duty—to make itself heard. After all, history may prove it to have been right.

It would be intolerable if every matter remitted to a committee were to result in two (or more) separate reports, yet

i

occasions arise where there are two strongly-held irreconcilable views and where it is desirable that both should be responsibly presented. One such case comes instantly to my mind. In the mid sixties the proposal that women should be eligible for ordination to the eldership was sent down by the General Assembly to be discussed and voted on in Presbyteries. In conformity with normal practice we in Glasgow appointed an *ad hoc* committee to consider the matter and to report. It was a subject on which there was clear division of opinion, with strong views firmly held on both sides, and many of our members had been at pains to let it be known on which side their sympathies lay. For that reason I deliberately arranged the membership of the committee to include both extremes along with a fair number from the centre. In the course of the meetings that followed, it became apparent that no kind of unanimity would ever be reached, and that, no matter which side ultimately prevailed, there would remain a strong and vociferous minority. It would be unfortunate if the side which carried the day in the committee were to prepare a report setting forth its arguments at full length and with considerable force, followed by its recommendation, and that this should be circulated in print in advance, while the minority were left to put their case in the form of a speech in support of a counter-motion on the floor of the Presbytery. Would it not be to every-one's advantage, and a more equitable arrangement all round, if the two sides were given the opportunity of presenting their respective cases under identical conditions? So I arranged that two separate reports would be printed—one (disclosed as carrying a fairly narrow majority) in favour of the proposal, and the other opposed to it, but that no recommendation would be made one way or the other. People would then vote for whichever side had convinced them, or, it has to be admitted, for whichever side they were determined to support, regardless of either report or debate.

I realise now that all this was in breach of the Assembly resolution of 1939. I didn't know that at the time, and could claim to have erred in ignorance, but honesty compels me to admit that it wouldn't have made all that much difference if I had. A minister challenged me on the propriety of this procedure—fortunately he shared my ignorance of the 1939 affair or he'd have had me by the short hairs! He said he thought it was 'disgraceful' (this, I remember, was his very word) that, on an issue of this significance, a Presbytery of the size and importance of Glasgow could not bring forward one single uncomplicated report and recommendation. 'Very good,' I said to him. 'If you had told me whether the recommendation should be For or Against I could easily have arranged for a committee to be chosen which would come forward with precisely that. But of this you may be certain—it would not be a reflection of the state of opinion within the Kirk in general or within the Presbytery of Glasgow in particular. Here we have an issue on which the Kirk is deeply and irreconcilably divided and any report which appears to indicate that there is among us some degree of unanimity will be to that extent completely false and misleading.' I am sure I was right in this.

Right or wrong, my method was followed. Those who had to vote on this crucial issue were supplied with a print of the best case that each side could advance, they were given time to consider the respective arguments, and we got what was, I believe, a true reflection of fairly well-informed opinion within the court. In the light of that experience I'd be happy at any time to present a Minority Report in favour of Minority Reports!

The reader would be correct in concluding that I have more than a little sympathy with minorities, and my sub-title to this book, 'Confessions of an Unrepentant Nonconformist', would confirm this particular view. If the reader knows anything of my track record as an Assembly commissioner, he (or she) will also know that over the years I have supported not a few lost causes. But I hope I am not prejudiced on that account, for when prejudice comes into the picture I am always satisfied it is the other fellow who is guilty of it! I surely don't imagine that minorities are always right, but neither do I think that mere lack of numerical support condemns an idea as necessarily wrong. I have a lot of sympathy with Carlyle's doctrine that folly multiplied by a thousand is still folly, whereas wisdom multiplied by one is still wisdom. At the Assembly a few years ago I intervened at eight separate points with amendments and I was successful in carrying no fewer than seven of these. I felt I must somehow be losing my grip! Writing too many Minority Reports can shake your confidence in your own wrongness.

Society owes a great debt to people who have been 'agin the government', who have refused to fall in with the majority, who have marched out of step, refused to sing in the choir, refused at times even to sing in tune, because they were convinced the majority was wrong, and who were prepared to face the loneliness and derision demanded of those who go their own way regardless. The minority path is rarely an easy one. I lose patience these days with many of the 'protest' groups who conceive they can break the law with impunity, yet complain of 'police brutality' after having deliberately created a situation where the law has been obliged to intervene and a in physical fashion. Taking part in a television discussion programme once, a certain course of action was being advocated and I took the opportunity to point out that there was a law forbidding it. Whereupon a young chap in the audience immediately chipped in with the claim, 'O but I'm not bound by that law: I have never approved of that law.' If our hostility to majority opinion takes us into the realm of law-breaking (as it can easily do) then we must be prepared to pay the price exacted of law-breakers—the fact that we think otherwise will afford us no protection. I may think it utterly wrong for us to adhere to our Keep Left rule on the roads instead of falling in with continental practice. As long as I confine my conviction to correspondence with my MP, stickers on my car window, letters to the Editor and the like, all will be well. But strong feelings on the subject, if I put my conviction into practice, will be poor defence against a charge of reckless driving. Martyrs' crowns don't come cheap.

In the following pages I have something to say on some of the issues which, from time to time, I have been at loggerheads with authority in one form or another; this is my account of some of the confrontations and the controversies that have come my way in the course of over half a century spent serving the Kirk as Parish Minister, Presbytery Clerk and Moderator of Assembly. Over these years I have, perhaps more often than most, found myself in situations where I had to decide very definitely and declare very specifically just where I stood on a variety of issues, and often when the count came to be taken I have found myself in a minority—sometimes of one. This book is about some of these situations. I know I'm going to enjoy telling the tales; I hope you derive some pleasure from hearing

Chapter 1
Alma Mater

THE LITERAL TRANSLATION of the term Alma Mater, the name we affectionately apply to the University where we received our training, is 'Bounteous Mother', and that is the kind of picture we like to entertain regarding the institution to which we owe so much. During two separate periods I have attended classes at Glasgow University: once in my early days when, straight out of school, I proceeded there to spend seven years graduating in Arts and Divinity, and then, some twenty years later when, as I explain in the chapter on 'Dabbling in the Law', I returned to take a degree in that Faculty. Each of these experiences in its own quite different way I much enjoyed; greatly enriched, I felt I had known something of the 'bounty' alluded to in the title. In very recent days that bounty has further expressed itself by the Senate awarding me a Degree in Divinity *honoris causa*.

It was in 1927 that I went up to Gilmorehill for the first time. That was the year immediately following the somewhat terrifying, and in many ways quite pathetic, experience of the General Strike, when trade unionism united forces to lend support to the coal miners, with disastrous results. They were hard times, unemployment was widespread, 'the dole' was bitterly resented, unrest was on every hand. My father was employed on the railway at a job which, while not over-well paid, was 'steady'. The General Strike, however, unsteadied many things, including railway employment, so that in its aftermath father found himself not only reduced to working three days a week, but downgraded into the bargain. Fortunately for us my mother was richly endowed with that virtue, so properly prized in those days, called 'thrift'. (It may still be a virtue, but it is not one that pays dividends in these days of constantly spiralling inflation.) Thanks to mother's ability to make do and mend, and to make a shilling spin out to the last bawbee, we managed to get through the bleak period without

1

undue distress. I was an only child and my parents had all the traditional Scots faith in the value of education. But just how my getting to a University was to be contrived in the economic situation presented a problem.

Problems have an odd way of resolving themselves, and, as it transpired, the same Strike that had so accentuated our problem led to a solution. One of the many services to be disrupted had been the newspaper industry, and in a day when radio was still in its infancy, the want of 'the paper' morning and evening was a serious affair. Messrs George Outram and Co, the proprietors of *The Glasgow Herald*, contrived to marshall a labour force of sorts and to produce a little paper called *The Emergency Press*. It was ill-produced and not very attractive, but it supplied a clamant need and commanded a large reader-ship. At the end of about a week a large-scale advertisement appeared in its pages to the effect that the staff of the newspaper, by having withdrawn their labour, were in breach of their contract of employment and that the said contract was being terminated there and then. The firm intended to resume business; they would do so this time as a non-union shop; they were interested to receive applications from would-be employees; preference would be given to former members of staff. By this time the strike was as good as over, so it was not long ere the *Herald* was appearing as usual with most of the old workers at their accustomed posts and with most of the vacancies filled. It was here that my opportunity arose, for I was able to secure one of these. The paper employed in their reading-room a number of people called copy-holders, each of whom assisted a reader in the important (at least that's how it was in those days) business of ensuring that mistakes did not appear in print. I was fortunate to secure an appointment, and this I held for the next seven years—with only one little interruption. The shift was from 5.30 in the evening until 1.30 next morning and was accordingly regarded as night work. Under the Factories Act only people of eighteen years of age and over can be thus employed. I had been there for many months before it was discovered that I had been only sixteen when I started. An early experience of being in a minority of one! So intense was the alarm when the discovery was made that I was sent home *instanter*, not even being allowed to finish the shift. They paid me for it, though, and they started me again a few months later on the day after my eighteenth birthday.

The job was well paid and I was able to make my contribution towards the household accounts. But I was still not well off. Four miles separated our house from the University and, except on the very coarsest of days, I used to walk both ways to save fourpence on tramway fares. And of course I walked the couple of miles home from the office in the early morning hours. The financial lot of the student of today must, if he is dependent on student grants, be far from an easy one. I get a little impatient, though, when I hear the impression given that for a student to have to scrape and pinch and do without is something new resulting from the harsh and uncaring attitude of government. I don't think I had it any easier, but I can honestly say I never grumbled.

I feel I should say a little about the job in the *Herald*. In a day before University Grants had been even thought of, this newspaper rendered an invaluable service to the cause of higher education by employing University students as copy-holders in their reading-room. A reader is a journeyman printer whose business it is to 'read' proofs: that is, to mark up the necessary corrections. This was the day of linotype printing, the day of 'hot metal', and at the speed at which we worked mistakes were inevitable. Now, as is well known, every journeyman needs his labourer—in this case someone to read aloud to him from the 'copy' while he concentrates on the proof. This was where we fitted in. We started at 5.30 pm, worked an eight-hour shift, six days a week, with no public holidays. Near the end of my spell there it was decided not to publish on New Year's Day—before that I had 'worked in' the New Year with consistent regularity. My father, incidentally, was so outraged at the idea of a day without a paper, he urged us to boycott the paper for the rest of the week in protest. Clearly he had learned nothing from the General Strike!

We students were employed on a half-time basis, working three of the six nights each week. Thus a pair of us were mated with each reader. During the summer—and for the *Herald* this lasted from May until September inclusive—we were taken on full time, thus providing the extra labour required to allow for holidays all round. The unfortunate bit about this was that the degree exams were held in May and September when we could well have done with less rather than more work. I remember a day when I sat from 9 to 12 and from 2 to 5 writing furiously at the Degree exam in History, then hurried to the office for 5.30; and when at length 1.30 came around, I was told to stay on because it was a General Election and the results were steadily pouring in. I was released at 5.30 and got home in time for an early breakfast, feeling I had had enough for one day! Yes, there were the occasional snags, but you can't expect plain sailing all the way, and from the point of view of people like myself the arrangement was an admirable one for which I personally have been eternally grateful. So much so I'd be prepared to elevate the *Herald* to the position of 'Bountiful Auntie'! (I'd give this in Latin if I only knew how!)

I am sure I'm overdoing it when I say, as I have often done, that I learned far more in the reading-room of the *Herald* than I did in the classrooms of Gilmorehill: but there is a very real element of truth in the observation. It is so easy in the sheltered atmosphere of a University to get things out of proportion, to lose touch with grim reality—so easy in fact to become an academic. And that, I am sure, is the worst possible training for the prospective minister, the ministry itself being so highly 'protected' an occupation. In the newspaper office I learned a lot about life and learned it in very simple but convincing terms. I learned too about how little I personally counted for in the divine scheme of things. They were lessons that were to stand me in good stead.

There were compensating disadvantages naturally, one of them being that one was left with little, if any, time for those extra-mural activities which for many are of the very essence of a University training. Not for me to knock about the Union after classes chatting with kindred souls, to return of an evening for a meeting of a debating society, to go off on hikes or climbs or sails at the weekends. For me, there was no temptation to become a professional University-attender. What I gained from my years at Gilmorehill was basically what I learned in the classrooms and little else.

By the standard of the times the student population in my first year was very high, not least in the Faculty of Arts. To take an Ordinary Degree in Arts there was a choice among, I think, five curricula, but whichever of these one followed it was necessary to secure a pass in either Logic or Moral Philosophy. To me this has always appeared a very proper provision, for I cannot imagine a liberal education which does not include some acquaintance with the business of thinking. In the course of a visit to Central Africa many years ago, I was shown around the up-and-coming College at Salisbury and was amazed to learn that they awarded degrees in Arts although they did not have a department of Mental Philosophy. At Glasgow these two classes were very popular, not perhaps because of their innate attraction but because of their position in the curricula. Of the two the Logic class was by far the more popular—so much so that it had to meet in two halves with roughly three hundred students at each sitting. By comparison Moral Philosophy was ill-attended, with just over three hundred altogether. The preference for Logic was, I understand, attributable to the fact that if you had a pass in that subject you were exempted from one of the classes at Jordanhill College of Education whither so many of our students were bound.

When I was preparing for University I was still just seventeen and not absolutely committed to any particular career although I had the ministry at the back of my mind—not too far back. My idea was to acquire a degree in Arts and then to decide finally on a destination. The curriculum business, though, presented me with something of a problem. The choices were cleverly designed to appear to offer a really wide selection, and yet they held you firmly to taking at least one language and one science. The science didn't worry me for I had always loved maths. The language was my stumbling-block. I have never had any facility for learning a language—I should know, for I had to battle with Latin and French at school and with Greek and Hebrew in Divinity. I just could not visualise myself mastering any foreign tongue to the extent of passing a degree exam in it. Having had a long-standing interest in philosophy I took the Moral Philosophy class in my first year—although this is definitely not recommended—and having found this enormously stimulating, and since my experience in the Latin class under Professor Rennie had confirmed my worst fears about my skill as a linguist, I decided at the end of that first year to switch to an Honours degree in Mental Philosophy and definitely to accept the Church as the destination towards which I was journeying—a decision I have never found cause to regret.

It was in this undramatic way that I 'answered the call' to the ministry. Not for me an experience on the Damascus Road, not even the experience of a Carlyle resolving his intellectual doubts in a blazing revelation on Leith Walk, converting the everlasting No to the everlasting Yea. My call was as simple —sordid if you will—an affair as a horror of languages and a profound interest in thinking. The Kirk is understandably concerned with recruitment these days, its intake of ministers being inadequate for current needs. The actual number of entrants is fairly high, but a large proportion are men and women who have been employed in other walks of life and whose ministry-expectancy must be relatively short. In the course of its enquiries the Committee concerned recently sent me a questionnaire based on the presumption that I had known a 'call' in the more dramatic sense of that term. Reared in a Christian household, trained in habits of church-going, imbibing faith with the air I breathed, I found it entirely natural to turn to the ministry as a way of exercising what talents the Lord had given and my Alma Mater had developed in me. For myself I think it is to this class that the Kirk should be directing its endeavours for recruitment—the folk who have had a 'call' will find their way without our needing to go in search of them. And I believe the ministry would be enriched by a measure of diversity in its ministry. Not all of us can fix a time and place for our calling. Even as John the Divine saw the Holy City with many gates, so I have always envisaged the ministry. There are many ways by which you can come in: what matters is what you do once you are in. If my entry was through the wrong turnstyle, it's a trifle late to be doing anything about it now!

In that first year in Moral Philosophy I instantly fell under the spell of Professor A A Bowman who had just moved to that chair and whom I have always regarded as one of the few really great men it has been my privilege to know. He exerted an enormous influence not only over me, but over a whole generation of Glasgow students. His lectures were listened to with breathless interest, even by the sharp lads usually so ready with their quips. They knew, I imagine, that their sorties would be more than adequately met. On an occasion when the

Professor had said that we all recognised there was a difference between the distinctions of right-and-wrong and of good-and-bad, one bold lad loudly challenged this. Fixing him with a cold stare, Bowman quietly remarked, 'One can only hope that by the end of term my friend's moral perceptiveness will have considerably sharpened'. We had no more trouble from him.

As it happened I did particularly well in the class, getting alphas for all my essays, high marks in the exams and a First Class ticket at the end of session. To me it seemed perfectly clear that I was the brilliant thinker whose arrival Glasgow had been long awaiting; I saw myself moving on to Oxford on the strength of a Newlands Fellowship; I wondered if I wouldn't be wasting my talents in the Church when so brilliant an academic career lay open at my feet. So convinced was I of my own brilliance that I came a cropper in the degree examination, which was by far the best thing that could possibly have happened to me. Like the prodigal son I 'came to myself', or, as we say in Glasgow, 'I ta'en a tummle tae masel', and I surely made certain I would not repeat the performance when the September resits came around. In the course of the summer I met one of my former school-teachers who asked how I was faring. Rather shamefacedly I told him I had been ploughed in Moral Phil. 'O,' he said, 'I shouldn't worry. It is all a matter of luck. They just toss a coin.' I said I didn't believe it, but he insisted that that was how it was. When the new term opened I had decided to move to the Honours course and so presented myself in the Higher Ordinary class. Professor Bowman took the class on that opening day and, on leaving the room, he came over to me and said, 'I was sorry to have to fail you in June. But it was your own fault, you know; you hadn't been doing any work—it was quite disgraceful. But it was obvious you had fairly pulled up your socks during the summer. Don't be stupid and let that kind of thing happen again.' How I wished I could meet that teacher to tell him how wrong he had been. Professor Bowman was most certainly a good friend and a great encourager to me during all my time in Arts.

Nor was he a mere cloistered academic, for he took a keen interest and an active part in the whole life of the community. I particularly remember a notable correspondence he conducted in the Letters column of the *Herald* with the ablest brains 'the trade' was able to employ on the implications of the nice distinction betwen the use and the abuse of alcohol. He was a formidable opponent. It was also understandable that, as a son of the manse, he made himself available as a preacher on many occasions, and that with great effect. He simply shed 'idealism' in the purest sense of that term—a city that is set on an hill cannot be hid.

The Logic class under Professor Herbert J Paton was for me a totally different affair, although I enjoyed it none the less. His lectures to the Ordinary Class, especially those in which he unravelled some of the mysteries of metaphysics were, in my view, of the highest order, and though it must have been quite an ordeal to have to deliver them twice a day, they never lost their freshness. It was, however, when we got beyond the Ordinary class that we got farther in our understanding of him. He was very much 'Oxford'—emphatically not 'Oxbridge'. He used to refer to a certain year (I don't remember which) when, he said contemptuously, 'Cambridge first began to think'. But it was the intensity of his devotion to his idol, Immanuel Kant, that so fascinated me. He appeared genuinely amazed that we in the Honours class were not all learning German, not with a view to holidaying in the Black Forest, but for the sheer thrill of being able to read the *Kritik of Pure Reason* in the original tongue and so grasp the proper nuances of the great man's thinking. Professor Kemp Smith in Edinburgh had suggested that Kant had allowed himself to be misled in some regards through his passion for getting his thinking neatly categorised in balancing patterns—'architectonic' Kemp Smith called it. I can still hear the utter disdain with which Paton pronounced the word. For myself I had a lot of sympathy with Kemp Smith's criticism, but I kept my thoughts to myself—a thing I've not always done successfully.

He used to have his Honours students three at a time at his house to read essays. He had a 'man', who I never saw in anything other than shirt sleeves and a green baize apron, who showed us up to a room furnished in great style and comfort, with a fireplace in which two huge pieces of coal leaned against one another like some enormous Coalhenge. In idle moments I found myself wondering what he did with all the dross. In my group there was a truly brilliant chap, John Brown, who one day was reading an essay on some part of the *Kritik* when he was interrupted by the professor: 'Tell me, Mr Brown, have you considered in this connection the terms of Section So-and-so?' John replied that he had read the passage over many times, had studied it carefully, had given it a lot of thought, but had to confess he had been quite unable to make any sense of it. 'How very interesting,' replied Paton, 'I have to confess that neither have I. This is just another example of Immanuel Kant's amazing subtlety.' For me that seemed a bit too much. A subtlety so profound as to defy understanding had for me no place in the business of communication. It was my turn to produce the essay for the following week. I managed, rather cleverly I thought, to involve Kant in a circular argument. 'To me,' I concluded, 'this seems quite simply to be arguing in a circle, but it may well be yet another example of Immanuel Kant's amazing subtlety.' I paused and waited for the comment. It didn't take long. 'But tell me, Mr Herron,' said the unruffled professor, 'is this not rather an example of your own amazing subtlety?'

There were, as I have explained, two sittings of the Ordinary Class, at three hundred a time, exactly the capacity of the classroom. That room, incidentally, is immediately above the room where Greek is taught, and it is said that on one occasion a great burst of foot-stamping in the upper room led to some plaster falling upon the students beneath, and to the comment from the Professor of Greek that, 'Apparently our premises will scarcely support Professor Jones' conclusions'. On the last day of term the two sections met as one for prizegiving and suchlike. The room was packed to suffocation. The professor appeared on the platform in full academic splendour and after handing over the prizes (of which I was fortunate enough to get one) he gave us a talk on 'Logic and Life'. The content I do not remember, but I do recollect that he ended by advising us, a fortnight before the degree exams, to lay aside our books and to go out into the country there 'to gaze upon cows and other natural objects'. Having concluded his address he lifted his mortarboard from the table and, turning towards the door, he added, '. . . and in conclusion I can do no other than wish you one and all the very best of luck in the forthcoming degree examinations'. The room positively erupted in cheering, clapping, foot-stamping, cat-calling. The professor paused, holding the door handle, and when the din had finally subsided added, '. . . for some of you will certainly need it'. And on that happy note he left us. On that same happy note I would end my comments on an intensely interesting personality. If Bowman impressed me, Paton intrigued me. The one inspired my affection, the other aroused my interest.

Two other subjects had to be taken as well as the Honours group and I had chosen History and English. Although from the examination point of view I managed to sail through these two with little difficulty, I have to admit that I remember remarkably little about either. English left the more vivid impression, especially of our contacts with the professor, W Macneile Dixon, although in all honesty I must say that the person who impressed me most in that class was Peter Alexander, then senior lecturer, who later succeeded to the chair and filled it with such distinction.

To conclude then, those four years that I spent in the Faculty of Arts represented some of the most enjoyable years in my life.

When in 1931 I moved from Arts to Divinity, I found myself in a totally different world. The Faculty had at that time a number of peculiarities which it owed to circumstances connected with events in the life of the national Church. It had been not so very long before this (in 1929) that the Church of Scotland had united with the United Free Church, and, following on from this, the Faculty had embraced what had been the UF teaching establishment, Trinity College, standing on the hilltop just across the River Kelvin from Gilmorehill. On the occurrence of the Disruption in 1843 the new Free Church was not prepared to have its students trained in divinity by professors who were committed to the Establishment and therefore under dominion of the State, and so they built their own colleges: New College in Edinburgh, Trinity College in Glasgow, and Christ's College in Aberdeen—and to these colleges their students proceeded at the end of their Arts course. Obviously the union of the Churches in 1929 created a completely new situation characterised by a wealth both of staff and of accommodation. The staffs were combined, and in Glasgow at least both buildings continued in use. We met at the

University for classes at 9 and 10 o'clock, then we walked across to Trinity where we grabbed a cup of tea before other classes at 11.30 and 12.30, followed at 1.30 by Common Lunch in the College dining-room, surrounded by a great cloud of witnesses, the walls being draped with the final-year photographs of all students every year from 1843. As one who had never been able to participate in the social life of the University, I certainly found this new fellowship a very precious thing.

The other aspect which I found so different—and so very advantageous—in Divinity was how close we were to the professors and how close they in turn were to the practical work of the ministry. Due to the fact of the Faculty and the College having united so recently, we had in effect two professors for each subject and there was no need of lecturers. What was most important, however, was that all our teachers were ministers of the Church of Scotland and, with one exception, had spent varying periods in the active pursuit of the parish ministry. They were to that extent well qualified to direct their instruction towards the production of parish ministers. This they did not set out deliberately to do, but the influence was inescapable. The position is vastly different today and in my view (possibly a minority one) we are the poorer for it. It has to be recognised that the present situation in the academic world has become such (and that even before the recent drastic cuts in staff numbers) that those who aspire to spend their lives in the ranks of University teachers just dare not allow themselves to get out of direct touch with the academic world. It is also a fact of life that there is no longer available the kind of quiet country parish where a man could do his job thoroughly and still have time to devote to research and scholarship. Those with an eye to an academic career keep close to a University, with a research scholarship, a modest appointment, leading to a less modest one, and so on. It may well be that this is producing a staff better equipped academically than ever before. But I doubt whether they in turn are producing ministers as well equipped for the rough and tumble of the parish ministry as was once the case. Certainly when I see a man appointed to a lectureship in Practical Theology who has never served in a parish, I marvel greatly. I've still to see the appointment of a professor of surgery who has never set foot in an operating theatre.

This matter of practical training is one about which many in the Kirk are today much exercised, for there is a widespread feeling that ministers coming to their first parish may be well educated but are ill-trained; they may be well versed in the theological implications of death, bereavement, the after-life—but ask them how to conduct a funeral? It must be conceded that the Universities are under no obligation to train students in the intricacies of ministering to a Church of Scotland congregation, but *they* should be so trained, and for this the Kirk itself must accept responsibility. Quite a few years ago a complete change was effected in the character of the BD which, from being a second degree taken only by graduates (usually in Arts), became a first degree taken after four years study. Thus the total University course for the straight-from-school student would have been reduced from six to four years. This was not acceptable to the Kirk, and so Diploma courses were tagged on to occupy the two years after graduation. My own idea (minority again?) is that one of these years could be taken over by the Church and coupled with the year's probation which all entrants have to serve in a parish, and could become the kind of apprenticeship with time off to attend classes which is the accepted pattern in so many disciplines today. There may well be a better solution. The discovery of some solution is, I think, a matter of the utmost urgency.

One physical advantage resulting from the move to Trinity was that we had desks at which to sit and do our notetaking with a degree of comfort—all very different from the oak benches and narrow ledges of Gilmorehill. But the real joy, the thrill, of the move to the College lay in the remarkable group of professors with whom we had the chance to mingle on terms of such intimacy, not only during lectures, but in the common room, in the library, and at common lunch. They were a truly distinguished company. In New Testament we had the great W M Macgregor, a quite wonderful man in so many ways, known affectionately as 'Williemac'; and at that time the appointment had just been made of George H C Macgregor (Garth) who, however, in my time seemed to feel himself overshadowed by his senior. In the Old Testament department we had a pair who complemented one another admirably: from the University, W B Stevenson whose passion for the intricacies of the Hebrew tongue was responsible for many a 'near-BD' in the ranks of the ministry; from Trinity, John E M'Fadyen, popular exponent of Old Testament thinking whose illustrations I feel sure enlivened many a sermon besides his own. The University teacher of Systematic Theology was William Fulton, a most erudite scholar and a fine gentleman, if perhaps not the most thrilling of lecturers. He shared the honours with A B Macaulay from whom I learned a great deal, a delightful soul to whom is credited the riposte when someone made the suggestion that we should let sleeping dogmas lie—'They generally do'. I find it hard to believe he could be so brutal. Church History was a strong field with Archie Main and W D Niven, each a master in his subject as well as an excellent communicator and man of practical good sense. And then we had Arthur Gossip giving us practical training, although a less practical individual it would have been hard to find. But he was an inspiration. He affected the old Free Church white bow tie (fixed in slovenly fashion) in preference to the Roman clerical collar, and I have a vivid picture of him opening the class with prayer, his right hand, on the fingers of which were balanced his pince-nez, stretched out heavenward in supplication. Rubbing shoulders and exchanging ideas with so distinctive and distinguished a company during these three years was a privilege indeed. We learned a great deal that was to fit us not only for our preaching, but also for our pastoral work in the parishes to which we hoped to be receiving calls. (It was the late Harry Donaldson who said that while the hymn assured us that 'the Church for you doth wait', it did not specify which Church.)

It was about halfway through my time in Divinity that I was able to exchange my method of earning a living from the newspaper business to an assistantship in Glasgow's biggest parish, that of Springburn Hill, with at that time a membership of over three thousand souls. The income was not so good, but the hours were more normal and more flexible, while the work was more interesting to the extent that it represented direct training for the job I had in view. I greatly missed the camaraderie of *The Glasgow Herald* where, by this time, I had served for close on seven years. It had been a wonderful experience and I had learned a lot of basic lessons that have stayed with me—an attention to detail, a stickiness for accuracy in things like the spelling of names, and perhaps most useful of all in view of my future position as Presbytery Clerk, a fairly intimate knowledge of how a newspaper is produced and of the pressures to which all concerned—reporters, editorial staff, printers—are constantly subject. The fact that over the years my relations with the Press have been of the friendliest I attribute in no small measure to my having had this close connection with their sphere of labour.

When on 6th April 1934, at a service in Glasgow Cathedral I, along with fifteen others, was licensed by the Presbytery of Glasgow as a Preacher of the Gospel, I could look back on seven years of attendance at Gilmorehill resulting in my acquiring the degrees of Master of Arts and Bachelor of Divinity, not to mention a gold medal and some other odds and ends. All of them in their own way had been happy years, all of them years from which I greatly profited, all of them years in which I could with all sincerity have referred to Alma Mater as 'Bounteous Mother'.

As I shall explain when I get around to 'Dabbling in the Law', my efforts at resisting a New Town at Houston took me back to Gilmorehill in 1950 to study Scots Law. Apart altogether from the New Town controversy, I had always had a notion to learn something about the law of Scotland, for legal questions always intrigued me. But it was nearly twenty years since last I had seen the inside of a classroom, or done any intensive studying, and I had no intention of taking the business too seriously. I learned that the Scots Law class met first thing in the morning which, in light of my parish commitments could not have suited me better. I also discovered that for practically the same fee I could enrol for three classes as for one. To a good Scot a bargain package like this was irresistible, so I duly enrolled for the three. It was only after I had got started on the course that I began to understand something of the problems confronting the person whom today we call the mature student.

Throughout all my University career I have found note-taking a dreary and profitless occupation. I have much sympathy with the description of it as a process whereby the notes of the reader become the notes of the hearer without passing through the mind of either. If the lecturer is holding my attention, the effort to scribble things down I find an intolerable distraction, and if I find him not at all interesting then there seems little point writing any of it down. Professor A A Bowman had a system whereby he read at dictation speed a carefully condensed paragraph, and then he filled it out, talked around it, illuminated it with telling illustrations, all at a normal racy pace. By writing carefully then listening intently, I found that, when later I came to study the notes, the *ad lib* stuff all came back to me. But then there aren't many Bowmans around. It seems to me that a long time has elapsed since Caxton brought to these shores the use of moveable types so that it might seem there should be simpler ways of conveying the text of a lecture to the members of a class than to assemble them all in one place, devoid of any proper facilities for writing, and read the lecture to them at a speed far too fast for accurate recording and far too slow to hold the interest of the non-recorder.

A long time later I delivered, for almost twenty years, a short course on 'The Courts of the Church'. My method was to print sheets with the bones of the material clearly and succinctly set out and then to talk in as interesting a way as I could by way of providing the flesh to clothe the bones. I was impressed by the number of students who still insisted on writing sixteen to the dozen. Is it just that deeply ingrained habits are hard to break, or is it that in my basic hostility to the practice of note-scribbling, I am in a minority?

To return to the difficulties peculiar to the mature student, and especially to the one who is holding down a full-time job. Quite early on I recognised that unless I was going to sit the degree examinations I would have little incentive to make the considerable effort required to keep up with the work. My difficulty was not so much rediscovering the ability to study as finding the time to do so. I did discover, of course, that where learning involves the amassing of factual information of an arbitrary character by sheer rote, a man in his forties is at a great disadvantage. I know nothing of the working of the human mind, but it seems to me that the memory is like a house which will hold a lot of furniture—once filled, will take in an extra item only if some other is thrown out to make way for it. On the other hand I found that, because of my experience of life and its problems, I had in some departments the edge on the young students because I could understand so very clearly the reasoning behind the judgments. I rarely forgot the salient points in an important case, although on occasion I was none too sure on which side the judgment had been given, and invariably I forgot the names of the parties involved. The business of finding time to study I solved by sitting the exams in September instead of in the spring and by getting up some summer mornings at 4.30 instead of 6. The other problems I had to contend with as best I could.

Having successfully completed the first year, having enjoyed enormously the class in Scots Law conducted with such consummate ease and skill—and panache—by Dewar Gibb, and, of all things unexpected, having been awarded a prize in Public International Law (a subject in which I had little interest), I was inspired to do a second year, largely to allow for taking the class on Evidence and Procedure, a subject that attracted me mightily. Once again the lure of three for the price of one prevailed, and I took two other classes as well. I was extremely interested in Jurisprudence, but the class met in an afternoon which for me was very difficult and I wasn't able to give the subject the attention I should have liked. Robert M'Donald, who was then Procurator Fiscal at Glasgow, and whose death as Sheriff of Dumfries soon afterwards was such a loss to the legal profession, took the Evidence and Procedure Class and did so with a verve, vivacity and vitality all too rarely encountered in University classrooms. I am inordinately proud of the fact that he presented me with a special prize for an essay on 'Relevance', the reason for this being not that I had displayed any great knowledge of the subject—for, as he was at pains to explain, I had not—but that I had consistently argued all my points from first principles. That, after all, was the kind of ability I was trying so hard to cultivate.

One subject which, in common I think with most students, I found positively fascinating was Forensic Medicine, partly because of its subject matter (after all it deals literally with matters of flesh and blood), but also and in no small part because of what I can only call the sparkling brilliance of Professor Glaister as a lecturer. There were times, however, when I thought he let his gifts as a showman outrun his responsibilities as a teacher. Not so very long before I attended the class he had been involved (along with Sydney Smith from Edinburgh although he did not over-emphasise the point) in what became the quite notorious Ruxton Case. Two dismembered bodies with many of the identifying features deliberately obliterated were found in a linn near Moffat, and thanks to brilliant forensic work they were identified as those of the wife and domestic servant of a Dr Ruxton in Lancaster. At the end of the day he was convicted of the double murder and hanged. The lectures were supplemented by a series of coloured slides disrespectfully referred to by the students as 'Dr Ruxton in Glorious Technicolour'.

The principal lecturer in the Department was Dr Edgar Rentoul—a very capable practitioner in the field of pathology, but with nothing of the flourish of his professor. Edgar's father had been minister in a Glasgow charge before coming to the former UF Church in Houston as a kind of semi-retirement which unfortunately he had enjoyed for only a year before suffering a fatal heart attack. When the two congregations in Houston united in 1949, the former UF Manse became redundant and Dr Rentoul took a lease of what had been (if only for a year) his family home, and moved in with his delightful Dutch wife and three young daughters. He was one of the most unassuming, kindly and gracious men I have ever met and we became very close friends. Added to which he was one of my elders.

When it came around to September and the degree exams were in view, I had an encounter of the most remarkable kind with the professor. It came about thus. The written examination was always held on a Saturday morning between the hours of 9 and 11, and I had, naturally, made timeous note of this in my diary. Unhappily one of my elders, for whom I had a profound regard, and who had been ailing for some time, died quite suddenly and an undertaker without any consultation with me managed to secure a 'spot' at the Paisley crematorium for the Saturday morning. This involved a service at the house at 10.45 and definitely put me on the spot, for at least half-an-hour was needed to get from Gilmorehill to Houston. Clearly the funeral was my priority, but I was most unwilling to withdraw from the exam, for, at Glasgow, law subjects have to be passed two at a time and I knew I had sat a very good paper in the other subject and would have been very sorry to see that go down the drain.

I had a brilliant idea. I told my friend Edgar Rentoul about the problem and about my solution. This was that I should approach Professor Glaister with a request to be allowed to begin the paper at 8.30 on condition that I would leave the hall by 10.15. This would reduce my time by fifteen minutes and would not in any way put me in a position of advantage vis-à-vis the other candidates. Edgar thought the idea an excellent one, and as he was to be invigilating assured me there would be no difficulty about letting me in at the earlier hour. Would I like him to speak to the professor on my behalf? Happily I accepted his offer and assumed the matter was as good as settled. When Edgar and I met the following evening he was looking very crestfallen. Glaister had never heard a suggestion so preposterous in all the years which, as man and boy, he had spent around the University, and he was shocked to think a member of his staff had become airt and pairt in a proposal so outrageous—and a lot more in the same extravagant strain. In short, it was not on!

To this day I cannot understand where the difficulty lay. I know, of course, that rules are rules, and I have never subscribed to the doctrine that they are made to be broken. They are, I believe, made to be observed, so that certain ends may be achieved. However, when a situation arises where these ends can be served only by a breach of the rules, then let the rules go hang. Is not this, after all, what a great part of the Sermon on the Mount is about? With a view to ensuring that the system will not get snarled up in its own regulations, men of acumen, clear vision, and sound judgment are put into positions of authority where they may use discretion to secure the wider good; and for a man in such a position to take shelter behind a rulebook has always appeared to me to be a shameful dereliction of duty. I recall an occasion when a civil servant of the highest ranking rejected a helpful and reasonable proposition of mine because, while admitting it would give a better service at less cost, it did not conform with standard practice as set out in a stencilled sheet from St Andrew's House—waving the said sheet around to prove his point. I was less than popular when I suggested that if all that was involved in his job was to administer sheets of paper without regard to the effects of their application in particular cases, then that could perfectly well be done by one of the wee lassies in the outer office at considerable saving to the national exchequer. I have little doubt that what worried him was the thought that, should my proposition go wrong, he would rather be found with the chit in his hand than with egg on his face. These chits are the rungs on the promotional ladder, and promotion is the name of the game.

The upshot of the Forensic affair was that I had to complete a two-hour paper in an hour and twenty minutes. It brought to my mind the tale of a student sitting one of those examinations where they print a dozen questions but assure you that 'Candidates should not attempt more than four questions'. The hero of our tale started on Question No 1 of his choice, filling many pages with neatly written, perfectly reasoned, im-maculately phrased material. Obviously time was catching up, so when he came to Question No 2, although he filled quite a few pages, the writing was deteriorating almost as rapidly as the literary style. The answer to Question No 3 consisted of the bones of what could have been, had time allowed, a very convincing answer. On turning the page the examiner found a square drawn enclosing in bold letters the message, 'Watch this Space in September'. The trouble in my case was that it was already September.

I was satisfied that I had made a really miserable job of the affair and had resigned myself to the fact that all was lost. If in the written paper you get within sight of scoring a pass you are given an oral, and, to my surprise, I had apparently managed that much. It was here that my 'maturity' came to my rescue, for I was able to put up quite a polished performance on a branch of the subject on which, as luck would have it, I was quite proficient. And so, fortunately for me, I got my two subjects that year. The ordinance, incidentally, says that every student is to be examined both in a written paper and orally, but the practice is that those who have indisputably passed, or equally indisputably failed, are not called for the oral. Tradition has it that a candidate in the Procedure class was not thus called. It was explained to him that his written paper was so bad that nothing he could possibly do in the oral could pull him through. Still he protested that in terms of the ordinance he was entitled to an oral, and an oral he would have—or else, in menacing tones, 'I will raise an action in the courts'. 'But of course Mr X. You would be perfectly within your rights. Tell me, what kind of action will you raise?' 'I'm not clear at the moment, but I'll find out,' was the reply. 'Well, Mr X,' said the examiner, 'I regret to inform you that you have now had your oral and that you have failed in that also.'

The following year, because of especially heavy parish commitments, I had to drop my classes. I was tempted to let the whole business go, but having passed in six of the eight subjects required for a degree I felt constrained to return the following year and take the two outstanding subjects—Conveyancing and Civil Law. They were subjects in which I had no consuming interest, they were both of the type where a good memory is of more help than an ability to think quickly (or to camouflage extemporising to pass for thinking), so I found that final year especially heavy going. Had I had any foreknowledge of what life held in store for me, I should surely have devoted myself more earnestly to the study of conveyancing, which was taught with the most patient, painstaking care by Donald M'Leish, whose health obliged him to retire quite soon afterwards, to his intense disappointment, for he loved both his conveyancing and his teaching of it. I could not say he was the most intensely interesting lecturer—but then I imagine even a Glaister would have been hard put to impart sparkle to such subject matter or to get any exciting slides to put on the screen. Had I, as I say, known that I was destined for the Clerkship at Glasgow, I should certainly have tried harder to gain some proficiency in the subject, for as Clerk I was to be brought into frequent and close contact with the whole business of the ownership of property. The best I can honestly say of my time in the Conveyancing class is that, while interested, I was not enthralled.

It was even worse with Civil Law for which, I regret to say, I could work up no enthusiasm whatsoever. Had I started off in my first year with Civil Law—as the curriculum expects you to do—I should most emphatically have proceeded no further. September came around and I had a feeling that, given a bit of luck, I might win through on Conveyancing, but I had little chance of success in both in the Degree examinations—with or without the help of an oral. As I mentioned earlier, the relevant regulations at Glasgow require that subjects be passed two at a time, so that even if you have scored an outstanding success in the one, it counts for nothing if you have failed in the other. Hanging around the quadrangle waiting to go into the hall for the exam in Civil Law, I was introduced to a fellow who was sitting the subject for the eighth time. He had in fact failed in it only five times already, but on the three occasions of his passing he had worked at it so hard as to neglect the other half and so he came down in that. I did not find that meeting greatly encouraging as I went in to sit an exam for which I was none too well prepared! As it transpired I passed in both subjects and went on to graduate LLB in 1956—which was perhaps fortunate for me, for the University, or for both of us! In the light of what follows I leave the reader to judge.

For, you see, in the event of accident I had something up my sleeve—an indispensable precaution for any worthwhile lawyer. What the ordinance literally said was that every candidate must pass in at least two subjects at one time of sitting. What I feel sure was intended (and what had always been accepted as being implied) was 'at *each* time of sitting'. But then surely in something as important as a University ordinance, words must be construed as meaning what they say, and not as what someone meant them to say or thought they ought to have said. Had the subject been Music or Spanish, one might have overlooked some carelessness of expression, but not, surely not, in the Faculty of Law! The BL ordinance was differently phrased, putting the matter beyond dispute, but that seemed only to strengthen my case, since the deliberate choice of a different form of words must surely be construed as implying a different intention. So far as the facts were concerned there could be no denying that I had passed two subjects at one time of sitting—for good measure I had done it on three separate occasions. As I saw it, there could be no more dramatic way of announcing one's arrival in the legal world than by having pursued a successful action against the University requiring to be taken on for graduation in Law. I still think it was fortunate for all concerned that my idea did not have to be put to the test.

And so my graduation in 1956 brought to a close—thirty years after it had begun—my direct connection with my Alma Mater. This last spell, whatever its difficulties, had taught me a great deal and had certainly done nothing to shake my view that Alma Mater could very fairly be translated 'Bounteous Mother'. I was happy to think that my connection with the University was at an end. My story would not be complete, though, were I to end it here, having told of the degrees for which I had to work mighty hard—a word has to be added about the degrees for which I did no work, the ones awarded *honoris causa*—for that's where 'bounty' really becomes big-hearted.

In 1975, for no very obvious reason, the University of St Andrews invited me to accept at their hand the Honorary Degree of Doctor of Divinity, and this I was more than proud to do—after all, St Andrews is our oldest university (with St Mary's College dating from 1539) and a distinction from them is indeed something to be treasured. It had been quite a bonus to be guests for the occasion of Matthew Black, Principal of St Mary's, and his wife, for Matt had gone through the Honours Philosophy course along with me nearly fifty years before. It had been a particular joy too that the actual capping had been done by my good friend Lord Ballantrae. Some three years later the University of Strathclyde—with which I have had occasional dealings of one sort and another, and which I have always regarded as the university of tomorrow, and with whose new Principal, Graham Hills, I had always got on extremely well—were so gracious as to invite me to accept the honorary degree of Doctor of Laws. The graduation duly took place at a most impressive service held in the nave of Glasgow Cathedral. Then towards the end of 1988 I received, to my intense surprise, a letter from Sir William Kerr Fraser, the new Principal at Glasgow University, whom I had met on a variety of occasions in connection with matters affecting the interests of the Kirk when he was Permanent Secretary at St Andrew's House, as well as informally at dinners and such like events, and whom I had come to hold in real affection as well as the highest regard, saying that the Senate had resolved I should be invited to receive the award of the honorary degree of Doctor of Divinity at the Graduation Ceremony on 21st June and expressing the hope that I would be able to accept the invitation. I had no difficulty in replying that I was both proud and happy to accept the Senate's invitation and that I looked forward with great satisfaction to receiving this distinction, however little deserved, from the University to which I owed so much and which I had always held in the greatest affection and respect.

Wednesday 21st June 1989 was a day of glorious sunshine, and everything about Gilmorehill was looking its incomparable best for this Day of Commemoration and Honorary Graduation. A company of eleven was to be honoured this day, men and women representing a wide range of interest and achievement, and the Chancellor, Sir Alexander Cairncross (a contemporary of my own) had come up from Oxford to do the honours. A most impressive Service of Commemoration of Benefactors held in the lovely war memorial chapel (which had been still a building in my Arts days) was followed by the conferring of degrees in the Bute Hall—the kind of colourful spectacle that we see only too rarely these days of drab uniformity. I am sure it meant a great deal to each one of us who was receiving an award, but to none, I feel confident, did it mean more than to myself. How little when I trudged these four miles to attend my first classes could I have imagined that it would all end thus.

Chapter 2
Minister Most Ordinary

WHAT exactly is involved in being Moderator of the General Assembly of the Church of Scotland? Since I had the distinction of filling the position in the year 1971-2, it might be expected that I would know the answer. The first thing to be said, obviously, is that it is a long title and it is also important it should be given in full. It is surprising in this day of abbreviations that we haven't come up with a group of initials —MOGA or some such monstrosity perhaps. Instead the title inclines to be shortened to 'Moderator of the Church of Scotland', which, as well as being quite wrong, is mischievously misleading. His sphere of office lies wholly within the Assembly. The little boy in Kirkcowan who described me, I believe, as 'the boss o' the Kirk' was quite wrong.

From time to time the General Administration Committee has addressed its thoughts towards producing something akin to a job specification for the Moderator. Invariably this has begun by being quite specific and then it has rambled off into generalities covering most of what in fact successive Moderators have done. The most recent such report (1962) ends with the masterpiece, 'to undertake such other duties as he may choose during his term of office.' You couldn't ask for a wider remit, could you? It is easy to be specific about the Moderator's position—properly his only position—in the chair at the Church court called the General Assembly; it is within that court alone that he has any clearly defined powers and duties, and his authority exists only so long as that court remains in session. Quite simply he is its chairman, with all the powers and responsibilities of a chairman in the matters of keeping order, putting matters to the vote, declaring judgments, and so on. His final duty is to dissolve the Assembly, to declare the date of the next Assembly, and to pronounce the benediction. That done, a totally new scene emerges. The Assembly rises towards the end of May and the Moderator is still to be found wandering around in his official guise until the following May when he has to return to constitute the next Assembly and see to the election of his successor. It is this long period which forms the grey area when it is far from easy to define what he is supposed to be doing—or why. Although, so far as his powers are concerned, that's an easy enough question—he hasn't any!

From its earliest days the Scottish Kirk has been insistent on the doctrine of the equality of the ministry—and has been able to shrug off the wisecrack about some ministers being more equal than others. But there is today a widespread desire —issuing partly from the demands of the media and partly from the example of other denominations operating under a different structure—to identify certain people as 'Church Leaders', and it is tempting to see the Moderator—and even ex-Moderators—in this exalted capacity. It has to be added that some would be happy to go along with the identification, although I am emphatically not of their number. A case can, of course, be made out for us having 'leaders'. Every other branch of the Church has them—why should we be the odd man out? This is the age of the summit conference—would it not be an advantage for us to have someone scaling the Ecclesiastical Everest? Today the media expect to find someone prepared, capable, and authorised to supply answers, instant answers, to questions about where the Church stands on each new crisis as it arises—why should they have to look further when there is a Moderator hanging around seeming to do nothing anyway? Our generation is geared to the person-to-person approach—why should we always be lumbered with a Committee? The argument carries some plausibility, and it appears to be collecting a following.

But I am convinced it is a case of making the worse appear the better reason. I am sure this is something which we Presbyterians must resist if we wish to remain Presbyterian. If change along such lines is effected we will not just be adding another item to the Moderator's workload, we will be radically altering the constitution of the Kirk. If the Assembly is to retain its position of supremacy, then a Moderator vested with powers such as those envisaged is going to have to give some account of how he has exercised them, and the Assembly is going to have the right of approving or otherwise. This presumably he will do at the following Assembly—when it will be too late to do anything about it anyway. Would this not detract enormously from the dignity of the Moderator's position? Picture the poor man in the two situations. First, when put on the spot by some crafty television interviewer, trying to think quickly and say the prudent thing, being goaded on until he says the wrong thing. Then at next Assembly standing—presumably at the bar —defending himself against the barbs which hindsight can so jubilantly fire. A humiliating spectacle bringing shame upon both the Assembly and its Moderator. For myself I have too high a regard for the Assembly as the supreme voice of the Kirk on every matter, and for the Moderator as the unchallengeable master of order within his court, to contemplate with any equanimity the possibility of the two coming to be at logger-heads, as sooner or later they would be bound to do.

So, when I had pronounced the benediction on that final session of 1971, I was prepared in the months that lay ahead to give myself without stint in the service of the Kirk, but the way in which I visualised that contribution was in the role of Minister Most Ordinary. I did not see myself as having the ability, I was sure I did not have the authority, and most emphatically I did not have the inclination to be anything more than that. Further, I am absolutely convinced that an extraordinarily worthwhile service can be rendered in a very ordinary kind of way by meeting the most ordinary folk (as well, of course, as the others) and saying to them a simple word of cheer and encouragement from the General Assembly. As Presbytery Clerk I have had frequent occasion to accompany Moderators on their 'Presbytery tours' and have seen at first hand just how much they can achieve. And that, and nothing more than that, was what I set out to do. So, as in the late autumn days of 1970 I sought to prepare myself for what lay ahead, it was my idea that I should travel around the country as a kind of low-profile public relations officer, conveying to people in many places and in many walks of life the greetings of the Kirk. I would try to convince them, young and old, gentle and simple, rich and poor, that they mattered to, and that they had a place within, the Kirk. And when it was all over and I had returned to my desk in the Presbytery Office, it was in so far as

my efforts had achieved anything in that direction that I felt
their effectiveness was to be measured.

In the following pages I propose to comment upon some of
the interesting situations into which my policy led me. But
before passing to that, I should like to say a few words on three
matters that, from time to time, arouse controversy—how the
Moderator is chosen, how he is dressed, and how lonely he can be.
First, then, how to select this so peculiar person entrusted with
these so nebulous responsibilities? Prior to the Union of the
Churches in 1929 the choosing was done by a so-called College
of ex-Moderators, being all former holders of the office. It was
done with the minimum of fuss and, if one may judge by results,
very well done; until the idea got around that the whole affair
was too closed-shop, and generally hush-hush, and that some
more obviously democratic process was called for. A new
arrangement was accordingly set up whereby the choice was
remitted to a large committee which, along with all ex-
Moderators, included representatives of all the Synods. In 1978,
following upon fresh expression of unrest, the matter was again
studied by an *ad hoc* Committee and the drill revised, the ex-
Moderatorial element being reduced to four, and the others,
while still geographically spread, being reduced in number.
Change was again made in 1983, however, so that today the
constitution of the Committee is the seven immediate past
Moderators, seven Assembly-appointed elders, and a minister or
elder from each of the home Presbyteries, a total of 61. There
can be no justification for talking of a caucus.

A novelty was introduced in the 1980 regulations, whereby
any member of a Presbytery could send up a name for consideration, all such names to be circulated in advance
throughout the Committee. This was intended as no more than a
way of ensuring that no likely person would be overlooked and
was certainly never meant as a system of nomination, that
remaining the exclusive business of the members of the
Committee. Unhappily it was seen by some as meaning that the
person suggested had actually been nominated and had become
a candidate. From this there emerged a spirit of candidature
which, according to the report to the next Assembly, 'led to
supporters of such candidates, or even the candidates
themselves, being encouraged to seek proposers and seconders

from among the members of the Committee, contrary to the tradition that there should be no canvassing'. In fact we had had a very vivid preview of the kind of thing to which a system of candidature could lead, and we had found the picture quite displeasing. With great enthusiasm the Assembly resolved to delete the provision.

I think it an admirable system that the Principal Clerk should in name of the Church approach a minister (or elder) and say that the Committee appointed for the purpose had chosen him (or her) to be nominated as next year's Moderator. Unless on grounds of health, or for some such compelling reason, I cannot imagine anyone rejecting the challenge represented by such an approach. On the other hand I can well imagine good men refusing to become candidates. Come to think of it, one of the most obvious grounds for turning a man down as utterly unsuitable is that he sees himself as supremely well fitted for the task and is simply dying to get started!

The Committee meets on the third Tuesday of October. To choose a man so far in advance may seem a bit premature, but in practical terms the time-margin is none too long for all that has to be done. Arrangements have to be made for one's normal duties to be carried on, and in my case this was a bit complicated. Some thought has to be given to the literally hundreds of speeches to be delivered and to the many sermons to be preached on special occasions. This aspect did not worry me unduly because I am constitutionally incapable of preparing work so far in advance. My mind seems to be void of ideas until the event is at least within sight, and my wits sharpen as the time-gap narrows. I heard of a highly distinguished Moderator-elect who, a week or so before his installation, showed a friend a pile of typed sheets more than a foot deep, being the text of every substantial address he knew he was to make. I cannot but enormously admire, even if I do not envy and could never in the proverbial month of Sundays emulate, ability of that kind.

Indeed I am heart sorry for anyone having to travel around as Moderator if he has no skill at all at *ex tempore* utterance. I remember an occasion when as Presbytery Clerk I attended a meeting of Deaconesses at which the Moderator's wife was giving the address—which she did exceedingly well. Her husband came along later to collect her, and on catching sight of

him the lady in the chair remarked that shortly we should hope
to hear 'a word from the Moderator'. Just at that moment I was
standing at the gentleman's side and was taken aback when,
turning to me in obvious alarm, he said he had not been told he
was to speak, he had nothing prepared, it was quite unfair, what
was he to say—and more in the same strain. I suggested he
might convey greetings, tell them a joke, convey more
greetings, and then take his wife home. He followed my advice
literally, including a not very funny joke which he told
remarkably badly. When in Shetland I was taken on a trip to the
lonely island of Foula, the 'edge of the world', where, I was
assured, we would visit some of the cottages and talk to the folk
at their own firesides. On arrival in the Loganair plane we found
the entire population—all thirty-two of them—standing around
outside the little church awaiting a service and a sermon. To
anyone so utterly clueless at *ad lib* utterance as my friend, a
year as Moderator must have been sheer misery.

All who knew Jim Longmuir, Principal Clerk and Secretary to the Moderator, will agree that he had his feet very
firmly planted on the ground. One day I was talking to him
when he had just come from a meeting with the current
Moderator. 'You know,' he said, 'some of these chaps get great
ideas about their own importance after they've been on the job
for a wee while.' He went on to explain that he had just been
telling the Moderator of a request that he attend a function the
following month and the Moderator wanted to know what it was
all about, who would be there, would it be covered on the
media, did he really need to go, would an 'Ex' not do, and so
on. 'I just said to him,' Jim continued, 'that in a few months'
time, after his year was over, he would be happy to go to the
Sunday School picnic and to attend the Woman's Guild social
and that he should not get any exalted ideas about his own
importance'. I often think it's a good thing that no matter how
we may have been chosen, no matter how we may have
performed, we go at the end of the year. Delusions-of-grandeur
is a most insidious disease that can afflict the humblest of us.

One last word before leaving this subject. For my own part
I have always disliked the tradition whereby ex-Moderators are
designed 'Very Reverend'. They are no more reverend than any
of their brethren. Strictly, of course, they never have been.

However, that during his year of office the Moderator should carry the distinctive title of 'Right Reverend' I accept (with no great enthusiasm) because during that year he occupies a position apart from, if not above, his brethren. But once his year is over, he returns to his parish or his desk and resumes the place to which he properly belongs and from which he was temporarily released. He will doubtless carry to the grave the scars of his year; the peculiar dignities of the office I think he should relinquish along with the breeches.

Talking of breeches brings me to my second point, the controversial subject of how the Moderator is to dress: in the traditional garb of cutaway court coat, breeches, black stockings, court shoes with silver buckles, and lace ruffles worn at the wrist and over the left lapel? Or, if not, in what? Whether or not he wishes to affect this distinctive dress is a decision which the Assembly in 1981 declared belongs entirely to the Moderator himself, although the report goes on to express the hope that no Moderator will 'depart radically and unilaterally from long-existing custom without prior consultation'. In 1987 for the first time, and I believe without prior consultation, a departure from standard practice was made by Dr Duncan Shaw, who elected for a dark lounge suit with, as his distinctive badge of office, a white silk stock. There were those—a considerable number, filling the space between collar and waistcoat, I am sure—who applauded this decision. There were also those, of whom I was one, who regretted the change and hoped the example would not be followed. The following year Professor James Whyte opted for a compromise—tradition from the waist up, but from there down plain black trousers. I have never had much faith in compromises which are generally neither one thing nor another, and this seemed to conform to pattern. It has, however, been adopted by Dr W J G M'Donald and will probably now be accepted as standard. I don't imagine it will spell the end of the Kirk, but I'm sorry about it for all that.

I myself was faced with this problem. Shortly after my nomination I had a letter from George MacLeod in which he pointed out that I had a reputation as a man not shackled by convention and it would be good were I to appear in normal attire and give the cost of the 'gear' towards feeding the poor. Having given the matter some thought I replied to the effect that

I did not think the Kirk would be swept into the twenty-first century by such a gesture on my part, nor did I think that an appreciable dent in world hunger would be made by the resulting contribution. On the other hand, I felt that a vast number of good simple Kirk folk would feel they had been deprived of a piece of very modest pageantry were I to follow his advice. And I duly got myself measured for the outfit —which, incidentally, although bought from a Scottish firm, could be made only in London. In my day the lace came from our mission station in Chingleput where the early missionaries had taught the skill of lacemaking to the native girls.

A distinctive office, as I see it, deserves, indeed demands, a distinctive dress, a uniform, and so if we are to abandon the court coat, breeches, lace and buckles we ought to devise something to put in their place, something more than a silk stock. There are those who say the dress looks ridiculous, makes the Moderator a laughing-stock—a description they are, presumably, prepared to extend to the Speaker in the House of Commons and to the Lord Mayor of London, both of whom wear, given the position of the odd button here and there, the identical attire. I refrain from asking what they think of copes and mitres. In my experience one great practical advantage of the dress was that when so attired you were dressed for every occasion, from a visit to the Miners' Welfare Institute to a visit to the Queen at Balmoral. In this I had a head-start on my wife, who was constantly wondering about a hat or not a hat, a long dress or a semi-informal one, and so on. Besides I was instantly identifiable. When, as Moderator, Leonard Small visited Glasgow, I arranged, thinking of his close connection with the game, to take him to Ibrox on the Saturday afternoon. As we approached the ground the crowd not only gave way, they formed a guard of honour—something they wouldn't have done for a white stock. And, of course, when you visited a school you instantly had the attention of every single child—what you did with that attention was your affair, but it was yours before you had even opened your mouth. When, as it often can do, tradition stands in the way of progress, I am the first to say, 'Ding it doon!'; but when it is as harmless as the breeches and the buckles, I am all for holding on to our symbolic links with the years that lie behind us.

A change that has overtaken the Assembly since my year in the chair is that the meetings are now encompassed within a single week, from a Saturday until the following Friday, whereas it used to constitute on a Tuesday and continue through until the following Wednesday. The change was made ostensibly so that it would be easier for the working elder to get time off to attend. How far this has been achieved I have no means of knowing, but I imagine the advantage can have been only slight. One advantage unquestionably followed on the change, and that was a very considerable financial saving. To maintain thirteen hundred commissioners in Edinburgh for even one day is a costly affair. So, I regret to say, the one-week Assembly has come to stay. I am sorry, because for one thing it has imposed a feeling of rush upon the whole proceedings, and this is to be deplored. There is a lot of business to be got through and time is short, so let's push on. Ah yes, but the main consideration surely is that the business should be dealt with adequately and fairly. The shortening has also curtailed, if not actually eliminated, what might be called the extra-mural activities, such as meetings of yearclubs and other societies, made possible in every case because so many people, normally far apart, were all together at one time. And this is a serious loss at the human level. It has created too an unfortunate predicament on the opening day. Each year the Lord High Commissioner gives a Garden Party in the grounds of the Palace of Holyroodhouse. This is an important social occasion attended by commissioners and their spouses, and by many it is looked forward to with keen anticipation. The most convenient afternoon for this event is the opening Saturday. So we present a rather poor image of ourselves as the supreme court of the Church, scampering through important business immediately after the formal opening so that commissioners may collect their spouses and get to the lawns in the shadow of Arthur's Seat for 3 o'clock. No great harm is done, probably, but it just doesn't look right.

Presiding over the deliberations of the Assembly I found—and still find—to be a most exhilarating, sometimes an entertaining, affair. My not inconsiderable experience of helping to guide debates in the Presbytery of Glasgow doubtless stands me in good stead here. The Assembly, though, I find much more terrifying than Glasgow Presbytery, even at its most belligerent —and that is pitching it pretty high!

One thing that particularly impressed me was the utter loneliness of the Moderator's position up there on the rostrum. Certainly there are lots of clever people close by to offer advice. Immediately in front of and below you, reading from your left there are the Procurator, the Principal Clerk, and the Clerk Depute—and a more impressive collection of ecclesiastical wiseacres it would be hard to find. But all you see of them from the chair are the backs of their heads, and that is far from encouraging. It is true that in the case of the Convener and Vice-Convener of the Business Committee you have an excellent side view, for they occupy opposite sides of the table, fortified frequently by the Solicitor of the Church, but they are quite a bit away, well beyond whispering range, and as you are mentally wrestling with some knotty problem of order, they give the impression of waiting with keen interest to see what kind of mess you are going to make of this one. To any Moderator who is not very sure of himself, I think this feeling of loneliness can only too easily develop into a feeling of helplessness, and even panic—although it has to be said it is generally well concealed. I think that, in any case, it is a pity if the Moderator is seen doing much consulting on points of order. I am sure it is good that he should at least give the impression of being perfectly clear and utterly confident in his rulings, however much he might welcome having them confirmed. If the trumpet has an uncertain sound, there are usually a few oboes, and even big drums, happy to render an obligato. When briefing new Moderators of Presbytery, I used to tell them that when giving rulings they should be clear, confident and firm—if they were right that was an added bonus!

The other aspect of this loneliness which much impressed me was the sheer impossibility of allowing concentration to flag for even a few moments. Esconced in one of the back benches, as my custom once was, I could allow my mind to wander. Indeed if some subject in which I had little concern was being debated in terms pedestrian and dreary, I found myself listening with half (or was it a tenth?) of an ear while busy with the rest of my faculties preparing a speech in support of an amendment I had it in mind to advance on some issue likely to arise later in the day. My wife accuses me of sleeping on such occasions, but that is nothing short of defamation—however much appearances may suggest otherwise. For one reason or another I have enjoyed a great many commissions to Assembly—Presbyteries generally send their Clerk every year and ex-Moderators are in a privileged category—and I think I am right in saying that I have been a commissioner on the last thirty-eight consecutive occasions. Is this a record? Record or not it is often enough to have enabled me to have developed a technique for tholing wearisome debates. But while, as I say, this may be fine for the back benches, it's no use in the chair where concentration has to be sustained at a high pitch throughout. You never know when you are going to be asked a question about something the speaker has said and it's a big help if you can remember hearing him saying it. Should you feel like forty winks—and in the persistent glare of the television lights it's little wonder if you do—it is advisable to get someone else into the chair and retire to the Moderator's room until the weariness passes.

It was the custom in my day for the Moderator to give a very substantial address at the closing session on the Wednesday, this being in effect a public meeting. I had put a lot of work into the preparation of my speech, but I don't remember clearly anything about delivering it—the only thing I remember was the heat. After more than a week in the chair I wasn't at my brightest; the temperature in the hall was already in the eighties when we started; to add to my Moderatorial gear I wore a heavy silk gown; television lights focused on me from every angle. I hope I managed to keep my head; I certainly didn't manage to keep my cool! Parched and sweating, I concluded my address; the closing formalities were got through; I pronounced the benediction; the General Assembly of 1971 moved into its slot as an incident in history; and my brief 'reign' came to an end—or did it?

Scarcely had I cooled down by the Saturday afternoon, when I had to 'open' a Fair on Leith Links in which all the congregations in that part of Edinburgh seemed to be involved, the whole affair being in the capable hands of David Graham, that prince of entrepreneurs. Each day of the previous week I had felt embarrassingly grand arriving on the Mound in a chauffeur-driven, ensign-bearing Rolls Royce, but that wasn't good enough for Leith—they had arranged for us to arrive in a helicoptor. Queenie, my wife, and I were duly uplifted—I suppose that would be the proper term—in the Queen's Park and given what I can only describe as a sweep's eye view of the capital as we skimmed Auld Reekie's lums to arrive in a great whirl of stoor in the midst of the fair. That had all been exciting enough to satisfy me, but not the organisers, who had arranged for me to leave in a hot-air balloon. Queenie was to be denied this privilege (spared this ordeal would have been another way of putting it), it being thought, apparently, that only the Moderator was expendable. Came the hour of departure and I was manhandled into the cage while hot air was being generated above my head. (The hot air above my head was no new experience after my eight days in the chair). But just as we were on the point of casting off, the police intervened with the plea that the wind was too high. So I was able loudly to protest my disappointment while inaudibly uttering a prayer of thanks-giving for merciful deliverance. Great the things a Moderator gets up to—nothing to what he gets up in! The Press, needless to say, immortalised the event with photographs under the caption, 'The Flight of the Herron'.

Our first official visits were to Shetland and to Orkney, each of which has a Presbytery. It proved to be a most interest-ing and enlightening time, for I knew little of these islands that are so near and yet in many ways so far away. I did know, however, that they came to us as a marriage dowry in 1468 when our James III wed the Princess Margaret, daughter of Christian I of Denmark and Norway. The fact that they are now part of Scotland does not yet seem to have been accepted by the native population who, when they refer to the mainland, mean the largest island of the group, Scotland being a distant land with which they enjoy friendly relations and from which settlers ('ferry-loupers') visit from time to time. I wonder how far this attitude is attributable to a dismal failure on our part to recognise the independent character, tradition and position of these islands and the unique nature of their problems. It might almost be seen as the Scottish/English relationship on a smaller scale, but characterised by the same hamfistedness—even if this time the fist is ours. It is so easy for the large body, when its small neighbour won't conform to its pat-terns, to decide that they blooming well ought to.

Whatever their views about their connection with Scotland, they seem proud to belong to its Kirk, and they are an extremely friendly and gracious people with a courtesy that belongs to a more leisurely age. During our stay we were loaded with kindness to the point of embarrassment. Normally on a Presbytery tour we were put up in a hotel and travelled around from there, but in Shetland we moved from manse to manse, living out of suitcases. Our journeying was done partly in Loganair planes, partly in little boats, and partly in ministers' cars, and it was not unusual for all three to be involved in one trip. The little boats were the worst. A fishy smell I don't find all that pleasant, but it is not improved by having superimposed on it a powerful odour of disinfectant, the vessel having been scoured in honour of carrying the Moderator and his lady. To get from the island of Yell to Whalsay, its neighbour, we had first a short journey in a missionary's car, followed by a sail in just such a boat, then a forty mile trip in the car of the minister of the mainland parish, then another little boat which (after a bit of tossing) put us safely ashore on Whalsay. I should dearly love the chance to revisit the islands today and try to assess what has been the long-term effect of North Sea oil, not so much on the economy as on the humanity. So easily a boom of this kind can serve only to make people discontented with a way of life they had found adequate and satisfying, while failing to provide any alternative to take its place. And when the oil dries up . . . what then? After all, I had a ring-side view of what the motor industry did to my first parish of Linwood.

Orkney is remarkably different from its northern neighbour. It is said that while the Shetlander is a fisherman with a croft, the Orcadian is a farmer with a boat. I certainly was amazed at the amount and the quality of arable land on the Orkney Islands, especially when compared with Shetland where the rock lies so near to the surface. This time we were housed in a hotel in Kirkwall and radiated from there, still with the help of Loganair and the local ministers' cars—but not so many wee boats. Unfortunately the magnificent Cathedral of St Magnus was in splints at the time of our visit, so the very well-attended Sunday service was held in the other church in town. We visited many institutions during our stay, but that which impressed me more than all the others was the school at Stromness, the standard of art in particular appealing to me as remarkably high. Altogether we had a wonderful time in these northern parts.

In the course of the late autumn we visited the three country Presbyteries of Perth, Auchterarder, and Wigtown and Stranraer. I had insisted on delaying these until after the harvest was expected in, for I could not imagine a rural community leaving the fields on 'a guid hearst nicht' to see or hear any Moderator—and I wouldn't blame them. As it transpired it was a fairly early harvest, so there was no clash of interest. I was more than happy that our programme included part of Galloway, a corner for which I have a deep affection. My father hailed from Kirkmaiden where his mother had run what must have been the most southerly trading establishment in Scotland—she had a wee shoppie beside the Southern School, a couple of miles south of Drummore and barely three from the lighthouse at the tip of the Mull. Among other enterprises, she operated a modest soup-kitchen for the schoolchildren, most of whom travelled a fair distance from farms and cot-houses scattered over a wide area. My own mother, who belonged to Kirkcaldy and for whom the country was a strange and rather terrifying place, used to tell of how the children came to the shop at lunchbreak and took their places on a wooden bench against the wall. Grannie went along the line collecting a half-penny from each. She made a second trip issuing a bowl and a spoon. A third round was devoted to removing all the boys' bonnets. Then a final trip with the goblet and the ladle. To mother it seemed remarkable that the boys never got around to removing their own bonnets; father found nothing strange about it—why should they when it was all part of the service?

Grannie had been widowed early, left with three young boys of whom my father was the middle one. Today we talk glibly about poverty, but I am sure we have little idea of what the reality behind that word must have been a hundred years ago in the case of a widow left with four mouths to feed and not a penny of income except what she herself could earn. Hence the converting of a room into a little shop; hence the daily goblet of broth and the collection of bawbees. When my father was ten, he and his elder brother were 'waged' by a local farmer as 'half-timers', which meant that each alternated at school for a half-day and worked on the farm for the other half. Thus the farmer got a full day's work—but nobody got a full day's schooling. When he was twelve, father left school altogether and was promoted to the charge of 'a pair o' horse'. Life was real, life was earnest in these good old days. At about seventeen he decided to move to Glasgow where he got a job in the service of the Glasgow and South Western Railway, and in that employ he continued for forty-six years. The work was 'steady', and while we never knew plenty, neither were we ever in want. While at 'Varsity I had frequently holidayed with friends at a farm near Stranraer, and often too with the shepherds in the Glen Trool country before forestry took it over, and if the herds had little to say, the dogs were wonderful company. For all these reasons our visit to that countryside was something of a homecoming.

Besides my youthful and ancestral connections with the country, I had myself spent twenty years ministering in a rural parish and had come to have a great affection for country folk, as well as some understanding of them, and even, I like to think, some ability to get alongside them. I understand—and relish—their pawky brand of humour, I am interested in their way of life, and even if my head is not 'fair fu' o' beasts', I do know something about livestock. So it was not wholly inappropriate that the first daytime engagement they had organised for me in Perth was a visit to the cattle-market. Here I was set down in a position of honour beside old Mr Harry Fraser of Macdonald, Fraser & Co, the well-known auctioneers. He did not have much to say to me, but I learned afterwards that he had remarked to one of his partners that 'the Moderator kens a Cheviot gimmer when he sees ane'. That shouldn't have surprised him—we ministers are supposed to be shepherds!

The Kirk is passing through a difficult time in its ministry to the country parish today, and the situation is not helped by the fact that we are just not getting any intake of ministers from these areas. Townsmen don't, as a general rule, fit too well into country parishes, and all too often they let it be known they are merely biding their time until they can get a city charge—which doesn't commend them greatly. While the farmworker in general may not have been kirk-greedy, the farmers' families were by and large reasonably dependable in their church attendance. In Houston I had many who were unfailingly regular, and many others who were pretty faithful. The situation today on the smaller farms has changed in that 'over the weekend' the farmer and his family are the only folk around the place to get on with the essential tasks, so that in many cases, with the best will in the world, they are tied. Linkings too have led to services being held at hours quite unsuitable for the farmer. This is a highly disturbing state of affairs, for, with ministers in short supply and finance in even shorter, it is inevitable that as attendances fall more and more country parishes are linked under one minister who cannot give them the pastoral care they so desperately need, consequently there is a further decline in both numbers and finance. So the vicious spiral goes on. I have to say, though, that there was little evidence of this decline during our tour of these country districts, but I know the problem is there and is growing more acute as the years pass.

In some ways the most memorable, in many ways the most depressing, of our Presbytery tours was to Lochcarron, which takes in most of Wester Ross. We went there in September when the autumn colourings were at their loveliest, and we were blessed with unusually good weather. Our first impression was of the leisurely pace at which everything moved. After weeks spent chasing schedules that always seemed to elude us, we got a real feeling of holiday in an area where we moved around in a cannie fashion and even had time to stop and talk to folk on the road. The West Highlander has a theory that when God made time he made an awful lot of it, and over the years they may have carried the implications of this a bit too far for their own good, but, believe me, it makes a nice change to live with it for a week or so.

For me a bonus to the tour was the opportunity I had to visit the little-known parish of Kilillan about five miles north of Dornie at the head of Loch Long. St Fillan, who died in 749 at Killellan in my old parish of Houston and Killellan (and whose name is perpetuated in both) after leaving Whithorn in company with his uncle St Comgan, travelled this far north and established a cell. Later he was followed by his mother, Kentigerna, who in turn settled on the other side of the loch. We paid a visit to the little two-teacher school, about the only thing you could visit in that tiny community—and my wife was greatly entertained by a small boy who beckoned her over to whisper, 'Miss, I fair like your hat!' Far from the busy haunts of men they may be, but they are still quite fashion-conscious at a tender age.

I am reminded of a class of little ones in the Auchterarder neighbourhood who had inflicted upon them the task of writing a composition about the Moderator. We were sent a selection of the results which I can only call interesting. One wrote, 'The woman had a nis hat'—Queenie's millinery seems to have gone over well. Of myself it was said that I had 'kind of orangy-coloured hair', that I had 'a mashtash below my nose', that I was 'nise but very oald', and that I wore 'funny kind of trowzers that came down to his waste'. Who would want to see himsel' as ithers see him? A humblin' sicht.

I have said that I found the visit to Wester Ross a depressing occasion, for one cannot be long in the district before finding oneself speculating on what the future may hold in store for such communities, and it is not easy to see it in a very hopeful light. Constantly there is the threat that the railway line that crosses Scotland from Inverness to Kyle of Lochalsh, to link with the ferry to Skye, will close, and I am sure that, had the question been decided on purely economic grounds, the trains would have stopped running long ago. One short stretch along the shore of Loch Carron is renowned as having been the most expensive few miles of track ever laid in Britain. It could well be that all of it is the most expensive stretch of line running in Britain today. There are other than profit-and-loss considerations to be put in the balance, though, and so far the line has been spared.

To hear some of the local people talk you might think that everything turned on the railway. But the railway is not the problem, it is just a symptom. Depopulation of remote areas is bound to occur in a day of mass production, and while a pulp mill at Corpach and an aluminium plant at Invergordon may offer employment to the Highlander a bit nearer home than Glasgow or Birmingham, they provide no kind of solution to the problem of what the young man reared in Wester Ross is to do for a living if he is to stay within sight of its lovely shores. Nor does it solve the problem of where he is to live when he gets married. As cottages come on the market they are snatched up as holiday houses or retirement homes by people from the south who have an appreciation of the great natural beauty and peace of the neighbourhood, but who belong to a tradition utterly foreign to the local ethos and who are likely to be interested in the latter, if at all, merely to the extent that it's always interesting, even amusing, to see how the other half lives.

Time was when the Highlands and Islands sent so many men into the ministry that they were able to fill all the northern pulpits and spill over to charm city congregations with the soft gentle lilt of their voices and their genius for preaching. Today there are not enough Gaelic-speaking ministers to supply those charges where a knowledge of the language of Eden is deemed essential.

A way of life, a distinctive culture, and a unique language—they are all disappearing into oblivion, while we stand anxiously by, helpless to save them.

I am not sure that the Presbytery of England is a 'home Presbytery'. Scottish Nationalists might think otherwise—but the practice has been for the Moderator to include as part of his home commitments a visit to London and possibly some other of the dwindling number of places south of the border where we have a charge, and the London trip is always timed for the period around St Andrew's Day. Of all the many varied and interesting things that happened to us during our time in the metropolis, my own most vivid memory is of staying for a few days actually within the Houses of Parliament. This happened at the invitation of the Sergeant at Arms, Rear Admiral A Gordon Lennox and his lady, for their residence lies within the precincts. To think you are actually lying there under the very roof where the great decisions are being reached is enough, even without the regular booming of Big Ben, to put you off your sleep! I also had the opportunity to conduct a service for Scots members in the Crypt chapel at Westminster and was much impressed by the significance which was obviously being accorded to our visit.

It was about this time that I became embroiled in an intriguing issue concerning this same Crypt Chapel. A Scottish member was to be married and he and his lady felt this would be the ideal place for the ceremony. On making enquiries he learned that, while there would be no difficulty about this, the actual marriage ceremony would have to be conducted by a minister of the Church of England. The Anglican minister involved was most anxious to be helpful, indicating that the groom's Presbyterian minister could take a large share in the event, only the legal part must remain with him. Having been consulted by the highly incensed Scottish member, I looked into the affair and found that it all stemmed from an Act of the sixteenth century, passed at the time when Henry VIII was setting himself up in place of the Pope as head of the English Church. I got very involved in exchanges with the Secretary to the Archbishop of Canterbury and got around to advancing the proposition that since Westminster was now a British, and not exclusively an English, preserve it should be seen as conferring rights on all the nations represented there and the Chapel should be available to any one of the Churches of these nations. I was in fact, I think, making some real progress when we were overtaken by the date of the wedding, the Anglican claim was grudgingly admitted, and the debate having lost all practical purpose was allowed to drop. A great pity, I thought.

Presiding over the Assembly, paying formal visits to home Presbyteries, the third main section of the Moderator's duties has to do with looking in on some part of the Kirk's work overseas. These days I am interested to read of the Moderator going to Nicosia, to South Africa and other such trouble spots, though as a Kirk we are offering no witness in these places, and this I can only see as a ramification of the 'Church Leader' doctrine to which I have never subscribed. In my day, I'm glad to say, the Moderator's touring confined itself to places with which we had a close connection built up over the years. It was organised on a three-year cycle, involving one of India, Africa, and either Europe, Israel or the Americas. I agreed to undertake Europe and Israel. The Scot having been the kind of gregarious creature he (or she) is, we have congregations in many cities throughout Europe, yet no systematic visitation of our continental charges had ever been undertaken by a Moderator. I had the idea that by driving my own car I could encompass all of our expatriate congregations on the continent, tag on a trip to Israel, and contrive to make something of a holiday out of it at the same time—and all within a couple of months. The suggestion commended itself greatly to Willie Marshall, that delightful, kindly soul who for many years was Secretary of the appropriate department—although he warned me that the holiday bit was likely to prove no more than a good idea —thereby showing himself as good a prophet as he was a secretary.

Lisbon being vacant, we felt it could be omitted, and in Gibraltar we had spent a week in January at the instigation of the War Office, staying as guests of the Governor at The Convent. We had met with our people in civilian occupations and in every branch of the Services, for they are all there. Among other engagements we had attended a Burns Supper at which I think Rabbie would have been hard pressed to recognise himself as guest of honour, but at which I feel he would have been mightily entertained. I learned a great deal during that week in Gibraltar. By thus cutting out Gibraltar and Lisbon we had considerably straightened our lines.

Our official overseas engagements began in Paris where we were to be guests of the Soames at the British Embassy. Here we spent a most enjoyable few days, preaching on the Sunday in the Scots Kirk associated with the adventures of the Tartan Pimpernel. The minister was now Mick Dempster who had been in charge of the Church's huts and canteens, and who was finding it increasingly difficult to maintain our cause at its former strength since so many young Scots serving apprenticeships in the French capital, who had been faithful members, were now going home on alternate weekends. My abiding memory of Paris has to do with a British Legion Dinner Dance at which Lady Soames (Mary Churchill) presided in the absence of her husband who had been suddenly recalled to London. She did so with a verve and a zest that I shall never forget. Perhaps second place in my recollection is taken by the Parisian motorists as I think of the verve and zest they put into overtaking on the wrong side of the road.

Leaving Paris we spent four pleasant days driving to Genoa where we were most graciously entertained by the consul and his wife, a delightful couple from Fife. For many years we have had a sailors' mission in that busy seaport, and the new minister, Dane Sherrard, had converted one of the rooms into a sanctuary which I was to dedicate. But our stay here had to be short for we were hurrying on to Rome where I had a full programme. From Genoa to Rome is, I think, some three hundred miles and, believe it or not, it took roughly as long to get from the outskirts of the city to our destination as it had taken to get there from Genoa. It had been in my mind that, after driving in Paris, I had nothing more to learn about continental motoring. But for driving in Rome I seemed badly in need of a 'crash course'!

We did finally make contact with Alex Maclean, our man in Rome, and Flora his wife. From them we learned that Canon Purdy from the Vatican had been trying to locate us. When he came on the line it was to suggest that I might like to seek an audience with His Holiness, which he assured me would be readily granted. I thanked him warmly for the gracious thought, but explained that my visit to the ancient city was designed merely to allow me to meet with our own people and that it did not carry any inter-Church significance. He still thought I should seek an audience. I persisted that I had no commission beyond our own Scots Kirk and people. He hoped I wasn't being put off by the formality of seeking an audience—that was the inescapable protocol, crowned heads were happy to seek an audience. I explained that mine was no crowned head, I was just a simple Scot visiting his ain folk. Would I, he wondered, accept an invitation? And of course I had to say I would think it a grave discourtesy not to accept such an approach. And thus it came about that a dyed-in-the-wool Presbyterian like myself visited St Peter's and had an audience with the Pope. From the fuss which the Press made of the occasion it might have been thought that this was the highlight of my year, although for myself I'm sure the cause of Christian unity was not noticeably advanced as a result of our very interesting talk. After about twenty minutes, my wife, the Macleans and the Canon were brought in, and on the Pope's suggestion we formed a semi-circle and each of us in our own tongue repeated the Lord's Prayer. This I found deeply moving.

Another day we visited the World Food and Agriculture Organisation. This, as may be remembered, was initiated under our own Lord Boyd Orr, Chancellor of Glasgow University, who drew a fair number of his staff from Scotland so that a very close link was forged between the Organisation and our Kirk, and although a new Dutch regime was now in control the link remained strong. We were to have lunch during our visit, but the arrangements were thrown into disarray by a strike of catering staff. Quite undaunted, our caterer had adjusted his menu to include only dishes that did not demand too much serving, and with some amateur help from the lady guests he, single-handed, laid on a very splendid meal. I could not but smile when I thought of how it would have looked had we been turned away hungry from the World Food Organisation!

Abandoning the car in the care of our host at Rome we took to the air for the flight to Tel Aviv, for we were to spend the next week, including Easter Sunday, in the Holy Land. Could anything have been more appropriate? On Easter Sunday I conducted Morning Worship in St Andrew's Church, which looks across the Valley of Hinnom to the Jaffa Gate and the walls of the old city. The church itself was erected and furnished as a memorial to Scots men who fell in Lord Allenby's campaign in Palestine during the First World War. It is a memorial also of something much older, for set in the floor is a plate which reads, 'In remembrance of the Pious Wish of King Robert the Bruce that his Heart should be Buried in Jerusalem. Given by the Citizens of Dunfermline and Melrose in Celebration of the Sixth Centenary of his Death'. It was a packed church, filled with pilgrims from every corner of the globe, and a memorable service—for I was so conscious when speaking of the Resurrection that it had all happened just over yonder. In the afternoon we were driven north through Samaria where I have an abiding picture of a man ploughing a pretty bare hillside with what must have been the biggest camel I have ever beheld, yoked with what must have been the smallest donkey—an ill-matched pair. In the evening I conducted a service in the little sanctuary at Tiberias amid the peace and quiet and glorious greenness of Galilee.

It was to be a busy week, travelling hither and yonder, meeting this company and that. One of its most remarkable features was the number of people I met whom I had known as a boy in Glasgow. In my schooldays the Jews in our city were starting to move south from what had been in effect a ghetto in Gorbals—a movement that took them to Langside, then to Giffnock, and now to Newton Mearns. The nearest school providing advanced education was Strathbungo which I myself attended. They were one and all diligent, clever children. We used to envy them not having to appear in the morning until 9.20 when the 'Bible lesson' was over, but were sorry for them having at 4 o'clock to troop away to the synagogue to master the silent shewas and other nice intricacies of the Hebrew language. Little did I then think the day would come when I too would have to make sense of such things. On our last evening in Jerusalem a great reception was laid on, attended by a number of the Jewish community, and for me it had something of the character of a school reunion.

In spite of that glorious Easter Sunday with all the spiritual uplift it brought, I am sorry to have to record that my abiding memory of the Holy Land is a far from happy one. One day we had been given a car to take us around the New Jerusalem and a guide to explain things to us. He was a man in his mid-thirties, well educated, speaking perfect English, highly cultured, with a keen sense of humour, completely charming in every way. He showed us many of the sights, giving us a most helpful and enlightening commentary, all in a free light-hearted fashion —until we came to Vad Ya'shem, the memorial to the six million Jews who perished in the Holocaust. Here I was to lay a wreath. As we got out of the car, our guide suddenly underwent the most terrifying transformation. He became hard, cold, bitter, and opinionative beyond all reason. Before we entered the shrine he told me the story of Samuel and Agag King of the Amalakites, and of how Samuel said to him, 'As your sword has made women childless, so shall your mother be childless among women', and of how Samuel hewed Agag to pieces before the Lord in Gilgal. He explained to me the difference between a mere battle to gain a victory and a war to achieve extermination. Then he told me of how each year every Jewish child is brought to the memorial and told what happened to their fathers in these awful years.

I tried to convince him that history has surely proved beyond all doubt that of itself hatred has never achieved any good thing, but he would have none of it. A debt in suffering had been incurred and it would be paid to the last drop of blood. Had he been himself a victim of the concentration camp I could have understood it better. In fact his father had been a lawyer in Berlin when Hitler came to power, and seeing the black clouds gathering he, with his family (and bank balance), had got out to

Israel in time. Our guide had no personal score to settle, but on vengeance he was bent—hell bent. There was no heat of anger to his attitude—what made it so terrifying was its sheer cold implacability, coupled with his determination that a new generation should be trained to follow his example. As these days I read about atrocities perpetrated on the West Bank and acts of terrorism in the Gaza Strip, I think of him, and the memory still has the power to send a cold shiver through my whole being.

The festival of the Passover was established among the Jews to be a constant reminder of the generations that had suffered persecution in Egypt, but its emphasis was concentrated on how the Lord had sent them deliverance—it was a festival of thanksgiving. And to me it has always seemed remarkable that it had not a solitary word to say about squaring accounts with the Egyptians. This new annual pilgrimage of the growing generation to Vad Ya'shem is very much a kind of Passover, but one where hatred and vengeance have taken the place of thanksgiving. Is this not unutterably sad? How far this is due to the fact that Israelism has taken over from Judaism, that the new nationalism has had religion stripped from its heart, I would not know. Surely the time has come when, for the preservation of the human race on the face of the globe, we have to break out of the fruitless cycle of meeting violence with greater violence, of answering atrocity with more brutal atrocity, of vengeance re-echoing vengeance, of bigger and still bigger bombs. Can we not at least try to make a new beginning with the slates wiped clean? And where better to start than here in Jerusalem, in the shadow of Golgotha and its Cross.

A word of which they are extremely fond in these parts is 'shalom'—peace. What hope is there of shalom when a rising generation is being indoctrinated in hatred. My last glimpse of the Holy Land as our plane taxied onto the runway at Tel Aviv, was a picture of soldiers standing guard on the roof of the terminal buildings, guns at the ready; my lasting memory of Israel will always be of our guide outside Vad Ya'shem relishing the memory of the annihilation of the Amalakites at the hand of Samuel. Shalom, forsooth. The Jews are surely to be con-gratulated on the many wonderful things they have achieved in Israel. But, they have still to begin to establish shalom. What an appalling way to go about it.

Our next stop was Nicosia and a few days on the island of Cyprus, torn at that time by strife in which there appeared to be three contestants—Greeks, Turks, and a United Nations peace-keeping force, the last-named taking most of the punishment. We hadn't been there for long when I was invited to sign a visitors' book and, taking from my pocket the first pen to come to hand, I found I had signed in red ink. O dear, I was told, I mustn't do that. Archbishop Makarios always signed in red. To me it surely appeared that he had done that over the contemporary page of the island's history—a terrible warning, I thought, of what can happen when the Church goes all political. However, we had a great time, not only with our congregation at Nicosia but with our RAF units in every corner of the island, particularly at Akrotiri. And from there back via Athens to Rome where we arrived on a miserably wet day. Flora Maclean, wife of our man at Rome, assured us that Italian rain is much wetter than any other national variety. I felt that, as a West Highlander, she should be well qualified to judge, and after driving through a relentless downpour all the way to Florence, I decided that she was. The weather mercifully improved for the next few days and we had a most impressive—indeed breath-taking—drive through the St Bernard Pass and on to Geneva, where the weather broke down once more. We were in that historic city for nearly a week during which we never once saw the hills, let alone the sun. On Sunday I preached in the Calvin Auditoire, sitting on John Calvin's own chair during the service.

Our next objective was Brussels, now very much an international city with a large American contingent attached to our congregation. Then on to Rotterdam and Amsterdam where we were able to relax a little before getting the ferry to Hull and home in time to discharge a few more functions before the Assembly of 1972 and my return to the comparative obscurity from which I had emerged just a year before.

I have said nothing about attending the Assemblies of the Presbyterian Churches of Ireland and England, of preaching at Crathie when I was guest of the Queen at Balmoral, of ten days spent in the company of Tom Nicol, Assistant Chaplain General, visiting our men (and often their wives and families) in the Army of the Rhine, of a trip to Runnymede in company with the American Bar Association, of the many foundation stones I laid and the new churches and halls I dedicated, of the thousands of children I addressed in school assemblies and church organisations, of the number of high-class suppers I consumed (and sang for afterwards), of the hospital wards I trod and the prisons that opened their gates to me, of the many sales and fêtes and bazaars either my wife or myself declared open. If all the people with whom we shook hands were to stand shoulder to shoulder, they'd cover a sizeable chunk of Scotland, if all the cups of tea we consumed were put together they would fill an enormous tank. That we spent a busy year no one could deny, that we spent ourselves without stint I should emphatically declare. But what did it all amount to so far as advancing the work of the Kingdom is concerned? Clearly it is a question I am ill-qualified to answer. I doubt if anyone could answer it. All I can do is to hope that some visit I paid, some word I was inspired to utter, brought comfort to someone in sorrow, caused a glimmer of light to break into some bewildered mind, came as a challenge to some youth swithering on the brink of faith, gave cheer and encouragement to some sair trauchled soul. And precisely that, surely, must be the prayer of every parish minister as he looks back over the years. Why should I as a minister most ordinary expect that my year would be any different? We can sow, we can even water, but it is God alone who gives the increase.

Chapter 3
'Wi' Champit Tatties . . .'

MODERATORS of Assembly are certainly given ample opportunity to exercise their gifts as public speakers, but it is, I imagine, one of the inescapable hazards faced by every minister that he should become involved in public speaking from platforms other than a pulpit, and not least that he should be invited to do some after-dinner speaking. But, of course, the daddy o' them a' is the Immortal Memory at the Burns Supper.

I wonder at just how many Burns Suppers I have spoken. While not astronomical the figure must be considerable. Not for a moment would I aspire to be in the same league with the late Revd James Currie of Dunlop, whose recently published biography claims that in one single year ('season' is, I think, a more appropriate term) Jim spoke at forty separate suppers. If the season lasts for a fortnight, this would give an average of three a day with obviously more some days than others. The strain on the imagination trying to conceive how it could possibly be done is nothing compared with the strain on the mental and gastronomical powers of the person who achieved it. The mind boggles. The withers are wrung. My own modest limit was four in a season—I simply refused invitations once I had that number in my diary—although more often than not I found myself taking on a fifth to help out in an emergency, to oblige a friend (the said Jim on occasion) who discovered he had double-booked, or whatever. I reckoned that was a more than adequate schedule.

It was on the occasion of just such a supper (the third that week and the fifth of the season), one at which my commitment was merely that of proposing 'The Lasses', that I got around to entertaining some new thoughts concerning this great festival—and that in itself is something of an achievement! I think it was because the principal speaker that evening seemed so remarkably uninspired, although it could have been that I

50

was suffering from a surfeit of haggis, or maybe just that the whisky was more potent than usual—whatever the cause, I found my mind straying off at a tangent. The incident that induced this change of direction was a chance remark by the chairman to the effect that we were met to celebrate a typically Scottish occasion. A typically Scottish occasion—but is it? I found that when I should have been following the speaker on a tedious and pedestrian journey from a cradle in a cothouse at Alloway to a graveyard in Dumfries, I was asking myself what it was that had led Scotsmen the world o'er to keep this particular feast, and to do so with such dedication, abandon, enjoyment and flair. The more I thought of it the more convinced I was that the Burns Supper is utterly un-Scottish in character, totally foreign to many of the dearest traditions of our race.

Had I had the courage to share my thoughts with the company, had I, when my turn came, instead of making all my neat little cracks about the lasses, told them that I saw the whole thing as something of a hoax, if not actually a fraud, I imagine it would have caused quite a sensation. It would certainly have been very much of a minority report. But at least I should have aroused the company to a pitch of interest which the principal speaker was signally failing to do. However, our worthy chairman looked already so red in the face that any unexpected shock could have had the most disastrous effects. So I held my peace on that theme and confined my remarks strictly to the charms of the fair sex—a much more welcome and less controversial topic! And the evening passed off without incident.

I take the opportunity now, however, of inviting my readers quite seriously to consider the proposition that the Burns Supper is a most un-Scottish occasion. Think, for example, of the fare provided, realising that if the menu were deviated from, the whole thing would be a flop. Haggis, champit tatties, mashed neeps, and bannocks—are these seen regularly on all Scottish tables in our calorie-conscious contemporary conditions? Furth of Scotland the vaguest notions abound about the haggis, this pivot around which the whole supper revolves. That it is something distinctively and exclusively Scottish is universally agreed, that it appears along with the Lion Rampant and the Bridie Couchant on the armorial bearings of the Archbishop of St Giles is generally admitted, that it may not be shot before the twelfth of August is well known (all, incidentally, very typically English jokes); but there familiarity with the subject ends. Few would care to answer even the first of the twenty questions and say confidently whether it is animal, vegetable or mineral. In Scotland, on the other hand, the haggis is well known by sight, many of us have explored its 'gushin' entrails bricht'—but haggis is far from being an everyday dish on many Scottish tables. Indeed how many Scottish stomachs of today can cope with more than a very modest spoonful? Even its culinary bedfellows, the champit tatties and the mashed neeps, are fast giving place to more exotic cauliflower au gratin, broccoli supreme, and what have you. 'Thanks, I'd love to; but potatoes are not for me; I've got to be so careful with my diet, don't you know.' It may still be true to say that 'auld Scotland wants nae skinkin' ware that jaups in luggies' (though when I scan the columns of today's menus I ha'e my doots), but it is, I fear, quite untrue to say that 'if ye wish her gratefu' prayer, gi'e her a haggis'. The Burns Supper menu may be traditionally Scottish, it may well be exclusively Scottish, but it most certainly is not 'typically Scottish'.

You may care to challenge my contention that the haggis is a rare occurrence on the everyday Scots dinner table, but you cannot but agree that the ritual connected with the Burns Supper is quite unparalleled in Scottish affairs. Just think of how much palaver and parade is involved. Think of the company rising and standing solemn-faced while the piper in full regalia marches among the tables (squeezing round many a tight corner), followed by the ashet-bearing chef in spotless white, carrying the offering aloft; hearken to the chairman address the sacrifice, making all the appropriate gestures to illustrate 'your hurdies like a distant hill', the grace 'as lang's my airm', and so on, culminating in the ritual stabbing of the offering; the glass extended to every member of the contingent from the kitchen and consumed in a oner; listen to the Selkirk grace; and later on to 'Tam o' Shanter—a Tale'; and so to 'Green grow the rashes, O', sung by the company in response to the toast to the lasses; and so on right through to the final joining of hands for 'Auld Lang Syne'. Think of all these ritual proceedings that have been scrupulously observed year after year until they have become positively sanctified. Don't let us be diverted by complaints that when rustic labour, with knife duly dichted, pierces the calorie-free haggis of today, there is nothing of dews distilling, nothing of amber bricht, nothing answering to the description of 'warm, reekin', rich', the general effect being much more as if a bag of sawdust had been torn apart. Don't, I say, let our attention be diverted by such irrelevances; let's rather stick to the point and ask whether there is anything distinctively Scottish in all this fal-de-ral—indeed in the very idea of the ritual which it exemplifies. Does it seem true to the character of a nation that threw its stool at the head of a bishop when he wanted to introduce a few set forms into worship, a nation that stained the heather with its blood rather than allow read prayers or permit any white-surpliced priest to impose the formulae of a prayer-book? The whole thing seems completely out of character. I find it exceedingly difficult to reconcile the set ritualistic forms of this annual ceremonial with the character of a people whose religion has been always marked by an austerity that identified set forms with superstition, ritual with idolatry.

And what are we to say about all the sheer sentimentality associated with the occasion? The Scot does not normally wear his heart on his sleeve—far from it. Actually he's rather ashamed of having a heart—and would strongly deny it on the least provocation. Yet given a few spoonfuls of haggis, a speech on Burns, a toast to the Lasses, a 'rendition' of Tam o' Shanter, and his heart is not merely on his sleeve, he has it laid out on the table for all to admire. The songs accelerate the process even more than the whisky, so that by the time we join hands for Auld Lang Syne we have reached a stage verging on the maudlin. I will argue elsewhere in these pages that the Scot is essentially a sentimentalist, but this normally he would stoutly deny; it is on the evening of the 25th of January that the fact becomes apparent beyond all possibility of denial. Nothing 'typically Scottish' here surely.

Another aspect of this evening that I have never been able to comprehend is the reverence accorded to the performance of Tam o' Shanter. Please don't misunderstand me—in many instances 'performance' is the only term one could use. The elocutionist may want a chair on which to stride his 'guid mare Meg' and even to stand on at some point, he (or she) may require a great area cleared so that he can cavort around, he may (as I have seen) have to change his raiment in course of the recital, he may need other members of the audience to be available for clapping on the back or shaking by the hand, he may require a guid blue bonnet alternately to haud fast and to wave around—and so on *ad nauseam*. And almost certainly the pace of his delivery will vary from racing headlong through some lovely passages to slow deliberate declamation elsewhere, and the tone may rise from the merest whisper to a roar that causes roof and rafters a' to dirl. To me Tam o' Shanter has always appeared a moderately funny tale of a fermer chiel who gat fou' on mercat nicht, a tale outrageously well told with the natural flow of the rhythm cantering along, whiles even galloping, in step with auld Meg; and to interfere with the natural flow of that rhythm, to underline, to gesticulate and to play-act, seems to me an insufferable affront to the work of a master of the craft of rhyming. The gloriously subtle humour of the text gets buried beneath the buffoonery of the reader. Yet no Burns Supper seems complete without it.

These thoughts and others like them were crowding my mind that night as I sat ostensibly listening to a dreary recital of Burns' biography. Psychologists assure us that repressed instincts will out, that in fact it is essential that they be given an outlet, an opportunity for expression, just as every steam engine must be fitted with a safety valve. Could it be, I found myself wondering, that the annual Burns Supper owes its popularity as a feature of Scottish life to the fact that it gives to a ritual-loving and a sentimental people a sorely needed outlet for pent-up inclinations and desires. I have heard it suggested that some part at least of the appeal of Freemasonry in Scotland is that it provides a platform for the kind of ritual parading upon, which our dour Presbyterianism has so consistently frowned. Or, I found myself asking, was it just that the unaccustomed haggis, along with the toasts (for we had already drunk a few and that right heartily) had been as bad for my mind as for my digestion, and that my brain was getting addled?

Seriously, though, there must be some logical explanation for the phenomenon of the Burns Supper. I know of no other literary figure whose birthday is so much as known, let alone honoured, in comparable (indeed in any) fashion. I feel sure that Shakespeare must have had a birthday, but who knows, or cares, when it was? The more I think of it, the more I feel the Chairman of our Supper was on to something when he described the event as 'typically Scottish', but what he ought to have said was that it was an 'essentially Scottish' occasion. Somehow or other, Rabbie has impressed himself upon us as being a kind of Scot *par excellence*, the kind of Scot we should all like to be, and we feel that in honouring his memory we are doing something for Scotland—not to say something for ourselves. None of us ever got round to telling our lass that she was a bonnie wee thing, a cannie wee thing, or that she resembled a red, red rose that's newly sprung in June—but we should have dearly loved to, if only we had the courage, and the skill, to do it. And even if we ourselves rarely employ it nowadays, it is greatly cheering to hear the guid Scots tongue spoken with a guid Scots accent. The Burns Supper is a kind of Scottish escape-hatch, if you like.

One thing about the Burns Supper which has always impressed me is the extent to which one varies from another in quality, and how utterly unpredictable they are in this respect. I have attended very grand affairs where the crockery, the cutlery and the cooking were all out of the top drawer, where the programme looked positively fascinating on its heavily embossed card, and where the speakers were all well-known national figures, but where the whole affair turned out to be unutterably dull. I could just picture Rabbie sitting unheeded in a corner scribbling some pithy lines about it on the back of the programme. At the other extreme I've been a guest at functions in some cheerless village hall where the food could literally be described as 'hamely fare' and the performers were amateur in the extreme, but which were a delight from start to finish and where I could imagine the guest of the evening being absolutely in his element.

Talking of the Supper in the village hall reminds me of what I've always thought a very funny story, and a parable into the bargain—I've even been tempted to use it as a Children's Address for the over-thirties—a story which comes from a Burns Supper in an Ayrshire country parish. The evening had gone well, the haggis had been in the best tradition of the puddin' race, the speeches had been racy, the singing excellent—all had been going splendidly when somebody rose to recite that supremely lovely 'Ode to a Mouse'. This he did extraordinarily well with deep feeling and telling effect. So much so that when he got to the bit about the poor creature being cast out to face November's sleety drizzle an' cranreuch cauld but hoose or ha', there was scarcely a dry eye in the hall. Unbeknown to the company a mouse had been lurking behind the wainscoting and, deeply touched by this expression of compassion, it decided to venture forth—after all it was among friends. Immediately it appeared, an agonised scream 'A moose!' arose from one of the ladies, who instantly leapt on to her chair, to be followed by other lassies, while the men of the company went stamping around in their tackety boots shouting, 'Get the . . .!' Ay, the moose in the poem is one thing, the moose at large in the hall is quite another. The black African groaning under the yoke of apartheid in Cape Province is one thing; the black African family having the effrontery to move into the house across the landing is something entirely different.

I would not have it thought that my whole speechifying activity was confined to attending Burns Suppers. Throughout the winter months for many a year I did my share—more, I think, than my fair share—of after-dinner speaking, mainly but far from exclusively, in Glasgow. There, inevitably, some part of this occurred in the Trades House, that very lovely hall in Ingram Street, and was in connection with one or other of the Incorporations. At the same time I was often involved in other reception halls at functions arranged by every type of organisation, and there can be few meeting-places in and around the city where I have not at some time 'performed'. The 'art'—I use the word advisedly—of after-dinner speaking is at something of a discount these days, and anyone who has any skill at it need never go hungry—there are so many organisers of dinners only too desperate to engage his or her services, although it is true that many of these functions remain exclusively masculine preserves, the last bastions of male chauvinism. It seems to me a pity that there are so few exponents of the art, for there is, in my view, nothing more delightful after a good meal enjoyed in pleasant company and restful surroundings, than to sit back and listen to an entertaining speech, or, better still, series of entertaining speeches, well delivered. But how very rarely one has the experience.

Given one, or at most two, first class speeches on the toast list
and you accept the rest of the drivel reckoning you have done
very well indeed. Once and once only in a long ministry have I
attended a wedding reception at which we had four toasts, four
replies, and a vote of thanks to the chair, and each was better
than the one that preceded it. It was an occasion never to be
forgotten—and has certainly never been repeated.

I tremble to think how much rubbish I have uttered over
the years at such functions. I could count on the fingers of one
hand the number of occasions at which I was not involved as a
participant at some point in the proceedings—busmen's
holidays were all too common. On these many and varied
occasions I have tried to bring some critical faculty to bear, to
make some assessment of what are the characteristics of a good
after-dinner speech, and, perhaps even more important, what are
the pitfalls to be avoided if you want to be invited back. Like
Jack Point in the Yeomen of the Guard, I find there are one or
two rules, half-a-dozen may be, that a Trades House buffoon of
whatever degree must observe if he loves his free dinners. Let
me try to set forth something about my findings.

First of all there is much to be said for, right at the very
outset, as soon as you open your mouth, capturing the attention
of your audience. Where there has been a fair amount of drink
taken, this can be absolutely essential. It can also be rather
important if you are a bit down the programme, or, even worse,
if you have to follow someone who has been an utter disaster.
Once the attention of an audience has been allowed to wander, it
is not easily recaptured. That is when you need something really
arresting to get you off your mark. I remember an occasion in
the Trades House when I had a bit of a brainwave—something
that doesn't happen too often. I was to propose, I think, 'The
City of Glasgow', but by the time I got to my feet it was clear
that the minds of my audience were on much further away
places. Now, at these functions the custom is as firmly
established as the laws of Medes and Persians that the Deacon
has to open his speech by naming in full a great list of important
dignatories, and it is not uncommon for other speakers to follow
his example. On this occasion I began, 'Mr Chairman and
Gentlemen . . .'. I paused, then added, 'and if anyone has been
omitted, the fault is not mine'. It took a minute for the penny to

drop, but when it did I had their attention. What I did with it thereafter was my affair, but at least I had it.

I am reminded of the story of the man who sold a mule. He gave strict instructions to the buyer that he must on no account shout or swear at the beast but must just speak to it quietly. In that way he would have no difficulty getting it to do what it was told. The next morning the new owner got his mule out of the stable, but he just could not get it yoked, let alone get any work done. Remembering his instructions he coaxed it in the most wheedling tones, even offered it bits of sugar, but altogether without success. It just stood and looked at him in a mulish fashion. He phoned the seller who undertook to come right over. Once he arrived on the scene, that gentleman took the situation in at a glance. Looking around the yard he saw a great stick which he lifted and he struck the recalcitrant creature a crack on its latter end with a force and ferocity that all but knocked it off its feet. 'Here,' said the new owner, 'you told me I was to speak to it very quietly.' 'Yes, that's right,' said the seller, 'but you must begin by capturing its attention.' I should say that the first of the rules that you must observe if you would be a successful after-dinner speaker is to begin by capturing the attention of your audience.

Second, I think it is important that you should have something intelligent and meaningful to say. I am not suggesting that you should set out to deliver a lecture, far from it, but there should be shape and form and purpose to your speech no matter how richly interlarded with stories and wise cracks. For myself I find few things less enjoyable, or indeed more aggravating, than the after-dinner speaker who stands rhyming off joke after joke without there being any link between one story and the next, or any connection between any of them and the subject of the toast he is supposed to be proposing. The man is obviously inordinately proud of having amassed a collection of new stories and he is determined to let the company have the benefit of them all, one on top of the other in rapid, quickfire succession, and, as I say, without rhyme or reason as to the order of their telling, and without any reason why in the prevailing circumstances any of them should be told at all. To me one of the first requirements of any speech, be it sermon, lecture, plea or after-dinner utterance, is that the speaker should address himself to his theme and that his remarks should follow a logical sequence—or, to put it another way, that there should be some kind of bone-structure. If he can illustrate each of his points with a yarn that has some relevance to it (and the more relevance the better) this is admirable and the mark of the true artist. He may even be permitted the odd digression to take in some pleasantry for its own sake, although this should be done sparingly. And, of course, if one of the points in his speech has been included for the sole purpose of giving a lead-in to a good story and not the other way round, who is to know—or care. The main thing is that we want a story book with telling illustrations, not a picture book devoid of text.

Third, I would advise speakers on all occasions to avoid smut of any description—it may get you a laugh of sorts, but it will cheapen your speech. I know very well that there are some companies that seem to expect it and enjoy it, even to demand it, but I'm sure they are better without it. A 'dirty' joke can be counted on to get a laugh, especially after a few drinks have been consumed, but observation leads me to say that the laugh is not the spontaneous reaction to amusement, but rather the awkward cover-up for embarrassment. I was at a dinner one evening—I cannot recall where it was or in what connection —and my contribution was a subsidiary one, the principal speaker being a very well-known and distinguished QC. I had heard him deliver a brilliant speech once before and was looking forward to hearing him again, but for some reason on this evening he told one doubtful story after another, interspersed with leering allusions, and generally brought himself down very considerably in my estimation, both as a speaker and a gentleman. It was all so uncalled for, because the man has enormous ability and could well have entertained us without any excursions into that field. He got plenty of laughs, all of them I thought to cover discomfort. I had the unenviable task of following him—but I did not follow his example. What interested me a lot was that, at the interval, I was approached by many people who thanked me for my contribution with some such remark as, 'It's awful nice to hear a good story that you can go home and tell the wife'. I've often noticed that when really good professional comedians start peddling smut it is because they are spent forces trying to delay the day of their final departure. Smut never pays—it cheapens the speech and it sullies the speaker.

Talking of sharing a platform with a QC reminds me of an occasion in Bothwell, when I not only shared the platform but enjoyed the company at table of a very distinguished and well-known QC who, throughout the very splendid meal, proved the most delightful partner, but who, shortly after the dishes had been cleared, contrived to fall sound asleep. Just as his turn was approaching I nudged him awake. By this time he was being introduced. Rising to his feet quite undismayed he delivered a most brilliant speech which was, deservedly, followed by round after round of applause. Ere the echo of the last round had subsided, he had resumed his interrupted slumbers, for all I know picking up his dream at the precise point where he had left it. I've never seen anything quite like it.

To return to our rules, it is clearly imperative that you be able to assess your audience. There are those, for example, upon whom any kind of subtlety is completely wasted—the smart aside, the partly hidden allusion are all to be avoided in favour of the obvious straightforward joke. Guffaws you can expect, but rarely smiles. There are those incapable of appreciating a good Scots story because it is told in a foreign tongue, but even more because it is founded upon a foreign way of thinking. There are those who will positively lap up what Fowler in his English Usage describes as the 'feeble pun', while others will respond to it with a far from feeble raspberry. And you are always well advised to think of possible personal susceptibilities. I remember once at a slater's dinner fearing I was going to be lynched because I told the old chestnut about the photographer who was engaged to take a picture of 'Slaters at Work', but unfortunately one of them moved and spoiled it. I had nobody to blame but myself—I should have had enough sense to centre the tale on a portrait of 'Plumbers at Work' and all would have been well.

My final point is that there is some value in having your closing sentences fairly well prepared. In the case of a toast, the matter is simplified for you since you have to call the company to their feet, to charge their glasses, and so on. I think it's a great pity when a good speech is allowed simply to peter out. I remember the great Professor Arthur Gossip lecturing to us on preaching one day and telling us of the efforts of some student he had heard who, he said, gave the impression of a boy learning to ride a bicycle—'he shot to one side of the road, then to the other, one moment he seemed about to stop and then the next he was off down the road at top speed, he wobbled for a while and then got straightened up, and this went on for about twenty minutes and then. . . and then he fell off the bicycle.' A rather inglorious way to end a sermon, or a good after-dinner speech. It is worth while ending up by giving the impression that there is lots more you could have said had only time permitted. In that way you may lead them to believe there is lots more they would have liked to hear! And that's always a nice way to finish.

To return for a little to the interesting business of assessing an audience. With the best will and all the experience in the world, there is just no way in which you can make a perfect advance assessment of how any particular audience is going to react to your effort at addressing them. To me, in fact, one of the great unresolved mysteries of after-dinner speaking is why audience reaction should vary so widely and should be so utterly unpredictable. Why is it that what sets one audience in stitches leaves another stone cold? Why is it that in one company you'll get a laugh every time you stop to draw breath, while in another you'll get scarcely a titter even when you've reached the punchline of what you thought your best joke? There must, I feel, be an explanation, but I'm hanged if I've been able to find it.

It is tempting to say the whole thing depends upon atmosphere—the shape of the hall, how the audience is seated relatively to one another and to the speaker, the comparative size of the gathering, whether it has been a good meal, the nature of the occasion, whether there are ladies present, and so on. Now, it is perfectly true that all these factors play their part—an important part at that. I have spoken at a function where the diners were spread through a series of small rooms so that in no way could you see your entire audience. There was a very excellent amplification system, and for anyone reading a lecture the arrangement would, I'm sure, have been admirable, but not for someone trying to give an after-dinner speech. Almost as bad is the pattern I met for the first time in London's

Dorchester—of all places—where right in front of, and running the length of, the top table is a square of polished floor for the dancing that is to follow. Directly opposite and across the square is a single row of small tables, while at either side and completely out of sight unless you turn directly towards one or the other, are tables seating hundreds of folk. It is unlikely the speaker will find himself much inspired by the sight of so much polished flooring while the audience is constantly being reminded of the pleasures that are awaiting them if only the fellow would dry up. I was in no way surprised that evening to be told that increasingly in London after-dinner speaking is being seen as a brief and formal prelude to the dancing.

You might not think so, but a party of less than forty can be a very difficult audience to address in an entertaining way—it falls half-way between the formal and the informal. This, as I say, may sound strange, for you might have thought there would be in such limited numbers a warm, friendly, homely atmosphere that would make speech-making easy, cosy, pleasant. But that is not so—the speech that would go well in a crowded hall just never seems to get off the ground in the comparative intimacy of the small group seated around a single table. Better far to sit and chat to them, but then that is a different technique altogether. Then, as must be obvious, if the company has been indifferently dined, they will not be in the most receptive frame of mind for listening to an address no matter how intrinsically entertaining. The same applies *mutatis mutandis* when they have been too well wined, only in that case you have the added complication that they may give vocal expression to their dissatisfaction, or, even worse, they may insist on giving you a hand in that glad spirit of bonhomie engendered of intoxication. O yes, there are many things to militate against the efforts of the would-be public wit.

Even allowing for all these things—and I'm sure they are all important considerations and affect the outcome—we have still not explained the phenomenon of the differing responses of different audiences. The complexity of the issue was brought home to me very forcibly by an incident that occurred while I was still minister of a parish with the frequent duty of proposing the health of the happy couple at a wedding reception. Weddings did not occur all that often in my parish so it was possible for me to make time to go to the reception and to preside thereat, when so invited—which was, I think, quite invariably. On one such occasion I had two wedding receptions on consecutive evenings. They were held in the same hostelry, the number of guests was almost equal, the two sets of families came from essentially the same social grouping, the one party of guests looked remarkably like the other, and, to complete the picture, we were treated to the identical menu. In short, the second reception might by all reasonable standards have been expected to be a fairly accurate replica of the first. I had given quite a bit of thought to my speech for the Tuesday evening and it came across exceedingly well, every subtlest inuendo was picked up, the more obvious jokes brought howls of merriment. Fortunately there was no guest common to both parties so, not unnaturally, I treated Wednesday's audience to a repeat performance. This time it fell flat on its face, my best jokes being hard put to elicit even a smile. Here clearly was a case where other things were equal and yet the response was vastly different. How to explain so different a reception for the identical speech delivered under identical conditions? In the end, I imagine, one has to fall back on the fact that no matter how funny your speech may be, 'there's nothing so funny as folk!'

Thinking about how people react to what is meant to be a funny speech leads inevitably to the subject of humour itself, a subject which I think deserves far more attention than has ever been paid to it. To fall back upon one of Fowler's 'feeble puns', humour might seem a funny subject for a PhD degree thesis —but why not? I'd love to write such a thesis—if only I could think of what to say! 'Who makes up all these jokes anyway?' is a question I have often been asked. I'd love to know the answer—if there is one. But it is a question which presupposes an answer to the earlier question, 'Is a joke made up?' It's easy to picture some solemn-looking soul sitting by his guttering candle in some lonely attic making up a series of side-splitting puns and wisecracks of the word-joke variety—and to hear some television funny programmes, it's easy to believe he has a ready market awaiting his product. But what I might call the 'situation-joke', like Topsy, was not made up, but just growed, emerged out of some chance unrehearsed incident. How often have I said of a gem of this kind that it simply had to be genuine, for no one could possibly have thought it up.

For myself I cannot claim to be in any manner or degree a maker-up of jokes. I confess to having been guilty of the odd—only too odd—pun in my time, and I would modestly claim to have considerably improved the quality of some stories I have heard others tell appallingly badly, but that's as far as it goes. What I can claim is a remarkable memory so far as jokes are concerned. Let me once hear a truly funny story or be involved in an amusing incident and without any deliberate act of will I can be counted upon to remember it ever afterwards. Not only so, I can generally recall from whom I heard it and the circumstances in which it was told. If only I had a comparable ability to remember names and faces, or to remember the errand I faithfully promised my wife to perform, or to remember the letter I put in my pocket with the intention of dropping it in the pillarbox, how much simpler life would be. If nature wished to endow me with one single spark of genius, why did it have to be such a useless one!

The late Dr W M Macgregor, Principal of Trinity College, Glasgow's theological school, and Professor of New Testament there, used to amaze his students by the way in which, without any scrap of notes, he could quote from the whole field of literature, classical, English, French. There he would stand, chatting on some theme, the references and the quotations and the illustrations simply dropping by the wayside. Someone once congratulated him on his remarkable memory, to which Williemac (as he was affectionately known) replied, 'I don't have a good memory; I've got a shocking bad memory, I can't forget a single thing'. I think I can understand what he meant, and within the strictly limited, and let it be confessed remarkably useless, field of the funny story, I can claim to have a shocking bad memory—I can never forget a single one.

While, then, I could not even begin to invent, conjure up, make up, think up, or whatever the process may be, a collection of funny stories, my memory would be subjected to no undue strain to compile a collection of 'Jokes I Have Heard', or, if you prefer it, of 'Jokes I Have Told'—and, let me freely confess it, they would be exactly the same jokes even if the former list were the longer of the two. In the domain of the after-dinner story, it has to be said, the ordinary rules about plagiarism do not apply. Perhaps they should apply, but it would be impossible to enforce them. I would, I know, be hard pressed to prove that some particular story was mine, but then you would have as big a job proving it was yours. The late Jim Currie could be honest to the point of embarrassment in acknowledging sources. He would introduce a tale by saying, 'This is one of Andrew Herron's stories', as though I had some copyright on it. And I'd be sitting there wanting to disclaim ownership, for I had picked it up from someone else just as he had picked it up from me. And so it was every bit as much his as it was mine. The day may come when you have to register a title to a joke (and maybe get royalties on it)—thank goodness it is not here yet!

How often does one hear it said, 'I'm one of those people who can never remember a joke'. I am sure the real trouble is that they have never understood the joke, haven't recognised what it is that makes it tick. Obviously I have no statistical information to back me up, but my impression is that almost half the population will assure you that they suffer from this inability to remember a funny story. What's more, they will usually report the fact as though they were recording some special virtue—much as they would tell you that they had never had measles. To me, as I have suggested, it has always appeared that the person who claims to be subject to this infirmity is suffering not so much from a defective memory as from an inadequate sense of humour, not primarily from an inability to remember the joke but from a failure properly to 'see' the joke. It's not that the joke registered and was subsequently scrubbed from his memory-tape; it's that it never truly registered on the tape at all. So when such a person tries to re-tell the joke, he is not faced with the problem of reproducing a piece of humour, but of repeating a word-form, the reason for whose construction is beyond him.

In this connection it is amazing what a mess some people can make of recounting the simplest joke. And that, as I have suggested, is because they are not reproducing a story whose structure is meaningful for them, but are attempting to reproduce a story which, when told in their hearing, seemed amusing. What they simply cannot understand is their own inability to make it mirth-provoking. A few summers ago my wife and I were all booked up for a fortnight in Switzerland, and a Kirk social at which I had to preside had had its date delayed to allow for our return. Very shortly before we were due to leave I suffered a fairly bad attack of flu, and then the day before we were due to depart my wife went to bed with an even more acute attack. So the whole affair had to be cancelled and the entire fortnight spent by both of us crawling in and out of bed. When the evening of the social arrived it was widely known that we were supposed to be just returned from our holiday, so I felt it proper to explain our lack of a suntan. I told of our misfortune, ending by saying that we had pinned to the door a notice saying, 'We have not flown: we have flu'. A few days later I overheard a lady who had been present and who had thought this an extraordinarily funny remark, repeating it to a friend. But the way she put it was, 'We have not flown: we have the flu'. Her friend, not unnaturally, didn't see anything to laugh at.

The same kind of failure to understand where the secret of the joke lies, what is the thing that makes it tick, is even better illustrated in the tale of Eustace the commuter. The bus was crowded as usual when Eustace boarded it on Monday morning bound for the office. He had hardly stepped into the gangway on the lower deck when the driver engaged gear in that engaging way they often do, and Eustace found himself hurled unceremoniously to the front of the vehicle, there to take refuge on the knees of a lady in the front seat. The situation was considerably relieved when a wag seated across the passage greeted him with, 'Good Morning, Laplander!' In the laughter that followed, Eustace was happy to regain his balance and some part of his composure. Restored to the bosom of his family, as they sat around the evening meal, he recounted his adventures of the morning. He got so far as the point where the fellow across the passage said, 'Good Morning, Eskimo!' and everybody had then burst out laughing. His wife, however, was a bit confused: 'What's so funny about that—*Good Morning, Eskimo*?' Long and earnestly Eustace pondered the matter. 'You know, now that you ask the question, I can't see what's so funny about it either. But, believe me, it sounded terribly funny at the time.'

One evening in London in a fairly large company at one of the Liveries, I heard the story of two men who had enjoyed a most successful night on the town. On meeting some days later, one had a rueful story to tell of how, just after their parting, he had been picked up by the police on a charge of 'drunk and disorderly' and had spent the night in the solitude of a cell. 'My, but you were lucky,' said his friend, 'I got home.' The tale was very well told, and the company erupted. By a very odd coincidence, I was present a few days later when one of those who had been at that earlier occasion, a television celebrity, retold the story. He completely missed out the phrase, 'My, but you were lucky', saying simply, 'O did you? I got home'. Needless to say his hearers were still waiting expectantly for the rest of the yarn. I'm sure my friend wondered what had gone wrong, because, like Eustace, he would have claimed that 'it sounded terribly funny at the time'. I may add that the hero of my tale was an actor, very well known and justly renowned, who had played many a humorous part on the stage. It set me wondering whether he has ever completely understood the words he has so successfully been putting across all these years.

I have wandered far from the champit tatties from which I began. Or have I? For surely there never has been, in Scotland at least, a more perfect exponent of humour than our own Rabbie Burns. They didn't maybe call it after-dinner speaking in his day, but whatever they called it he was its master. For the exposition of its own peculiar brand of humour, Scotland owes to Robert Burns a debt which it can never hope to repay. It could begin, though, to honour its debt by trying to keep that humour alive as a distinctively national attribute. Even if we let the haggis go, let's hang on to the humour.

Chapter 4
The Clerk's Tale

NOVEMBER 1st 1959 saw me take up my duties as full-time Clerk to the Presbytery of Glasgow. For the first two months I was to be acting as Assistant to John Sinclair who was due to retire at the close of the year. This gave me an admirable opportunity to look about me and see just what was what before accepting the full responsibilities of office. At that time there were in the Kirk some sixty Presbyteries, only three of which employed full-time Clerks, and Glasgow was alone in having its own office premises, the others being served by parish ministers as an extra duty performed from their manses. For the previous seven years I had myself acted in this capacity in the Presbytery of Paisley while I was minister at Houston and Killellan, so the work was not wholly new to me. Glasgow, however, was unique among Presbyteries—largely on account of its size. It embraced in that year 263 charges and 62 other ministers entitled to seats, giving a total membership of exactly 650, and being responsible for 203,208 Church members. By the time of my retirement (almost 22 years later) the number of charges was down to 172, the total membership to 528, and the Church membership to 108,500. Hardly a success story, you would be entitled to conclude. But I beg of you to reserve judgment until the end of this tale.

Throughout the whole of my ministry I had been intensely interested in the business of the Presbytery, had taken my full share in the work of its Committees, and, as I have said, had served for seven years as a part-time Clerk. The ordinary day-to-day business of my new job presented me, therefore, with little novelty—just the same old story, only more of it! The move to the city, though, was another matter, for we had so much enjoyed living in the country. But both my wife and I had been brought up in Glasgow, so we quickly adjusted to the new life in the very pleasant villa provided for us in Pollokshields, while our four daughters, who were either attending colleges or working in the city, found the move a great convenience. Keeping to office hours was for me something of a change from the rather shapeless pattern of the parish minister's day, but I have always inclined to an orderly way of living, and my experience when serving an apprenticeship in law had accustomed me to the workings of an office. As I have indicated above, what Queenie and I most acutely missed was the country pattern of life, not being able to stop and speak to everyone you met on the street, having to shop from shelves in a supermarket instead of learning the latest news at the local store, not having every door opening wide to welcome you, not even knowing who your neighbours were or what they did, having to lock your car door every time you got out of it, being a mere unit in, instead of a member of, the community. But we got used to it, and the transition to the new way of life was effected quickly and painlessly.

The more formal part of a Presbytery Clerk's work, the preparing and keeping of minutes, the supervision of the work of committees, the arranging of this and the organising of that, the making of yourself available to listen to worries and to advise on problems, were all familiar enough to me, even if the scale was now much magnified. But my arrival in Glasgow coincided with something quite abnormal, something unprecedented, I'm sure, in the history of any comparable city—for Glasgow was being completely replanned and rebuilt. At no time during the eight hundred years of its history has 'the dear green place' undergone so complete a transformation, so traumatic an experience, as it did in my twenty years as Clerk. The work was already in progress when I arrived, a section of Hutchesontown re-development being a *fait accomplit* by that time, Pollokshaws being far advanced at the blueprint stage, Anderston already on the drawing board. What we had seen happening in Hutchesontown was something entirely new and quite frightening. We had been accustomed to see the odd building knocked down and in due course a new one arising in its place, but this was something entirely different. Here a bulldozer started at Point A and drove relentlessly forward until it reached Point B a hundred or more yards away, and then it turned and came back triumphantly obliterating everything in its path, and justifying, surely, my remark once in the Assembly, that Glasgow's new coat of arms was a bulldozer rampant and its slogan 'Let Glasgow Perish'! It was not blocks, it was not streets, it was whole areas that were being swept into oblivion to leave cleared sites on which redevelopment could take place on a really massive scale. About this there was to be nothing haphazard, it would all conform exactly to a design prepared by the planners.

As soon as I had recovered from the first shock of seeing old landmarks vanish in a cloud of dust and had begun to grasp what was afoot and to form some idea of its implications, I said to myself that the Kirk must get itself involved in replanning and rebuilding for the next century. Were we to wait to see what the planners made of the new city, we should find ourselves left well behind and our long-established Church pattern would be wholly out of date. It was imperative that we get right in on the act, and get there quickly. It was time somebody was getting going.

Standard practice within the Kirk (as, I imagine, within most comparable bodies) is that if you happen to suffer from a bright idea you begin by selling it to the Presbytery which will then appoint a committee to take charge of the whole affair. I've worked both with and on a great many committees in my time and I am not without respect for the careful, painstaking way in which they can carry through their remits, but I have rarely found them to be either inspiring or inspired, and they don't move quickly. In my experience, renaming them 'working parties' has made no significant difference—why not be honest and call them talking parties? True, if you are not very sure of your own judgment it can be comforting to have a committee behind you to help carry the can should events prove you wrong. But in an area where decisions have to be reached fairly smartly and decisively, where deliberations with outside bodies can progress only if the representative carries some authority, where a number of balls have to be kept in the air simultaneously, where responsibility has to be assumed, a committee can be a positive millstone. In any case I had no doubt about the rightness of my own judgment here and I was prepared to carry any cans I might collect on the way. I decided that, in the situation of the city at that time, the simple and effective plan was for the Presbytery Clerk to appoint himself sole Planning

Officer for the Kirk, and, having duly made the appointment, I set myself to study with diligent care the blueprints for the new city, to get to know the people who, at that time in a modest enough office in High Street, were in charge of planning, and to get on to terms of familiarity with the Estates Department which had to do with the cash side of affairs. And let me pause here to say that from all these people, at all times, I received the utmost help, advice, encouragement, and courtesy. I was always made welcome in the office where we had many unscripted discussions, and I was kept *au fait* with all that was afoot.

I had also, however—and this lay at the heart of the whole project—to get Church people alerted to what was happening, prepared for the kind of changes that were coming. So ere long I found myself very busily occupied addressing evening meetings of all sorts of groups on the subject of 'The Church in the Changing City'. It was, I felt, desperately important that people should appreciate the magnitude of the operation that was afoot, should therefore recognise the need for the Kirk to adjust her agencies to meet the altered situation, and even should visualise the part they themselves might of necessity have to play if the vision were to be realised.

The plan centred (literally) on a Ring Road that was to encircle the inner city, crossing the Clyde by a new high-level bridge to be built at Kingston in the west, and again by a bridge near Glasgow Cross in the east. From this road, expressways would branch off in every direction—to Dumbarton, Aberfoyle, Kirkintilloch, Stirling, Edinburgh, Carlisle, Kilmarnock. The pattern with which this would present us would be that of the hub and spokes of a wheel, or, as I used to say, of a great half grapefruit all segmented. Opportunity would be taken to use these basic divisions to create real self-conscious communities within the city. To achieve this there were to be twenty-nine Comprehensive Development Areas. Each of these would be a complete self-contained unit with, at its centre, the necessary services—shopping, school, medical services, and so on—and its boundaries would be the natural ones created by the major expressways, for these would constitute the kind of barriers the railways had served in the past. When vehicular traffic consisted of the tramcar and the horse-drawn coal lorry, the tendency had been for the busier streets to attract the shops, the churches

—and the crowds. But with traffic of today's density this is a ridiculous pattern. We should be drawing people away from the busy perimeter roads to a pedestrianised centre. It was, it seemed clear to me, in a strategic place in this pedestrianised centre that we wanted the Kirk to be. And, given that, there seemed a chance that we might be able to recapture something that had been lost with the sprawl of the Industrial Revolution—a real parish church at the heart of a real community. But if any of this vision was to be realised we had certainly to move—at once, smartly, decisively, and constructively.

The question sharply presented itself—where was 'the siller' to come from? Two possible sources suggested themselves. First there were a few of our churches occupying strategic sites for commercial development—although not nearly as many as might have been wished for. And second there were those church buildings which would have to be demolished to make way for the new plans to go forward. They would therefore have to be bought by the local authority, in terms of legislation governing compulsory purchase. Interesting legislation! It provides that where any subjects are to be acquired under a Compulsory Purchase Order, the acquiring authority is to pay the price which such subjects might expect to fetch in the normal market. But what of subjects for which there is no normal market? In such cases, provided there is a *bona fide* intention on the part of the owners to continue functioning, the compensation is to be the reasonable cost of equivalent reinstatement. Here, as I saw it, lay our chance to move into the new century, to drive there in a carriage and pair, if I may mix my centuries! How far could we persuade the City Fathers that our buildings stood in the way of progress? And how far could we persuade congregations that so far from throwing away their heritage they would, to mix metaphors, be giving that heritage a new lease of life by transporting it to where the people were now living? These were the burning questions. Only time would reveal the answers.

By a fortunate coincidence I had already been over this particular course while still in Paisley. A church in George Street in that town stood in the way of a large-scale development of the area and so was made the subject of a Compulsory Purchase Order. A vast new housing scheme to the south of the town, Glenburn, was in process of being developed and we badly needed a church there. I managed to persuade the congregation of George Street to adopt a *bona fide* intention of carrying on their existence in this new field—which was no fiction, for many of them were now resident in that part of the town. Oddly enough, the first claim, I think, to be raised under the new legislation had come from a golf club quite close by. Clearly there is no ordinary market for trading in golf courses, and the local authority had accepted its responsibility to meet the reasonable cost of creating a new course slightly higher up Gleniffer Braes. I wondered how we would fare with our claim in respect of a church. It might be remarked in passing that my earlier suspicions that committees would be of little help was amply borne out here, for when I (of necessity) went to the Edinburgh committees concerned in the case, I was advised from every side to 'forget it', told that I 'hadn't a hope' and so on. I was so persistent, however, that it was finally agreed we should take opinion of counsel in regard to our prospects. As a result of further consideration the legal department agreed we should hold on to counsel's fee until we ran into difficulties, and in the meantime we should press on with our claim. I had had, I should say, a great deal of help in framing our case from Mr William Hall, now of the Lands Appeal Tribunal, then a property agent in Paisley, a man of infinite skill, experience, and patience. At the end of the day we were successful, the Town not contesting the validity of the claim, and the District Valuer accepting the work we proposed to do at Glenburn as fair equivalent reinstatement. I had had my worries, I must confess, about moving so far away from the site which was being acquired, but no difficulty was raised on that score. Nor was any objection raised when some years later we reinstated a church that had stood in the way of the southern approaches to the Kingston Bridge some miles away at Mearns Castle.

As I said, by the time I came to Glasgow the regeneration of Hutchesontown was too far advanced for us to do anything there. The district had been completely bulldozed and ten-storey flats, for which the architect received many awards (although the tenants never understood why), were already occupied. Pollokshaws also, where I am sure something really imaginative could have been achieved, had crossed its Rubicon on the basis that existing churches, of which we had three, were to remain untouched. Needless to say this gave great delight to the three congregations, but not to me, for Pollokshaws was supremely a case where you had a real community, separated geographically, traditionally, and you might almost say ethnically, from its neighbours. It was the very place that should have had a new modern church complex at its heart. We are now, in fact, down to one single congregation, worshipping in a building which, while central, is old-fashioned (erected in 1843) and inadequate in respect of hall accommodation. It is, incidentally, the sole church building of the former Original Secession denomination still in service.

The area that was giving most concern at this time was Anderston. Hard to credit though it may be, Anderston was once a village of weavers situated on the river a good distance west of Glasgow. When the first church, a Relief cause, was built in 1769, it is recorded that Anderston was separated from the city by the two villages of Brownfield and Grahamston, and that 'the walk from Anderston to the Tontine was along a genuine country road skirted by hedgerows and trees'. In the years that followed, the area grew to be one of the most densely populated, and many congregations flourished therein. By the time I found myself taking an interest in it, Anderston was 'spent' so far as housing was concerned, the charges had been reduced to three, and the Ring Road with its northern approaches to the Kingston Bridge was going to take a great deal of land at its heart, including one of the churches, the one situated in Heddle Place, just at Anderston Cross. Here, then, we had a situation where Glasgow Corporation (as it then was) was clearly 'in for a penny' and it seemed to me they might as well be 'in for a pound'. Here was a case for discovering just how much we could achieve in the way of constructive planning.

It would, I felt, be foolish to begin the discussion with the people who would have to foot the bill, invariably and understandably the toughest line of defence. Rather let's begin with those likely to be most advantaged by our proposals. So I met unofficially with the planners, pointing out to them the disadvantage of having to plan around the two churches that were to remain, neither of them a thing of great beauty. If, on the other hand, these were out of the way, they would have a fully cleared site ready for redeveloping. We would be prepared to throw in the two additional churches if the replacement value that was going to have to be provided in any case for the Heddle Place Church were calculated on a generous scale. They were all very enthusiastically on my side, which made it all the easier when I got to the Estates Department for me to secure their agreement in principle. That naturally took us to an architect whom we supplied with a brief to prepare drawings. Then in due course, accompanied by these drawings, we visited the District Valuer whom we managed to persuade that the proposals represented 'equivalent reinstatement', and, if he got rather a shock when later he heard the price, he accepted the deal with a good grace and the very fine new complex was put in hand, to be dedicated by the Moderator of Assembly, the Very Revd James B Longmuir, on 18th December 1968. But that was still a long way off.

I had managed to persuade the purchaser, but would I be equally successful with the sellers? Evening after evening I spent in the vestry of the church in Heddle Place (invariably with my back to a roaring coal fire) telling the ministers and representative office-bearers of the three congregations about this new road that was going to come across the river, go underneath St Vincent Street, proceed in a cutting past the Mitchell Library and so underneath Bath Street and Charing Cross. I'm sure they thought I was imagining it all. There were times when I wondered myself. So many things we had always thought of as part of the very essence of Glasgow seemed to be standing in the way. I did persuade them, though, that they had no future as independent entities in the new Anderston that was going to emerge, and that their one hope—and a glorious hope at that—lay in uniting in the new premises that were to be erected.

It was typical of the kind of irony that seems to go with perfect planning, that changes effected at the last moment in road patterns (after our plans were being put into effect) resulted in the very grand front entrance designed for the new church becoming almost inaccessible to pedestrians. Thus the principal access to the premises has had perforce to be what was originally intended as the back door! Mere trifles of that kind, however, were completely forgotten on that memorable evening in December 1968 when the Moderator of Assembly came to the church to declare the union of the three congregations and to dedicate the new building. Our good friend, the Revd Ronald Falconer, Director of Religious Broadcasting, had agreed to have the service televised and excitement ran high among the members of the new congregation. On the day before the big event a rehearsal was staged and I slipped into a back seat to hear how it was all going. An electronic organ had been installed about whose quality I had had some misgivings. As it led the singing of Psalm 100 my doubts were completely dispelled. The effects produced by the instrument were quite incredible, particularly its reproduction of brass. It was only as the service was breaking up that I discovered that the efforts of the new organ were being supplemented by the Boys' Brigade brass band tucked away in a corner where I hadn't been able to see them. Nothing can reproduce brass so well as brass!

I was very contented that evening. I felt we had established an acceptable pattern. I had a mental picture of twenty-nine Comprehensive Development Areas all being regenerated, if not on quite so grand a scale, at least on the same pattern. In the event we did manage to accomplish something comparable to the Anderston Story in a few cases, so that when I retired in 1981 I was able to report that in my twenty-one years' Clerk-ship, I had been involved in the erection of no fewer than twenty-five new churches and seventeen cases of massive hall extension (on average two new buildings a year), and, in the case of the churches, seven had been wholly paid for out of compensation and four through a straight commercial deal.

However, I had hoped to have accomplished much more than that. What went wrong? Very largely, I think, one has to accept Burns' simple if fatalistic philosophy that 'the best laid schemes o' mice and men gang aft agley'. For one reason or another much of the planners' dream has remained a vision, and since our future depended on their progress we fared even worse than they did. Even today, more than thirty years on, many crucial features of the plan still exist only on paper. The Inner Ring Road, for example, around which it all literally turned, is still incomplete—and likely to be so for many a year to come. Once the west and north flanks were in operation, the heaviest of the traffic was diverted out of the city centre. The urgency being thus relieved, progress just came to a halt. Difficulties about how the east flank would affect the Cathedral Precinct provided an admirable excuse for endless delay, doubts about the early stages of the Carlisle Road provided another . . . and so on. When it came to the expressways that were to radiate out from the Ring Road, there was constant changing of the line to be followed; at one moment a church was to be compulsorily acquired, some months later I would discover (usually by accident) that this was no longer the case. In one instance a housing complex of very considerable extent was to be built on a certain site. I had an architect prepare an elaborate plan for a church and a suite of halls to serve the area, only to learn there had been a change of plan and only a few hundred people were now to be housed on the site. A fundamental change of policy occurred after the worst of the slums had been cleared away and after the most appalling examples of massive high-rise blocks had been perpetrated in the thirty-storey monstrosities of the Red Road and in the tenements (now demolished) in Crown Street. Gone was the zeal for the March of the Bulldozer. Why not rather conserve some of the splendid domestic architecture of our Victorian forbears. It was solid and substantial, it looked good, it was already there with all necessary services laid on—given re-roofing, stone-cleaning, internal modernisation and we were equipped with good housing for a long time to come. I have to agree that the idea was sound, but it was not the radical pattern around which my whole policy had been centred. And so, for one reason or another, the planners' plans have shrunk with the passing of the years, and the vision some of us had of a church completely rejuvenated in respect of her property, and of the position of that property relative to the people, has been realised only to a very partial extent.

In view of the lavish funds made available to private house owners (not impoverished ones) to carry on this work of rejuvenation of the flats, I made soundings as to how far it might be possible to have the grants extended to the Church so that she might be in a financial position to undertake the repairing and refreshing of her neighbouring properties, but I was assured that since no votes were likely to be gained by grants of that kind there was no chance of my suggestion being taken up. I think it's a pity. In relation to the amount of government funds being spent on upgrading the city (not to mention

what has been squandered on ill-considered ventures) the total
sum involved would have been a trifle, and it would have been
to everyone's advantage to have the Church's property brought
up to the same standard as that of the flats among which it
stands and whose inhabitants it seeks to serve.

The story of these years of replanning would not be
complete without some reference to the events that led to the
creation of the Renfield Church Centre at the west end of Bath
Street. It was away back in 1847 that a group of people left the
UP congregation in Regent Place in Dennistoun to establish a
cause farther west whither, they were convinced, their members
were steadily drifting. A site was secured on the south-west
corner of Renfield and Sauchiehall Streets, being, a contemporary account assures us, 'elevated, clean, and healthy, in the
centre of a populous district and with no other church in the
immediate neighbourhood'. Little could they have known just
how busy their corner was destined to become. For a long time
the church was very much a preaching-station attracting vast
crowds to its evening services, and for this a busy corner had
obvious advantages. It also had its drawbacks—it was all but
impossible for a be-ribboned limousine to stop for long enough
to disgorge its bride, let alone to accommodate the guests, and
even on a Sunday the congregation skailing from a service
found themselves swept along in the flow of pedestrian traffic.
With increasing insistence the question came to be asked,
whether this was indeed the most profitable use that could be
made of such a site?

The congregation was formerly UP, and its temporal affairs
were in the hands of a small group of managers, all of them
fairly long-headed men of affairs. The membership roll was
steadily dwindling and they were constantly being approached
by developers interested in making them an offer. In the nearby
Garnethill district, a number of unions had taken place
culminating in the creation of the congregation of Milton St
Stephen's which worshipped in a church in Shamrock Street.
This building had been scheduled for demolition in connection
with the Ring Road. A union of this congregation with that of
Renfield Street was effected to form the new charge of
'Renfield'. Some idea of the rate at which Glasgow had
expanded westwards is to be gleaned from the fact that in 1849

the Shamrock Street church had been erected in green fields 'on the furthest outskirts of Glasgow to the west', and already in 1964 it was being demolished to make way for the Inner-Ring Road.

The minister of the newly united charge was an adventurous and far-seeing young man, Campbell Gillon. It was his conviction that it was for the Kirk to establish a fellowship centre in the city centre: 'the Kirk,' he maintained, 'should be at, and should be seen to be at, the heart of the community'. What followed is a long and complicated story, but it is worth telling quite briefly. Agreement was finally reached for the sale of the Renfield Street site to British Home Stores for what was then an astronomical sum, and it was further agreed that the free proceeds would be available for the creation of a Church centre in the city centre. The original idea was to secure a site somewhere near Charing Cross and to erect thereon a complete suite of buildings which would include a sanctuary. Vividly I remember going around with Campbell Gillon looking at possible sites, having meetings in solicitors' offices, consulting planners and architects, and so on. The kind of site we had in mind, we discovered, was not going to be easy to find, still less to pay for.

We had a bright idea. The former St Matthew's Blythswood Church at the west end of Bath Street, a handsome structure with a truly magnificent spire, was lying empty and steadily deteriorating structurally, and an adjoining office block might be acquired. So the Trustees began by buying the Church, which had been erected around 1850 as an Independent Chapel, purchased some years later by James Baird of Cambusdoon and presented to the Church of Scotland for use as a parish church. Then they turned their attention to the business of acquiring the offices, a more intricate and time-consuming exercise which, however, was successfully carried to a conclusion in eighteen months when the last of the tenants departed and the work of demolition began. While waiting for the offices to be vacated, work had gone ahead in preparation of plans for the whole project and on repairs to the church. The stonework was cleaned inside and out, the very fine pipe organ from Renfield Street was installed, pulpit and communion table were brought from Maxwell across the river (another church awaiting demolition to make way for the Kingston Bridge), and the crypt was developed to provide ancillary hall accommodation. On 28th June 1968 the restored church was rededicated, the congregation moved in, and the first stage of the dream was now a reality.

The whole affair reached completion two years later, being dedicated on 4th September 1970 by the Very Revd Hugh O Douglas, Moderator of Assembly. It was built around three sides of an open patio. On one side was the church with, alongside of it, a very lovely chapel seating roughly a hundred in which it was thought daily services might be held; straight ahead was a public restaurant, 'The Patio', run on a commercial basis, with a lounge above it; on the other side was a large, well-equipped, modern hall, above that a suite of offices let to the Presbytery for the use of its Clerk, and above that again a gymnasium. Altogether a scheme imaginative in its conception, vast in its extent, and costly in its execution. Probably never in its history has the Kirk been able to mount so ambitious a project. One wonders whether it ever will again.

Sadly it has to be admitted that the experiment has not fulfilled the high hopes centred upon it. The Patio Restaurant has closed, the gymnasium has gone, the daily services never got off the ground, the congregation has remained small and its activities restricted. The theory, propounded by Campbell Gillon, was the one behind the entire project—that fellowship centred around worship should be the crucial thing in the life of a congregation, and that accordingly a church should be for seven days of the week and not exclusively for the seventh. Could it be that we in Glasgow have not yet come to terms with such an idea, that Campbell was a prophet in advance of his time? Let there be no misunderstanding, the premises are in constant use and fulfil a very necessary function in the city centre and in the life of the Kirk generally—it's just that it is not a Church centre in terms of the vision that inspired it.

From what I have been recounting the reader might well imagine that all my working days in the Presbytery were spent in the company of planners, architects, district valuers. Far from it. This aspect of things was only one of many that made heavy claims on my time and attention. Another call which not only made inroads on time, but could also take heavy toll emotion- ally and spiritually was in the field of what is nowadays generally referred to as 'counselling', 'personal episkope', being pastor pastorum, acting as adviser, friend and comforter to ministers—and others. In the ecumenical debate we Presbyterians are often unfavourably contrasted with our Episcopal brethren under whose system, we are assured, if a minister finds himself in difficulty or trouble, the bishop is always on hand to advise, help, correct. In our case, so the story goes, the unhappy brother has to await a visit from the Superintendence Committee of the Presbytery some weeks later! The one picture, so far as I have been able to discover, is quite as remote from reality as the other. It is, I think, generally accepted among ministers that the Presbytery Clerk is the person to whom to turn in difficulty, but this need not be so, each minister being free to go to whom he will; and it has always seemed to me that the real strength of our position as Clerks in this regard lies in the fact that a man is free to tell us, if he feels that way inclined, where to stuff our advice. The suggestion is occasionally advanced that a senior minister, perhaps retired, might be appointed in each Presbytery as official pastor pastorum. This, I think, would be a grave error. The moment the concept of 'official' creeps in, something of unique value goes out. The man to whom you must go is the man to whom you do not want to go.

I have never been impressed, I must say, by the moving picture sometimes painted of the lonely young minister deep in trouble and not knowing whither to turn for comfort and counsel in his hour of need. What does worry me is the case occurring only too frequently of the lonely young minister deep in trouble, who, if the Angel Gabriel appeared at the manse door, all expenses paid, would respond to his offer of help in some such terms as, 'Good of you to call, but I'm managing very nicely thank you. Do remember me to Mrs Gabriel when you get home'. There is no one more difficult to help than the person who does not need help—at least in his (or her) own judgment. How you get through to such people I just don't know—all I know is that these are the ones in the most desperate need. Only too often, by the time it is possible to intervene in any way, the situation in the congregation has deteriorated far beyond the point where advice can be of much help. Blood-letting is the only remedy.

Requests for advice come in all shapes and sizes. First

there are the straightforward cases of those who simply want information on some matter of fact, or guidance on some question of procedure. Usually the information could have been obtained fairly easily by reference to the Year-Book or to Cox's manual of procedure, but it is less bother to lift the phone and ask the Clerk—after all, what is he paid for? Less bother it may be, but I used to think that if people would just take the trouble to look for the answers to some of their queries, they would in course of their searching find the answers to a lot of other questions. And I did rather resent the man who phoned me at home at night after 11 o'clock to ask some silly unimportant question that wasn't worth asking in the first place. The following yarn has to do not with seeking advice so much as with seeking confrontation. It was at a time when Archbishop Winning had contributed a piece to the evening paper on the subject of football hooliganism, and a number of us had been approached for our reactions, some of which had found their way into print. It was 3.15 in the morning when the phone rang and I found myself (as one does) in the middle of the bedroom floor wondering where I was, and even more urgently wondering where my spectacles were, for without them I am incapable of coherent thought. 'Are you the Mr Herron that had that bit in the paper aboot the fitba'?' was the question. I granted this was so. 'Well, I would like to discuss with you, man to man . . . .' 'Look,' I interrupted, 'I'm not prepared to discuss anything with you at this hour of the morning. Away home and go to your bed.' 'You mean to say you are not prepared to discuss with me, man to man . . . ?' Again I interrupted to say he had got my message right. 'Well,' said he with an air of sad resignation, 'I consider that a very ignorant attitude for you to adopt.' 'You're probably right,' I conceded, 'I'll away to bed and sleep on it. Good morning.' And I hung up. He must have run out of small change or I'm sure he would have rung me back—man to man!

Then there is the minister or office-bearer who comes to you with a problem—which may have to do with the running of an organisation, with the state of the property, with the possibility of buying a new manse, with the proposal to open a betting shop in the middle of the parish, or with any of a host of other subjects. There is no 'personal' element in the equation, it is just a straightforward question of what is the best course to follow. In this field the Clerk can often be of real help. He may well know of a similar situation that occurred somewhere else—it is only very rarely that the problems which beset us are unprecedented—or he may know the proper legal steps to take, or he may be able to indicate where specialist or professional advice may be obtained. At the very least he can often help just by listening to the details of the story, and by skilful questioning can bring out the essential factors in the situation, thereby extricating from the mass of interesting irrelevance what is the real issue to be resolved. I have had many an interesting discussion of this kind.

And then there are the really sticky ones, the problems where personalities are involved, where in truth personalities lie at the heart of the case, where there have been rows, where elders, leaders of organisations, members, have been offended, or, worse still, where the minister's 'dignity' has suffered hurt. Yes, here we move into a much more difficult area. For one thing the Clerk is liable to be approached by both sides. More than once it has happened to me that, while I have been listening to an elder sitting at my desk giving me an account of last night's Session meeting, the minister has come on the phone to discover when I'd be free to see him—'I'd like to have a word with you about a wee thing that arose at last night's Session meeting'. I've even had a buzz from the outer office that the minister was in the waiting room! The saddest case of all is when you have the lady of the manse in your office and her husband in the waiting room. Every Presbytery Clerk's office should be fitted with two doors leading to different passages. However, in that connection it can be both interesting and instructive to hear the same incident described by two opposing parties, each of them doubtless telling the truth. Until you have heard both you are in no position to form a true picture of what actually occurred and therefore to reach any kind of judgment or offer any useful advice.

If this kind of double approach happens to a lawyer he immediately directs one of the parties to another firm. I suppose everyone knows the unkind (and unlikely) story of the sheep farmer near Perth who, on market day, went to see a lawyer in town to consult him about an injustice he had suffered at the hands of a neighbour. The lawyer explained that as it happened the neighbour was a client of his and had just been to see him about this very matter. His visitor seemed dejected. 'If you're worried about whom to consult,' the lawyer said, 'I can give you a note of introduction to a friend of mine who will look after your interests very well.' The offer was gratefully accepted, the note was written and handed over in a sealed envelope. Finding legal interviews drouthy work our farmer decided a dram was called for before venturing on a second go. Under the influence of inspiring bold John Barleycorn he thought he'd have a preview of the letter of introduction. He found that after briefly outlining the facts of the case the couplet had been added, 'Twa woolly hoggs frae the Braes o' Balquhidder; you fleece the ane an' I'll fleece the ither'. Apart from the fact that there was no fleecing to be done in my case, there was the more disturbing fact that there was no obvious person to whom to direct the other party.

There are two quite different motives that may bring a minister to see his Presbytery Clerk in a case of disagreement of this sort. The former is to get an independent, informed, and fair assessment of the situation with a judgment whether he had been right or wrong, and in either case to discuss what the next step should be with a view to restoring peace and amity. The other is to get a defence for what he has done, irrespective of whether it was right or wrong. It is that latter motive that generally takes people to their lawyers. And, I'm sorry to have to say, that is the one that generally brings them to see their Presbytery Clerk. I remember saying once of a certain minister that he came regularly ostensibly to seek my advice, when in fact all he wanted was confirmation of his own stupidity. The most extreme example of this kind of thing in my experience had to do with a minister who one afternoon breezed into the office to tell me he was on his way to see his solicitor to instruct him to buy him a certain house that had just come on the market. I expressed surprise that in his present circumstances he should be thinking about buying a house at all and in particular that house. I lined up all the reasons against such a move, which struck me as the height of madness. He was utterly unconvinced. At length in exasperation I said to him, 'Well, since your mind is obviously made up, the best thing you can do is to get away to your solicitor and get your house bought'. He went and did just that—as he was perfectly entitled to do. What he was not entitled to do, as I learned afterwards from his solicitor, was to say he was doing so on my advice. Although in a literal sense, I suppose, he was right.

In all cases where I recognised a responsibility towards both parties, whether or not I had been consulted by both, my own invariable custom was to give the most honest and impartial opinion I could of the rights and wrongs of the situation, to act as judge rather than as counsel for either side. It didn't come easy, for I would make a better counsel than a judge. Two things in this field have never failed to impress me—how difficult it is to persuade the person in the wrong to admit fault, and how ready the party in the right generally is to forgive fault, even to find excuses for it, if it is freely admitted. The passion for saving face is as intense as it is misguided. We exalt, not demean ourselves, when we frankly confess we have been in the wrong, and that is a lesson we Christians of all people should find easy to learn.

Still another class of suppliant is the person who says he wants advice, but who in truth wants only an ear into which to pour his worries and a shoulder on to which to shed his tears. That is when you have to play a purely passive role, just to listen and to make the odd sympathetic noise. But not to keep looking impatiently at your watch, even although you may be thinking of all the day's work still waiting to be done. The late James Longmuir, our distinguished Assembly Clerk of yesteryear, told me of an occasion when a lady came to seek his advice. She poured out her woes and he listened. When at length she had finished, she thanked him very warmly for his advice; yes, it was clever of him, she saw it all so much more clearly now. The latter part of her message was doubtless true, but it was due not to any far-seeing quality in Jim's advice, since he had never got around to offering any, but just to the fact that she had been obliged to set the whole business forth in some kind of orderly fashion, and in doing so had seen through to the heart of the matter in a way that had eluded her before. The only way in which I personally can ever solve an anagram is to write out the letters in alphabetical order, vowels in one line, consonants in another. Often even before I've finished writing I've seen the answer—something I had been quite incapable of so long as I gazed at the original word.

I think one of the nicest compliments ever paid me came from a minister who had spent a few years with us in Glasgow and who was leaving for a charge in a distant part of the country. He was one of those people who attract trouble, who have an eye for detecting trouble when none is there, and who have no ability for coping with trouble when they do meet it. He had been a frequent visitor to the office. Before leaving us for good he dropped in one morning to say goodbye, and to thank me, because, he said, 'you have always managed to make me feel that my wee problem was the most interesting and important thing you had come across for weeks'. It's the odd remark like that which can make you feel your job has been worth doing.

In connection with the people with personal problems, I used to feel that very often it all ran back into a want of faith—of faith that God is still in command of His world. Myself, I have always found great encouragement in the words of Browning's Pippa who, you remember, greeted the morning with her song that 'God's in His heaven, all's right with the world'. I know very well that this can be seen as sheer blind stupid optimism. But it isn't, you know. For if you can affirm with absolute conviction that God's in His heaven, then you have no alternative but to believe that all's right with His world. If, on the other hand, you conceive an absentee God who has deserted His heaven, then you're bound to see His world going to hell. There is so much wrong in the world, and since God is no longer there we see ourselves in the role of the Salvage Department responsible for putting all things to right from the National Debt to the spread of AIDS, and taking in apartheid in South Africa and civil war in Nicaragua along the way. How often have I said to a man, 'Just you get on and do to the very best of your ability the job for which you were inducted to your parish. Leave something for the Presbytery to do. And leave something for God to do'. It is not an attitude of 'couldn't care less', but a spirit of caring far too intensely, that is causing breakdown in the ministry today.

We hear a great deal about 'ministerial burnout' these days, and indeed a Church group was specially appointed to study the subject. I have my doubts about 'burnout'. As Editor of the Church of Scotland Year-Book, I have to print each year a list of 'Unattached Ministers'—that is, ministers who have demitted their parishes and are now employed as laymen outwith the service of the Church. (It does not mean, as a spinster daughter of the Manse once suggested to me, ministers looking for wives.) It is a list which grows longer each year, and at a rate which I find disturbing. At the moment there are 283 ministers in secular employment, as against 1289 in parishes. Of the former, 54 had given from five to ten years' service, and 67 five years or less. In no fewer than 15 cases, students had been ordained as Assistants and had opted out of the ministry without ever holding a charge. This is a situation demanding careful study, but I don't believe it has anything to do with burnout. It would, I think, be fair comment that if a man is burned out within five years of ordination, he couldn't have had much spiritual fuel in the cellar to start with. Not burnout but disillusion is the trouble in many cases. For the ministry can be a most discouraging task. In this materialist age when all our tests are based on figures, it would be nice to be able, as you go on with your ministry, to feed figures of hours spent and miles travelled, of sermons preached and prayers offered, of visits paid and counsel given, into some glorified computer and come out with an index of efficiency. But, as we all know, in the ministry this is something we cannot do. When I was nominated as Moderator I was interviewed by Dorothy Grace Elder. She quoted me as follows: 'I think it is not surprising that in a technological age such as ours, when it is possible to assess things fairly accurately in material terms, it is very very difficult to believe sometimes that you are achieving much in the ministry. You cannot feed the results of twenty years' ministry into a computer and come out with anything very encouraging,' he said, rather wistfully, then added, with typical Herron humour, 'But it could be that when the Great Computer issues its figures on the judgment day it will appear that it has not been wholly wasted time. At least that is the faith in which some of us plod on'. *Typical Herron humour*, my foot!—I was never more serious in my life.

By far the most difficult and distressing problem that comes the way of the Presbytery Clerk is represented by the case where he is consulted by a minister who has become the subject of what in the Kirk is called a fama, a scandalous report, where, in short, he is being accused of some grave moral fault. Let it be that he has been charged by the police with drunk-driving, or with embezzlement of some fund of which he was treasurer, or that he has become amorously attached to the lady organist, or that he is alleged to have been involved in some homosexual misdemeanour, and that he approaches the Clerk for advice. This is a very dangerous area—a positive mine-field—for there is every likelihood that action will have to be taken against him, a libel raised in the Presbytery, and if that is so the Clerk will in normal circumstances have to lead the prosecution. Obviously it would be shamefully contrary to justice for one who in the end is to act as prosecutor, acting at the outset as confidant. In a situation of this kind, it has been my own custom to tell the person concerned, as soon as I dis-covered the nature of the problem, that I was in this position, and that while I should be happy to guide him in relation to the procedure that would be followed, and so on, if he wanted someone in whom to confide or someone to help with the preparation of his defence, he should turn elsewhere.

It is never a pleasant task being prosecutor, particularly when the accused has been a friend, and yet I think it is most important that the task should be undertaken and faithfully discharged, for I am sure that in these cases we should be more diligent than we often are in carrying to a proper conclusion the trial of those who are believed to have been guilty of grievous fault. I know, of course, that we will be told about Christian charity and all that, but my recollection of the Sermon on the Mount is that Christian charity comes into the picture after, and not instead, of the application of the law; that the second mile begins only when the 1760th yard of the first mile has been traversed, that love is a supplement to and not a substitute for the law.

What in fact almost invariably happens in these cases is roughly this. A minister obviously guilty of some grievous fault offers to resign his charge and to slip quietly out of the picture on some plea of ill-health backed up by a certificate from his doctor saying he has been under stress. It is very tempting to accept the offer—no fuss, no nasty trial, no reporters hanging around, no dirty linen. I am not satisfied that these arguments should persuade us to neglect our obvious duty. It has always been a contention of mine that there is no shame in having dirty linen, the shame lies in never being seen going to the laundry. If the person is prepared to make an admission, then there need be no trial, but there will be a judgment and that will go on to the record. If he denies all guilt then he is entitled to a trial, for that is the only way to clear his name. We can be weaving a very tangled web when we take the cowardly way out of a difficult situation.

Things inevitably assume a different complexion when the charge likely to be involved is one of heresy, for in such a case the issue to be determined by the Presbytery will be one of relevance rather than a question of fact. Not, Was the statement made? but, Is it heretical? What exactly he said or wrote will generally be admitted (if not actually loudly and even proudly proclaimed) by the accused; but it will be his contention that what he said represents the truth as revealed in Scripture, while it is the Church, in so far as it differs from this, which is in error. There can be little harm in the Clerk freely discussing such matters with any of his people. It is a long time now since the Assembly was last seriously exercised with a heresy trial—the nearest thing being when a year or two ago the question of 'second baptism' arose. The cynic would say that, in the present state of uncertainty as to what is orthodoxy, it would be quite impossible to prove that anything was heretical. That is not quite true, for a situation can arise where some overt act is involved—such as a member being baptized a second time, or a minister refusing to ordain a woman elder—and here the issue takes on sharp lines and, in defence of the rights of other people as well as in self-defence, the most liberal of Church courts is bound to take action.

From all of the foregoing it will be apparent that for the Presbytery Clerk the field of counselling can be both wide and interesting, beset with pitfalls as well as offering rich rewards. Indeed I was intrigued at a recent conference of Presbytery Clerks to be told by some that the pastoral side of the job is becoming the biggest and the most demanding part. It is good that in a day when the mechanical side of the job seems to be demanding more attention, the human element should still command top place.

I remarked earlier that in my time in Glasgow I had been involved in the opening of twenty-five new churches. In that same period of twenty-one years I was involved in the closing of nearly a hundred. About each one of these it could be said, in the words of the Psalmist, that for some its very dust to them was dear. But honesty compels me to add that in some of the cases the dust had lain undisturbed for quite some time. I am reminded of an application form for a fabric grant which explained that there was a serious outbreak of dry rot in the vestibule and they had decided to put down new linoleum! The demands of readjustment have constituted one of the most urgent and acute problems confronting us in the Presbytery over these years. It was bound to be so, for we were grossly over-stocked with churches.

At the turn of the century when the UP and the Free Churches united to form the United Free Church, there were usually at least three Presbyterian denominations with a place of worship in each district—there was the old Parish church, usually a quoad sacra dating from the latter half of last century, there was the UP church, descendant of one of the eighteenth century secessions, and there was the Free church, child of the Disruption of 1843. So long as people still felt bitterly about the issues that had divided them in an earlier day, all three churches were needed. But the Union of 1900 bringing Free and UP together, was followed by the Union of 1929 gathering all three into the fellowship of one reunited Church of Scotland. So there was no longer any justification on doctrinal grounds for the continuance of all three. But I am afraid our divisions are often founded on personal rather than doctrinal differences and congregations still looked across the street at one another with suspicion, even if they no longer glowered with the open hostility they had once shown. From the population point of view, the situation was positively alarming. I remember as a schoolboy being proud to know that Glasgow was 'the Second City' with a population of a million and a quarter. We are today talking in terms of 800,000—of two where there had been three. But since my time at school, vast housing schemes have been developed in the fields to which we used to travel by train for our Sunday School picnic, and it is estimated that some 400,000 of our people are now living in these far-flung places. This reduces today's population in the old city and its suburbs to 400,000—where there had been three there is now one. If, then, we were grossly overchurched in 1929, what is the position today when the catchment area for these congregations contains only one-third of what it once did? And that is taking no account whatsoever of the fact, generally conceded, that a smaller proportion of the people is within the membership of the Church. Can anyone deny that some kind of re-appraisal, re-arrangement, rationalisation, readjustment—call it what you will—is a must.

Not very long after I came to Glasgow I was approached by Peter Bissett, who was then minister of one of the Dennistoun congregations, regarding a meeting he was organising of all the office-bearers of local congregations, to discuss the future prospects in the area generally. He wanted me to set Dennistoun in its place in the city scene. It was a well-attended gathering at which, I think I am right in saying, eleven congregations—all good healthy congregations—were represented. By this time, though, the rot was beginning to set in, the character of Dennistoun was changing radically. I pointed out that in the previous year they had among them lost something like 900 members. That really meant the loss of one whole congregation, even if it was spread over the eleven of them. Given a continuance of the trend for a couple of years more, they would be down effectively to eleven congregations with the proper membership for eight, each of them struggling for survival against steadily increasing odds. It was clear that all this was new thinking for them and we were beginning to get a very useful discussion launched as to what might be done, until one elder arose and made an impassioned (and carefully prepared) speech to the effect that come hell, high water, depopulation, Presbytery Readjustment Committee or whatever, his congregation would certainly continue—his congregation being at that time, incidentally, the weakest of the eleven! This inevitably led others to stake a claim in the future for their particular cause and the worthwhile part of the meeting was at an end. There are today three congregations in place of the eleven—and even so they are having their difficulties. I don't know that there was anything we could have done to stop this, the forces being beyond our control, but we could certainly have taken steps to make the transition less painful for those involved and less hurtful to the cause of the Kirk.

Some time later I myself convened a meeting to which I invited eight congregations in the more or less immediate neighbourhood of Kelvingrove Park to send a couple of representatives each. With the relentless spread westward of city office premises, the resident population was disappearing and things were becoming very difficult for these congregations. After I had outlined the problem as I saw it, and indicated certain aspects of it that I felt we could profitably discuss, I threw the meeting open for contributions. One elder, a very able man from whom I would have expected better things, took the floor and read us a long prepared speech designed to show that his congregation was completely immune from any of the difficulties outlined and that it had a future that would extend for ever and ever, Amen. The pattern being thus set, we had similar, if more off-the-cuff, performances all round and the meeting closed to the satisfaction of all concerned—with the exception of the Presbytery Clerk. It would have been so much easier to discuss these situations when all the congregations had ministers and none of them felt under threat. Today, of these eight congregations, only one remains.

It is a well-established fact that in our gardens it is pruning that inspires growth and makes for health, but it is a lesson we in the Kirk are sweirt to learn. It is sad that our people so utterly refuse to recognise the advantages that can come from the union of two congregations, advantages that accrue only if the union is undertaken early enough, when both are still relatively strong. This is a theme on which I can speak from experience. In 1949, while I was minister at Houston, we in the former Parish church had a union with what had been the Free church in the village. Certainly they had lost their building by fire some years earlier, so the question of which building would be used did not create the usual bitterness. Both sides were at heart happy to accept the inevitable (even if some felt bound to make symbolic noises of protest) and we both went into the venture determined to make it work—and it did. In my opinion that union was one of the best things that ever happened in the religious life of the community. The trouble so often is that people put off uniting until they are too weak and too weary to resist any longer, and, the other half being in the same unhappy state of exhaustion, the inevitable result is that they have no strength left to make the thing work. Thus instead of two congregations crumbling into the ground, you find yourself with one nominally larger congregation doing just that.

Up until now the driving force behind the call for readjustment has come from the shortage of ministers. It would be my guess that from now on the impetus will be supplied by the deteriorating condition of church property. The Church of Scotland is today facing a major fabric crisis. Some idea of its extent may be gained from considering that in our Presbytery alone, in the first six months of a recent year, applications for permission to carry out major repairs to Church property came to a total of just under £1 million. When you realise that outlays of under £6000 do not need to be reported, you end up with a figure well over the million mark—for half a year! This works out at rather more than £20 per annum for every nominal member on our books, and that is just about one half of the total giving per nominal member for all purposes. We are, then, spending half of our income in supporting what are all too often tottering properties, which in many cases are really not needed —and it is difficult indeed to see how such a proposition can be justified. It would seem essential that some of that property —buildings which are no longer truly necessary for the ongoing work and witness of the Kirk—should be unloaded, and any capital recovered therefrom invested to form a Fabric Fund for the maintenance of the buildings that remain. It is not a cheering prospect. In fact, I'm rather relieved to be retired.

A town planner, a father-confessor for ministers, an ecclesiastical marriage broker for congregations—the Clerk is also expected in his idle moments to be a Clerk in the traditional sense, to keep minutes, to prepare agendas, to arrange meetings, to organise special services for the licensing of students, for the induction of ministers, for the commissioning of deaconesses, for the dedication of new buildings, to attend to correspondence. All of that can add up to quite something, and I have done my full share of it all. I look now at a shelf which carries ten fat volumes of minutes of the Presbytery covering these years, and realise that I wrote every word that is there, and I was involved—usually to a greater rather than a lesser extent—in every item of business that is recorded there, I feel that I must have been kept fairly busy! The record of it surely makes up in bulk what it lacks in literary excellence.

They were for me twenty-two memorable years, and if in the course of them, I was enabled to do something to advance the work of the Kirk in this city of my birth, and to help its hard-wrought ministers, I have certainly been more than adequately rewarded.

Chapter 5
The Cost of Conservation

ENVIRONMENT-CONSCIOUS is a term that has recently entered our vocabulary; it describes a condition widespread today as never before. Not only have we become acutely alive to the extent to which environment affects our characters and shapes our lives, we have come also to appreciate that environment is, to a considerable extent, what we are determined to make it—if only we are sufficiently determined. No longer will we permit our pleasant green places to be cluttered with the senseless sprawl of urban development, no longer will we allow our atmosphere to be polluted with the smoke from factory chimneys, or our rivers with the filth of industrial effluent. Our fathers were a bit fatalistic about the whole affair, allowing economic considerations to dictate the pattern of development; we have come to treasure the earth's resources—those which nature itself provides ready-made and free of charge, and those that are man-made at a price. It is good that it should be so.

In practical terms there are two sides to this movement—the new cannot be left to develop in haphazard fashion, neither can the old be left at the mercy of the principles that determine survival in a hard competitive world. The best from the past has to be deliberately preserved. So the local authority cannot be just a planning body with an eye to the future, it must also be a conservation authority with an eye on the past. And to encourage authority in this latter activity, voluntary societies of one sort and another have sprung up—a conservation lobby—and these have acquired a degree of influence far beyond anything to which I personally think they are entitled. Influence without obligation I have always seen as a highly dangerous thing.

Legislation has also been introduced whereby buildings of particular architectural or historic significance may be 'listed', thus enormously restricting the power of the owner to alter or to

95

dispose of his property without the say-so of the local authority (and in the last resort of the Secretary of State), and creating for the unfortunate owner all kinds of problems when he has no longer any use for his property.

This was a field in which during my years as Presbytery Clerk, I often found my views at variance with those of authority, and still more often with those of the 'lobby' (if you can have a lobby in a field!), a field in which I was only too often in open hostility even with popular opinion. It was a field in which inevitably I had a very real and deep concern, for the great bulk of Scotland's listed buildings are Church buildings, and Glasgow has its full share of them. There were times when I felt it had more than its fair share. And with the rapidly and radically changing character of the city during that period, the future of these buildings often presented truly baffling problems. Movement of population would leave a church of considerable architectural importance without a congregation. For us it had no continuing use, but it was still of great architectural significance—what was to be done with it? Controversy would erupt, and I seemed invariably to appear on the side of the Philistines—indeed I was, I'm sure, seen by many of the self-appointed Davids as Goliath, chief of the Philistines!

Let me at this early stage seek to make clear just where I stand in relation to this important principle of conservation, this determination to preserve all that is best in our heritage, whether in the natural world of God's creating where so many agencies are busy corrupting and polluting, or in the artistic world of man's designing where the often senseless demand for change ('progress' those who have a vested interest call it) can lead to the destruction of priceless treasures. I should say right away and without hesitation that I am whole-heartedly in favour of preservation.

I am, I say, wholly with the conservationists in declaring that no thing of beauty, whether in nature or art, should be allowed to be wantonly destroyed. Unhappily this, like so many statements of principle, can be entirely acceptable without being very helpful. And even after we have accepted it, we have to go a stage further. We have to declare that the thing of beauty shall not be the subject of careless neglect, for in the case of buildings at least, moth and rust, dry rot and nail sickness, broken gutters and choked rones are vandals every whit as ruthless as any gang of city desperados. Now it has to be granted that property owners can be careless, selfish, unconcerned; they can even be unaware of the treasure that is in their keeping; or (as more often happens) keenly aware and deeply concerned but too impoverished to do anything about it.

It is at this point that conservation enters upon the scene with its demand that things of beauty, significance and historic interest shall be maintained in a proper state of repair and shall not be demolished or drastically altered at the whim of the owner. He, willy-nilly, is appointed a kind of trustee of the property, the true beneficial owner being the public at large. As such they are awarded rights far in excess of those they would enjoy under any normal trust deed. It is precisely here that I find myself with grave reservations. The ultimate goal I am still happy to accept, but I am not satisfied that we are achieving it in a way that will be crowned with success. In any case I believe that our methods are neither fair nor equitable from the point of view of the owner—the trustee-in-spite-of-himself. By shutting our eyes to important implications we have been able to over-simplify the problem. We have not, I am sure, thought the business through in all its implications, and I am convinced it is high time we were making a deliberate and constructive attempt to do just that.

It is true, I imagine, of any city that its churches will be among the most prominent and distinctive of all its buildings, that church steeples, pinnacles, and towers will be the outstanding features of its skyline. I imagine, further, that people with an interest in some famous architect will be keen to see preserved some example of how this man of genius tackled the brief of designing a church. It will also be inevitable that fragments of pre-Reformation architecture will be almost wholly confined within the ecclesiastical sphere. Thus the Church will always be at the receiving end of the activities of the conservationists. In short, the Church has a major interest. Yet, so far as I know, she has never been consulted on the issue as a whole.

While the Church will be happy to accept realistic claims by the conservationists and to co-operate in helpful schemes, she has at all times to insist that for her the ultimate question

must be how far any proposal contributes to advancing the ends
of the Kingdom of God. Architectural excellence must be for
her a secondary consideration. As I have reiterated *ad nauseam*
over the years, ours is a Ministry of the Word, not a Ministry of
Works; we exist to build up living congregations, not to shore
up dying buildings; our concern is with people, not with stone
and mortar. So that when, for example, a choice has to be made
between two buildings, the former a fine cruciform gothic
structure with unique fenestration, comfortless and unheatable,
with scant hall accommodation, set on top of a hill, and the
latter a couthy but shapeless building, with lots of halls stuck on
at odd corners, situated on a main street near the centre of the
parish, there is little doubt that the Presbytery will go for the
latter, however great the annoyance caused to the conservationists who extol the artistic merits of the former. The
same kind of situation can arise when a building with claims to
be preserved is no longer suited as a place of worship for the
people of that district, for the suitability of a place of worship
can alter with the changing years and can vary between one
community and another.

A striking example of what I have in mind was provided
by the church of St George's in the Fields at the top of St
George's Road, close to the Round Toll.

Until early in the nineteenth century, Glasgow's western
extremity was to all intents and purposes represented by the line
of Buchanan Street—beyond that lay the wilderness! When in
1807 St George's Church (now commonly referred to as 'The
Tron') was opened in that street, a contemporary writer put on
record that it was 'upon the extreme verge of the city—all
beyond was entirely rural', and hinted that 'it being so far in the
country it could not be expected that the inhabitants of the town
could venture for worship there in dark nights.' It was not
strictly true that all beyond was rural, for to the north west
stretched a series of quarries that, in their day, had supplied the
stone for the building of the city. By 1824, however, the
development had spread as far as the top of St George's Road
and a church was built there in that year—it was an offshoot of
St George's in Buchanan Street and, appropriately, was called St
George's in the Fields. It was erected on what was known as the
Black Quarry. A small village lay to the north, but it was

surrounded by fields. Some sixty years later (in 1866) when the fields were no more than a fragrant memory, Hugh and David Barclay designed and built the imposing structure that was to serve the congregation for the next century. A massive affair standing away above the level of the road, with its six enormous pillars crowned with sculptured pediment, it has been described as the last great work of *ancient régime* classicism. Seated for perhaps 1200, it was for many years well supported and very well attended. It also constituted a formidable local landmark.

But, as we all know, fifty years can change a district out of all recognition with a corresponding effect on its parish church. In the thirties the congregation of St George's in the Fields had been in the 1300 member bracket; by the seventies it had fallen to one-tenth of that figure. The writing on the wall was as clear as the graffiti contributed by the vandals. The inevitable happened in June 1980 when what was left of the congregation sought dissolution.

What to do with the building? Ruthlessly to demolish so grand a stucture, to remove so conspicuous a landmark, was a possibility to be considered only as a last resort; planning permission would certainly be refused, and in any case the cost of demolition would far surpass the value of the cleared site, and, anyway, who would foot the bill? The first suggestion made to us was, predictably, that we should continue to use it as a place of worship. Now it was true that a certain amount of house building had occurred in the near vicinity. Why should we not tidy the place up and make a fresh start? To the 'lobby' this seemed the obvious solution. What the lobby did not, or would not, recognise was that the people who were living in these new flats were not of the sort to take kindly to massive pillars and embossed pediments and *ancient régime* classicism—they wanted their religion in homelier terms. There are people like that. In the course of a television interview on the site, at the stage when the controversy had reached 'the box', I remarked that the local man would feel a bowler hat and a rolled umbrella were *de rigeur* for passing through these lofty portals—and as his wardrobe did not rise to such refinements he would stay at home. I went on to say in all seriousness that if you built me a modest hut on the patch of muddy ground at the side of the church, I'd be prepared to conduct a mission there with some hope of success, but never—no, never—in that splendid morgue behind the pillars. In any case it was far too big, at least three times too big. As a sanctuary it had conclusively established itself as a failure. Why not accept that?

Nor would it readily lend itself to conversion. A number of clubs, businesses and individuals inspected the property, but all for one reason or another decided it was not for them. And it was not the price that frightened them, for we were offering it for nothing. It need hardly be added that, while all this inspecting was going on, the condition of the property was steadily deteriorating. Oddly enough the church had not been too badly vandalised—even the vandals, it seemed, were over-awed by its grandeur (witness how the adjoining hall had been torn to shreds).

I have, I hope, established my point that an acute problem arises regarding the cost of maintaining a building specifically designed as a church when, in its particular location, it can no longer be advantageously used in that capacity. And I must insist that it is the Church and not the planning authority—still less the conservation society—that is to be the final arbiter on what is 'suitable'. It appears to me that there should be provision whereby, except in the most exceptional circum-stances, such a building may be demolished, but not, of course, until a full photographic and other record has been made for the interest and information of future generations. A derelict building is a credit to no one, a gothic church converted into a furniture store, a cash-and-carry, a garage, is a shoddy memorial to the genius of any great architect.

Although, as I say, I think I have established my point, I feel I should not leave the story of St George's in the Fields without adding an intriguing postscript regarding an incident which had its amusing aspect, but which had also a sinister side and could well have landed me at the wrong end of a prosecution.

The interior of the church was plain to the point of drabness, although it is true that the materials were all of a high quality. One feature which stood out was a beautifully carved oak pulpit of the free-standing egg-cup variety. The pews were solid, of good hardwood and had rather attractive haffets. While we were still looking for a user, I had a visit at my office from a minister of a Free Church congregation on one of the western isles, who wondered whether we could sell him a few pews from a disused church. I took him up to St George's in the Fields and he was thrilled at the idea that he could remove half a dozen pews free of charge and with our blessing. What, I went on to ask, were his chances of finding a home for the pulpit? The joiner who was there to advise about the pew removal was all enthusiasm, pointing out that the pulpit had been so masterfully constructed that when a certain key panel was removed the whole affair would come apart. It would be simplicity itself to dismantle, transport and re-erect. As I was at this time daily expecting to hear that the whole place had been set on fire, I readily agreed to removing the pulpit, and six—maybe eight—pews.

Imagine my surprise when, only a few days later, I was the recipient from the appropriate department of the District Council of a formal document informing me that certain articles of furnishing were missing from this listed building and that it was understood they had been removed with my authority, wanting to know what steps I proposed to take to have them restored, and enquiring whether I had anything to say regarding why they should not institute proceedings against me in terms of the relevant Act so-and-so, Section such-and-such. It gave me a lot of satisfaction in replying to point out that the Act which they quoted was not in fact the 'relevant Act'. Apart from that, my reply amounted to 'Prosecute and be Damned!' In view of the very close and friendly fashion in which I had always worked with the planners in a host of difficult cases over the years—not least in the present case—it seemed to me a peculiar way of proceeding. Had some official come to see me and 'torn strips off me' I should have taken no offence—even if reserving the right to do some strip-tearing in return. But to threaten me with an action and to do so by Recorded Delivery! Why must some officials be so officious? I had some words off the record in the right quarter and in the event it was decided that since the articles removed were continuing in ecclesiastical use, my misdemeanour would be overlooked. They didn't disclose which section of which Act they were invoking here. I had up my sleeve what I considered a sound defence and would have welcomed a forum from which to expound some of my way-out views on conservation. But that's not really the way I like to do business.

In the course of these observations about our difficulties with St George's in the Fields, I have spoken of the impossibility of using an otherwise adequate church building in the place where it happens to be situated. It is there that so often the rub can lie. The building is admirable in every way if only it were somewhere else. I have often said that if we could find a contractor with a big enough low-loader, and a plant hirer with a heavy enough crane, and if our roads were just that wee bit wider, we could solve a lot of our building problems to the complete satisfaction of all concerned. Yet even without these advantages, a church can be moved—stone by stone if needs be—and this has twice been proved within our own Presbytery. It occurred before my time in Glasgow, but I remember the events clearly and the facts are well recorded.

In 1895 H E Clifford, who designed so much of Pollokshields, was responsible for a very fine structure erected for the Church of Scotland in that area. The ground, which had been a farmyard, was the gift of Sir John Stirling Maxwell. It stood back to back with a UP Church, was less than two hundred yards from a Free Church, and was within a quarter of a mile of the Parish Church of Pollokshields—a degree of proximity at that time quite acceptable. The cause, 'Titwood', had been functioning from an iron building since its inception nine years earlier. Of necessity the congregation had a very restricted catchment area which became distinctly more limited after the Union of the Churches in 1929. By 1941 a union was effected with the Parish Church and the building became superfluous to requirements. In March 1943 the Alexander (Greek) Thomson church in Langside Road was completely destroyed by fire as a result of enemy action and the homeless congregation found shelter in the vacant Titwood building where they continued for three years until they went to Camphill, leaving the fine premises once more unoccupied.

In 1948 the Presbytery, with the backing of National Church Extension, established a new charge in temporary hall accommodation in the vast housing area that had grown up to the south of the city in Pollok, and the following year it was resolved to move the empty buildings to the site which the Corporation had made available there. This was a completely new idea, quite a venture of faith, and the exercise occupied all of three years and cost a great deal of money, considerably more than a new suite of buildings would have done. On the other hand, it provided magnificent premises in which the new congregation could spread itself, it set up a landmark in an otherwise dreary scene, and it had a life expectancy far in excess of anything we could possibly have put there in contemporary idiom and materials. Today the building stands proudly, the one thing of architectural significance in a housing wilderness, a tribute to the vision and faith of those who thought up the unthinkable.

The second case also had its starting point in Pollokshields. At the western end of that district, the Church of Scotland erected, as recently as 1908, at the junction of Sherbrooke and Hamilton Avenues, a splendid suite of buildings in red sandstone, 'St Gilbert's'. A couple of hundred yards away was a Free Church, and it is not surprising that the people of St Gilbert's in due time found their way down the hill to unite with their near neighbours, leaving their fine building untenanted. Away back in 1925 there had been a proposal to erect a church in Burnside, that fast growing suburb on the fringe of Rutherglen. Difficulties arose, and it was after many vicissitudes that, in 1939, plans for a church were finally prepared and approved. But the outbreak of war brought the whole venture to an end. In 1947 negotiations were begun for the transportation of the St Gilbert's buildings to a most prominent site in Burnside, and, although it was not until 1954 that the Church was ready for dedication, it stands there today, a thing of great dignity and beauty—and of real Christian usefulness. And although it cost a lot of money, it has been worth every penny.

These two experiences had inspired confidence in the feasibility, as well as the economic viability, of transporting a good suite of buildings to a new location where there was a job for them to do. And it was the success of these ventures which led me into what proved to be an abortive effort to solve the problem of the future of the Greek Thomson church in Caledonia Road. The story of that building is intensely interesting. It began almost two hundred years ago and its final chapter has yet to be written.

In the year 1799, as the land on the south side of the Clyde was beginning to be developed for residential purposes, the Relief Church set up business in Hospital Street. By the early

1850s, this building was in need of considerable repairs. There arose, it would seem, difference of opinion within the congregation (which by that time was of the United Presbyterian persuasion), some favouring repair while others advocated the erection of a new church on a fresh site. The former group carried the day and set about their task with such effect that, when it was completed, it was said of it, 'there is no church on the south side more cheerful or comfortable, although externally it still wears something of its original aspect'. Meanwhile the defeated minority approached the Presbytery with a petition for permission to form a new charge, and this being granted the congregation of Caledonia Road, as it was to become, came into being. They engaged the services of Alexander (Greek) Thomson to design a church to fill the gusset site bounded by Cathcart Road, Hospital Street and Caledonia Road, with a fairly narrow frontage on to the last named. This was to be the first of three Glasgow churches which this so distinctive architect would design (St Vincent Street and Queen's Park St George's being the others) and some would say it was his best. It was dedicated on 22nd March 1857.

By anyone's standards the church was of impressive and original design, flanked by a great square tower of Lombardic pattern and carrying a row of massive pillars over the portico. It is known that Thomson devoted a great deal of study to this work, which has been declared as one of the great monuments of nineteenth century architecture. It has to be added, though, that while the interior of the church was attractive, bright, commodious and out of the ordinary, the ancillary accommodation was scant and inadequate, the main hall being (by reason of the gusset site) almost triangular in shape.

As the nineteenth century moved over into the twentieth, the whole character of Gorbals deteriorated, so that by 1924 the congregation was happy to be joined by what had been its parent body and had by then become 'Hutchesontown', and the new congregation struggled on in the face of difficulties and adversities. In 1960, shortly after I became Clerk, thieves one night raided the roof of the church, stripping off and removing all the lead, of which there was a substantial amount. Undaunted, the congregation scraped together the funds needed to have the whole roof repaired and the lead replaced, this time with copper. On their return some weeks later to do a repeat job, the thieves were so incensed at the deception practised on them that they stripped off all the copper, throwing it down into a neighbouring backyard. And they didn't think it was worth their while to remove it. The congregation took the view that enough was enough and approached the Presbytery with a plea to be dissolved, which they were at the close of 1963.

The Presbytery now found itself in the position of having on its hands a quite unique listed building with no congregation to occupy it and no hope of ever establishing one, and with the rain literally falling direct into the interior. I considered I had done a very good job when I persuaded the Corporation that this truly remarkable building, being in such parlous condition and there being no funds with which to carry out repairs, should be purchased by themselves and protective action taken. This they did, paying us a nominal purchase price. Without delay they proceeded—at considerable cost—to make the structure water-tight. They also tried very hard indeed to find a user, all kinds of suggestions—from a small theatre (taking in part of the adjoining tenement property in Hospital Street for backstage facilities) to a kickabout pitch for a local boys' club—being explored, with a signal lack of success.

This was when I approached the officials with a pro-position. There were, around the fringe of the city, I suggested, many dreary, featureless housing estates, some of them still awaiting the erection of a church which would likely be dull enough architecturally to match admirably its surroundings. Why, I asked, could the Corporation not do what we had done with such success at Pollok and Burnside, and move the Greek Thomson building stone by stone to a site in an area where a church was desperately needed. They could then lease the property to us and we would undertake to keep it in use and to maintain it in good repair. We would also undertake to erect a range of halls in the same idiom and materials so that it would 'read in' with the church, spending as much on these as we would normally do on an entire project. In this way we should have a church in use for the purpose for which it was designed by one of the nation's greatest architects, in an area where it was needed and in a position where it would lend character to an otherwise drab environment. And we wouldn't really be saving money, merely spending money to save a masterpiece

The officials were interested—intensely so—and I was invited to present my case to 'the politicians' at a meeting of the Planning Committee. This I did with all the eloquence at my command, only to be laughed out of court as an idle dreamer. I wasn't so much as asked a single question. I am sorry to have to record that I have rarely been treated with such discourtesy, being nodded rather than bowed out of the chamber within ten minutes of entering it. I did pause long enough on the threshold to remind them that the Greek Thomson building in Caledonia Road was their problem, not mine. It is still their problem, and twenty-five years later still waiting to be solved.

It was not long after this fruitless meeting (in 1965) that vandals set fire to the church, which was completely gutted, leaving only the great square Lombardic tower and the pillars that stand above the portico. I find it interesting when, from time to time, the suggestion is quite seriously advanced that the building should be transported and re-erected simply as a monument in the 'culture area' that is to be created around the north end of Buchanan Street. Meantime the gaunt ruin stands there, a pathetic monument to architectural genius and to official indecision.

I am still convinced that my proposal was sound in every way. The building is so distinctive in character that it could find a future only as a church. There was no need, and no hope of creating a need, for a church in that particular place— incidentally the site is now part of a vast traffic island. If then the building is of supreme importance, and I am sure it is, public funds could have been properly spent in moving the structure to a new site where it could have brought distinction and beauty to a whole area. The ways of alleviating deprivation are many and varied.

To revert to this business of the listing of buildings, it has always been my contention that some opportunity should be provided for the owner, or indeed for any other party having an interest, to contest the issue before the listing order is put on. As things are, the decision to list your property is made without any consultation with you. Now the law (rightly) requires that you be officially notified and given an opportunity to make representations before your neighbour can make any alterations to his premises. Yet your property may be far more seriously and detrimentally affected by listing than by the worst your neighbour could do. Yet you are given no comparable opportunity to object. One of the effects of listing can be, for example, to make it difficult, if not impossible, to obtain planning permission for its demolition, thus locking what may be a very valuable site so that the owner can in no way realise its value. For this to happen without his being given so much as the chance of bidding farewell to his asset, has always to me seemed less than just.

The listing seems to be done in a completely peremptory, if not cavalier, fashion. I am not sure that the owner needs to be informed that it is happening, only that it has happened! Listing also has the effect of locking everything inside the building (witness my experience with the pews) yet it appears to be done without the need even to examine the interior to see what it contains: many of our buildings that are listed have got into that state without our being approached for access. Strictly speaking, of course, it is the Secretary of State who does the listing, but he does it on the representation of the local authority which reaches its decision, so far as I know, without the need to consult anyone. When, as has frequently happened, I have expressed misgivings about this kind of procedure, I have been assured that the owner can appeal later to have his property taken off the list—to become, presumably, a 'Delisted building'—we already have A, B and C. To turn things around in this way, to put sentence before trial, I had always thought of as 'Jeddart justice', a system never held in high esteem in the best legal circles. I must repeat that for my asset to be frozen in this fashion, without my being given a chance so much as to state a case, seems to me to be grossly unfair. *Audi alterem partem* and all that! What about the principles of natural justice?

For argument's sake suppose that the Park Church in Lynedoch Place (of which I shall have more to say hereunder) had belonged to an individual, let's say to an impoverished elderly lady. When at long last permission was obtained for its development, it realised a tidy £125,000 (a lot of money in the mid sixties) so that our elderly lady was not so impoverished—she was on the contrary a very wealthy citizen. Yet while the conservationists were arguing about whether her property was to go into deep freeze or just into the fridge, she could have died of hypothermia for want of the price of a bag of coal.

In fairness I have to concede that no matter what opportunity was provided for resisting having your property listed, it would have been unlikely to have saved the Park Church from that fate. That, however, does not apply in every case and I am sure there are many instances of buildings going on the list when they do not deserve such treatment. In that context there was the case of Gorbals John Knox Church in Carlton Place facing the river, which in my view should never have been listed and which caused us a great deal of needless difficulty and brought on our heads a load of unmerited criticism. To pick up the beginnings of the Gorbals Saga, one has to dig fairly deep into Glasgow's history.

It was away back in 1450 that, at the instance of Lady Lochnawe, there was founded on the south side of the river, at what was later to become Hospital Street, a hospital for lepers dedicated to St Ninian, and there until the early part of the seventeenth century charitable work continued to be done. It is hard to understand why it should not have been until the early nineteenth century that the parish of Gorbals first began to attract housing, but it is clear that the development once begun proceeded apace. A Chapel of Ease had been established in 1730, but it was during the ministry of James M'Lean that the population flocked across the river—it was said that his forty years' ministry saw the population increase from 500 to 35,000.

In 1810 they got around to building a new church in Carlton Place, a reasonably attractive affair with a fine steeple, internally furnished in lavish style, and here the congregation grew steadily. It would seem, though, that at the Disruption in 1843 a great number went over to the Free Church, so that those who were left experienced a particularly hard time—so much so, apparently, that the feu duty, which was unusually high, fell into arrears, with the result that in 1852, at the insistance of the superior, the building was adjudicated and put up for public roup. A number of gentlemen of the Free persuasion clubbed together, bought the property (for £2800), and handed it over to be the place of worship of the new (Free) East Gorbals Territorial congregation. Ten years later the original congregation, whose fortunes had by now considerably revived, exercised its right to clear its debts and buy back the church. Understandably enough this was disputed, but it was upheld in the Court of Session and the property in Carlton Place became once again Gorbals Parish Church, spiritual home of a bien congregation of dwellers in the very grand spacious homes in and around Abbotsford Place. As a matter of interest it might be added that the dispossessed Free Church congregation moved south and built themselves a fine church in the gusset at Eglinton Toll formed by Victoria and Pollokshaws Roads, a building that was burned to the ground in March 1929. To this last fact I can bear personal testimony. Walking home from my work in the *Herald* in the early hours of that morning, I formed, for a little time, part of the group of interested spectators at the blaze.

That year, 1929, was an unhappy one for Gorbals churches, for on the night of Sunday 8th December the steeple of the church in Carlton Place was struck by lightning and partially demolished. It was a considerably truncated affair that was substituted when rebuilding was undertaken. In these years too a suite of halls had been added at the side of the church building, reproducing more or less the Church's gable frontage on to the street, so that there were now twin gables, one of which was surmounted by a stumpy tower, the result being a decidedly lop-sided affair. It was never, in my view, a specially lovely building, although, admittedly, what was left of the steeple did stand out against the long level line of the roofs of Carlton Place, a 'punctuation mark' we were told. I doubt very much if its listing would have stood up in face of serious challenge.

By 1943 the fortunes of the congregation were sinking, due to a complete change in the population of the parish, and the congregation entered into union with their near neighbours of Tradeston John Knox, itself, as the name implies, a union of some thirty years earlier. The new body adopted the name of Gorbals John Knox. The early seventies saw the area declining even more rapidly (one of its streets had earned the name of 'the Burmah Road') and the congregation was in very poor shape with a building that was crumbling fast. Not only was it listed, it was listing! We had reason to believe there was a plan to build a new Sheriff Courthouse on a large site that would embrace the church, so I approached the Court Commissioners to see if an early sale could be effected, and they manifested considerable interest. The conservationists, however, had other ideas. The tower, they said, must be preserved at all costs and must be incorporated in any new structure that was to go up. The idea of a grand new Sheriff Courthouse with the truncated steeple of an old church arising out of its midst seemed to me to have little to commend it—but who was I to judge?

The problem was resolved in our favour when in 1976 we were served with an order to demolish on grounds of public safety. Even then the argument was continued on the plea that it was the church and not the steeple that was a cause of danger, and that the former could be demolished while leaving the latter standing. I'm not sure that we ever succeeded in demolishing that argument, but we certainly managed to demolish the building in its entirety. The price obtained from the Court Commissioners helped considerably to put up the fine modern church in the new Gorbals—already, as I write, under threat if the southern flank of the Inner Ring Road is to be resurrected.

Clearly an architectural masterpiece is a work of art, but there are at least two very significant ways in which such an artistic expression differs from all other art manifestations. First it is costly to maintain. The Venus de Milo can indefinitely adorn a gallery without incurring great expense, a magnificent carved communion chalice can stand in a glass case for ever, giving pleasure to all who behold it, but without attracting moth, rust, deathwatch beetle. Not so the beautiful church superfluous to current needs, standing empty and unfired, uncared for. Apart altogether from the vandals who, apparently for the sheer hell of the thing, will tear the whole place to bits; apart from the back lane scrap metal merchant who, for private profit, will reset the haul of those who rip out pipes, whip lead out of valley gutters, wrench brass fittings off walls, haul up cast-iron railings; apart from the children who smash the windows and throw lighted matches around, and so on—apart altogether from these there is the simple fact that a building which is not being regularly heated, ventilated, and cared for, where the systematic carrying-out of repairs to roofs, seasonal cleaning of gutters, periodic painting of outside woodwork, occasional attention to pointing —where these and all the other multifarious (and mighty expensive) things are being neglected, will quickly deteriorate, and in a quite remarkably short space of time in the interest of public safety, the whole affair may have to be demolished. Once you have paid the purchase price for the masterpiece in oils or in marble, you will have little to spend; a masterpiece in stone and lime you may get for a song, but the real financial music has still to be played. If you are wise you won't accept it in a gift. I should know, for I have offered more such gifts than I have ever found takers!

The second peculiarity about the work of art that takes the form of a fine building is that it is occupying a particular plot of land. And, in the centre of our cities at least, a plot of land will always be very much at a premium. The engine of the Flying Scotsman is in no one's way in the museum at York—it would be vastly different were it left standing on the main line just outside King's Cross. A complication of this feature, especially in today's world, is that the very changes in the character of a locality which frustrate the use of the church for the purpose for which it was designed, can create an urgent demand for the piece of land on which it is sitting. Thus to the problem of a building surplus to your requirements you have the added factor that if it were out of the way, the sale of the site would bring in enough to meet the clamant need for the building of a new church somewhere else.

Salvador Dali's 'Christ on the Cross' has no particular purpose to serve apart from making an impression on its viewers. It is not expensive to maintain, and it does not occupy a valuable site. However, the Rennie Mackintosh church at Queen's Cross differs in all three of these respects.

All of these considerations featured in the famous (or should I say notorious?) controversy that raged over the future of the Park Church. It is a fascinating story well worth the telling.

When in 1843 the Disruption had more or less split the Church of Scotland in two, the new Free Church which emerged was not content for its Divinity students to receive their training in the Universities. After all, these, just as completely as the Established Kirk itself, were under the domination of the State—and in any case who would want to mix with the Auld Kirk students attending there. So they erected their own colleges—in Edinburgh, Glasgow and Aberdeen. In Glasgow it was in 1856 that work was begun on a site in Lynedoch Place to create a massive structure incorporating a great Lombardic tower that dominated the whole Park hilltop, and that, some would have maintained, proclaimed to all and sundry that the Free Kirk was here to stay. The following year the neighbouring site farther down Lynedoch Street was developed as a church (including twin Lombard towers) for a new Free Church congregation called 'College'. This church was destroyed by fire in 1903, but six years later was restored and given a very splendid ceiling as the library of the college. So we have the conspicuous hilltop dominated by the three Lombard towers of Trinity College—three-quarters of the famous Park skyline.

Such a declaration of strength could not be allowed to pass unchallenged, and it is not surprising, therefore, that the Parish Church acquired a site directly opposite the college, and, under the inspired direction of J T Rochead, erected a very grand building with clerestory gablets, pointed arches, and a most magnificent square tower—all in the gothic manner. The nave it was generally agreed was a very ordinary if adequate affair; the tower on the other hand was a masterpiece. It represented the fourth quarter of the famous Park skyline. Perhaps it is less than fair to see this exercise in stone as a mere answer to the Free Kirk's declaration across the way, for there was a real need for a church in the area to serve the population that had moved into the mansions forming the magnificent terraces that now covered the entire hill, for the parish church was far away—both geographically and culturally—in Kelvinhaugh. In its day the Park Church played a meaningful part in the life of that community and played it well. It was all very grand, all very self-assured, there was a profound conviction that the future was theirs, and the Park skyline was its outward symbol, its public declaration.

But already between the wars the rot had begun to set in. These great vast houses had been admirable residences in a day when domestic servants were easy to find and easy to pay. Now they were far too large, too ridiculously inconvenient, for the family home. So one after another they fell into the commercial bracket, the frontage being retained with scrupulous care and the interior converted for use as offices of the highest quality. By 1960 the only residents in an area now entirely given over to offices were the students in one University hall of residence, the very occasional on-the-premises caretaker, and, I think I am right in saying, one solitary example of what might be called a normal family, although if I am correct in my suspicion that it was George MacLeod and his household, I'm not sure the description is very apt! Members of the congregation now resident in Bearsden, Newton Mearns, Cambuslang continued in their fellowship largely because of sentimental ties, but they were growing relentlessly older and their numbers were dwindling, so that by the early sixties we in the Presbytery were talking very seriously with the office-bearers about what the future might hold in store.

Obviously one question which bulked very largely in our thinking had to do with the future of the building, and more especially of the tower which made so outstanding a contribution to the city skyline. It was a question that was going to arouse widespread interest—of that at least we could be certain.

We considered the matter long and earnestly from every angle—not forgetting the financial one, the site being one of the most prestigious in the city. We came up with a specific proposal. We engaged a highly distinguished architect to design a new eleven-storey tower block of offices which would occupy the whole site of the church, and which would offset—in a different and quite striking (startling, if you will) fashion—the Lombard towers. We had a great model prepared and mock-up photographs taken showing from many angles how it would all appear *in situ*. One morning the *Glasgow Herald* appeared with one of these montages on its front page—and the repercussion had to be felt to be believed. Practically everyone was agreed that our proposed tower represented a fine piece of architecture; but they were no less unanimous that it wasn't going to be built in Lynedoch Place! It was remarkable to learn over just how many dead bodies it was going to be erected!

As we had anticipated all along, our application for planning permission was turned down. The planners, however, indicated a willingness to meet us to discuss the whole situation, and at the close of a really healthy get-together we were led to believe that sympathetic consideration might well be given to a scheme for the development of the nave, retaining the tower as it was and restricting the height of the new office block to match that of the neighbouring terraces. A new plan was accordingly prepared embodying these various features and this secured considerable favour in some quarters and got us the approval of the planning people themselves. It was strenuously opposed though by a number of conservation bodies, with the result that authority had second thoughts. They decided to consider purchasing the church themselves, provided some municipal or other public use could be found for it. Delighted with this outcome the conservationists set to, with an enthusiasm unsurpassed by police combing the woods for the murder weapon, to find an acceptable use for the building. Suggestions included an extension to Kelvingrove Museum to house the armour section, a shopping centre, an eating place for office workers—but all with a conspicuous lack of response when it came to finding 'takers'.

We in the Presbytery were not so enamoured with the prospect of a sale to the Corporation, since the offer we had reason to believe they were proposing was less than a quarter of what might be expected from a very modest office development. As this income was already earmarked for the erection of two new churches in developing areas on the perimeter of the city where they were urgently needed, the aspect of price was one we could not responsibly ignore. It has to be said, too, that in undertaking, as we were doing, to put the tower into a good state of repair at our own expense (estimated at £20,000) and to write into the conditions of sale a requirement that the said tower be maintained in good repair in all time coming (estimated loss £15,000), we were putting up a lot of money for no other purpose than that the citizens might enjoy the skyline. It would have been nice to think that some of our critics were making comparable—or indeed any—contributions.

At the end of the day the Corporation granted planning permission for the modified scheme, and the office block stands there today, tagged on to the great gothic tower to which it bears no conceivable relationship and which makes no contribution to its life or usefulness. It is my experience that compromises are usually accepted because they are not positive enough to offend anybody. It is overlooked that neither are they positive enough to please anybody.

In respect of the bald contrast which it incorporates, the scheme might be thought to be in line with much else in the

Park Circus complex. The façade of the area is generally perhaps the most magnificent piece of Victorian splendour you will find anywhere today, and certainly it is as eye-catching as it was the day it was built. Or almost so, for it demands a lady in a crinoline and carrying a parasol, being handed out of a landau by a liveried footman, to give it the vitality it originally enjoyed —two motorists angrily competing for a spot of parking is totally out of character! But look behind the façade. Open one of the doors and see how the beautiful interior has been torn apart to make way for the stairs and passages and emergency exits which conform to today's office requirements. Or, worse still, take a turn round to the mews at the rear and admire the fire escape stairs, the broken out windows, the suspended toilets. The lady in the crinoline would avert her eyes in horror, the very horses would shy, at the spectacle.

I am still opinionative enough to regret that our original proposal for the eleven-decker office tower was turned down. It would have changed the skyline, but it would not in my opinion have ruined it. And we could well have got three new kirks out of the price. It would at least have given a building designed from podium to attics to serve its purpose, instead of the compromise affair that impresses the stranger as a church that somewhere along the line has gone wrong—when in fact it was the planners who went wrong.

I feel I should not leave the story of the Park Church without adding a couple of postscripts—amusing, alarming, or pathetic, as you care to see them. The former has to do with the fate that overtook the Park pipe organ. The danger of damage and depredation to a church obviously out of use is of course very considerable, and the Park people had continued to employ their Church Officer with instructions to come about the church daily, to keep the grounds tidy, and generally to make the place look inhabited. In spite of this they had their organ stolen. It was an unusually fine instrument and it had been our intention to have it installed in one of the new churches that would ultimately be established with the proceeds of sale. With this in mind the congregation had continued their contract with the organ tuner who, on his arrival one day, was unable by pressing the keys at the consol to produce any sound—in or out of tune. Examination revealed that the organ chamber had been stripped of every single pipe. This job must have involved at least a couple of men with a lorry for well over an hour, and must have been carried out during normal business hours when lots of people were around. Yet no one saw anything untoward. If the job was done with a sufficiently confident air, nobody would. Quite a piece of 'derring-do' you might think, worthy, surely, of a better reward than the £30 which I am assured would be the scrap metal value of their haul. I find it hard to believe that a second-hand sale was effected, though, who knows, some congregation may in all innocence be happily singing the Lord's praises to the leading of organ pipes to which they have no valid title!

A no less blatant, and even more impudent, piece of thuggery had been perpetrated at Caledonia Road. The wife of the beadle, out shopping one afternoon, turned a corner near the church in time to see a group of children swinging on the gate, an enormously heavy cast-iron affair that matched the railings and had been designed by Greek Thomson himself. While she watched, the hinge apparently gave way and the great mass of metal crashed to the pavement. Mercifully none of the children was hurt, and with her in pursuit they dashed off. Soon she gave up the unequal contest and returned to the church to find no sign of a gate, either on its hinges or on the pavement. She had a shrewd suspicion where it might have gone and, when she reached the nearby scrapyard, there, sure enough, was her gate propped against a wall. 'Naw, mistress, ye must be makin' a mistake. That gate's been lyin' there for mair nor a week—that canna be your gate.' After a few exchanges she relinquished her second unequal contest of the afternoon. When her man got home from work and had had his dinner, she took him along to corroborate her identification. When they got to the yard they could find no sign of a gate anywhere. 'Naw, mistress, you must have got mixed up, it wasna this yaird ye were at. This efternin, ye say? Naw, I've never clapped eyes on ye afore. An' I've never seen yer gate. It must be some ither yaird ye're thinkin' aboot.' So convincing was the act that, on the way home, the church officer asked his wife if she was quite sure that this was the yard she had visited earlier!

To return to the Park. It was following on the discovery of the organ theft that I had a talk with one of the officials at George Square about the danger to the building when it was possible for a thing like this to occur. The risk of fire seemed to me only too real and terrifying. The official agreed most heartily and to my surprise undertook to mount a round-the-clock watch which would be housed in the vestry. This was done and maintained right through to the end—and must have cost a packet. There was a fireplace in the vestry, so a great load of gas cinders was dumped at the rear for the comfort of the lonely watch. It was only after the planning issue had been settled and the watch had been discontinued that I had occasion to visit the back premises, and discovered that the ashes from the vestry fire had been consistently dumped in a corner of the session house next door—on a wooden floor! Not, you might have thought, the best way to guard against a possible outbreak of fire. But it is incidents like these that lend a bit of interest to what can often be the dull life of a conservation challenger.

My final example represents probably the nearest I ever got to a success story in my incursions into the field of conservation. Not that it has been all that near, but it is coming along nicely, and the story is worth telling.

In the pre-Reformation sixteenth century, the Parish of St Mungo included along with the city of Glasgow the adjoining vast estate of the Archbishop, covering most of what today we call 'the west end'. As a consequence of the Reformation this property was granted by charter as a feudal holding entitled 'The Barony of Glasgow'. In 1595 the lands were disjoined from St Mungo's and erected into a separate parish called, not unnaturally, 'The Barony'. We Scots have always been reluctant to put up a new building if an existing structure can be found to serve our needs, so the new congregation worshipped in the undercroft of the cathedral while the mother congregation was using the choir. A contemporary account describes The Barony sanctuary as being 'of an arched roof which is low, and supp-orted by a large number of pillars, it is exceedingly dark, dirty and incommodious'. Even today when these closing strictures do not apply, it is difficult to conceive the crypt as a place suited to the ongoing worship of a congregation. Why they should have chosen this part of the building when the nave was not in use is a question to which I do not know the answer. (It was not until 1648 that the East congregation was housed in the nave and became the 'Outer High'.) What is known is that, for all its obvious disadvantages, the undercroft apparently supplied the needs of The Barony congregation for almost two centuries.

Then in 1798 the congregation moved to new quarters in a church they had built in what is now part of Cathedral Square, directly east of the present church. Having waited so long 'doon in the darkness o' a dunnie' (in Cocker's phrase) the congregation might have been expected to emerge with some flamboyance and flourish. Instead of which the new church was plain to a fault. 'The church was faced with dressed corner stones, but the whole frontage was plastered over in the rude style known as "rough hairling", and the edifice thus presented a very mean and commonplace appearance. The interior was similarly antiquated and inconvenient, having galleries clumsily fixed on three sides and an awkward pulpit reached by a plain wooden stair.' Nestor refers to the building as 'that strange abortion of architecture which stood as a foil, or in mockery, beside the classic cathedral'. An abortion it may have been, but it must have been a vast improvement on the crypt, and it was to serve its people throughout the next century.

The congregation's third home was to be a vastly different affair, nothing less than the best this time. The design was put out to competition adjudicated by John Pearson, the successful candidates being Sir John Burnet and John A Campbell, and succeeding generations have speculated on which contributed what to the magnificent structure, embracing not only the church but hall, ancillary rooms and church-officer's house, which appeared on the site in the years 1886-89. Truly an outstanding piece of architecture.

The fact is well enough established, even if it is often ignored, that a magnificent building in the proportions of the new Barony is near impossible to heat and extremely costly to maintain in any proper condition of repair. For example, when a light bulb 'went', a scaffolding tower had to be erected to effect its replacement—two men busily occupied for at least half a day. As the congregation dwindles the property inevitably deteriorates, and the day comes when it is clear that something drastic will have to be done if it is not to be too late. Seeing such a day fast approaching, I had an idea at least twenty years ago that the burgeoning University of Strathclyde must have a use to which they could put the spacious, imposing hall accommodation which the church could easily be converted to provide. They had nothing to compare with the Bute Hall at Gilmorehill, and in order to cope with the numbers involved at graduations they were reduced to holding these in a series of ceremonies.

So I approached the appropriate official. The proposition was enormously attractive, but two major difficulties stood in the way. First, that they had just concluded negotiations with the Corporation whereby the City Hall in Candleriggs was to be restored as a concert hall and they were to have the use of it for graduations. The second difficulty was even more formidable. No one knew exactly where the eastern flank of the Inner Ring Road was to be located. This line of motorway that was to link the Townhead Interchange with a river crossing east of Salt-market, was subject to three possibilities—it might go to the east of The Barony (and that would suit admirably); it might go to the west and be encased in a tunnel (and that too would be fine); or it might go to the west in an open cutting (and that would be fatal). So the proposition had to be put on ice until this other issue was resolved.

The congregation bravely and doggedly battled on, but the situation steadily worsened. The neighbouring congregation of St David's Ramshorn, in Ingram Street, sold their building to Strathclyde University. The latter body was keen to acquire this particular property because of its associations. The first minister of the parish in 1718 had been John Anderson, later buried in the little adjoining graveyard, and it was one of his grandsons, also John Anderson, who founded the Anderson College which later became the Royal Technical College and in turn the University of Strathclyde. The Ramshorn congregation were then united with the Barony in the hope that this might strengthen the fellowship there. In fact, of course, the Ramshorn had been largely a gathered congregation and, once their treasured building was no longer theirs, they took the opportunity of transferring to places of worship nearer their own doors. And so the inevitable happened. The struggling congregation admitted defeat and the Presbytery found itself confronted with the problem of the future of the building, now in urgent and desperate need of repairs running to vast sums. Unless the really essential work was put in hand immediately, the whole affair could get beyond redemption. My successor, Alex Cunningham, took the matter in hand, got together a special committee representative of many different interests, and finally the University of Strathclyde—which was very keen to acquire but had not the necessary funds—found itself in a position where it simply had to take over the building which, of course, was made over free of charge. The work of restoration is proceeding slowly, but at least the rot has been halted.

I await with interest the ultimate outcome, but in general terms the solution which from the very outset had appeared to me to represent the ideal one has come to be accepted. I do feel, though, that public funds could have been released to allow all of this to happen a long time ago, when the cost would have been a fraction of what it now is, and when it could have been done more smoothly and without the financial embarrassment that has been caused. Considering the position of the building, on the very fringe of the Cathedral Precinct on which so much money is shortly to be lavished, it simply had to be preserved. So why put off taking action until the whole thing is threatening to fall apart? We have all along been unanimous about the need to conserve, but so long as there is an owner, the responsibility for meeting the cost will be held to be his, and if he has no funds, the bills will get bigger and bigger.

Where is all this leading us? What is the moral of it all? Well, arising out of the foregoing, and out of the multitude of other cases in which I have been involved over the years, there are three positive proposals which I should like to advance, three things which I think would at once simplify conservation procedure, increase its fruitfulness, and reduce its frustrations.

My first suggestion is that the 'list' should be ruthlessly purged. It would seem to me that when the list was initially prepared, the tendency must have been to include every building for whose preservation a case could possibly be made out. Claims for inclusion were never properly tested since there was no devil's advocate to present the other side. Clearly I recall a day when I met a group of planners in Cowcaddens to discuss a problem that had arisen there—still unresolved today, twenty years later. One of the company observed that it would be imperative to include in the preservation a piece of adjoining property. On my asking what claim to immortality the (to me very plain) building enjoyed, he replied that it was a pleasant, well-proportioned building; and he seemed hurt when I suggested that if that alone was to be a sufficient criterion for preservation there would never be many vacant sites in the city.

What I believe we need is a list of those properties which by common consent must be preserved, preserved at all costs —and at all costs to the community and not just to the owners. And let these owners be brought in for consultation from the very outset with a view to winning their support instead of arousing their hostility. Once such an expurgated edition has been prepared, the other buildings could obviously be freed from the carping restrictions which listing imposes—the ordinary planning procedures give them all the protection they require. In this way, as I see it, it would be possible in any given area to assess the precise extent and proportions of the problem and to seek to find a comprehensive solution rather than having to deal with the whole thing in bits and pieces at the dictation of a series of crises. It would also be possible to make some rough assessment of the total cost involved and to see just how the spending could be spread out over a period of years.

Second, I think steps should immediately be taken to compile an exhaustive record of all the buildings which had been on the list or which have any claim to fame. Let's get our hands on the plans and specifications, let's take lots of photographs outside and in, let's get down the details of all the peculiar features and historical data—in other words, let's build up a complete dossier on every interesting structure, be it church, factory or dwelling house. And let it be done now while the premises are still in use, or at least in a fairly good condition. Don't wait until dry rot and vandalism have done their worst. If there isn't room in any of our libraries or museums to stock all this material, and provide facilities for easy reference to it (and it could demand a lot of space), then here, surely, is an admirable opportunity to revitalise one of our redundant buildings—St George's in the Fields could have fitted the bill to perfection. Had this been done in the past then we should now have complete information on, for example, the Greek Thomson masterpieces in Caledonia and Langside Roads, John Street Church with its quite incomparable stucco work interior, the old St Andrew's Halls, the Peel of Drumry, and so on, and so on.

My third suggestion is that the whole machinery for compulsory acquisition by the local authority should be completely revised with a view to speeding up its operation, to making it positive and constructive instead of a last resort, and, above all, to ensuring that funds will be available to an extent adequate enough to cope with what will of necessity be a fairly large scale and expensive exercise. As the law stands, the local authority is under obligation to purchase listed property only when it has been shown that there is no possibility of finding a buyer. But how do you prove a negative? How long do you persist in looking before you agree that a taker is not to be found? And in a world of moth, rust and vandals, what happens to your architectural masterpiece in the meantime? What, as I see it, is needed in such cases is an application of first aid, not an administration of last rites. Money is going to have to be spent on the property sooner or later, and clearly a lot less will be needed sooner rather than later. So why not get the formalities out of the way and get on with the work *instanter*? And if the money is being spent in the national interest, let it come out of the national exchequer.

To me it appears eminently reasonable that those properties which are worthy of preservation in the public interest should be held in public ownership and maintained out of the public purse. They can then be leased either to the present user or to some other, and at a rent which is fair from his or her point of view, even if it can never be economic from the Council's. The Art Galleries will expend an astronomical sum in acquiring a masterpiece on canvas which the average citizen will see and admire once or perhaps twice in a lifetime. Why then should we be so reluctant to spend what is by comparison a modest sum on the maintenance of a skyline which thousands can admire—and at the time of the Park controversy we were confidently assured *do* admire—every day of every week?

I am, of course, well aware that a suggestion of this kind will strike terror into the hearts of a District Council. I have no access to figures, but I have a fair idea of what it must have cost the Corporation to put the Greek Thomson church in St Vincent Street into good order, and what it costs their successors in the District Council to keep it in that condition, and of how that figure compares with the paltry sum received in rent. It would be interesting to know what has been spent and is being spent on the Royal Exchange building in Queen Street. The bills must be enormous, but why should it be only when the Council has to meet them that they become prohibitive? The nation owns Glasgow Cathedral. Why should the City not own St Andrew's Church, and quite a few other of its historic buildings?

If a congregation has provided a building of outstanding beauty, and maintained it for the citizens to admire completely free of charge for over a century, it seems a poor reward to tell them that they'll jolly well keep on providing it at their own expense for the next century. I remember a friend, who had grown rather bitter about the whole thing, saying to me, 'The moral here is surely very plain. What you must do when you have a new church to build is to engage an unknown architect, get him to sign an undertaking that he'll remain unknown, and invite him, please, to keep the design fairly ugly. In that way, when you have no further need for the building, you'll have no difficulty securing permission to demolish it (you may even qualify for a grant), and so, having realised the full value of your asset, you'll be in a position to look for another unknown architect to put up another ugly building somewhere else'. Even if I regretted his cynicism I could find no logical fallacy in his argument—especially not when I recalled that we had had two redundant churches fairly close to one another in Maryhill. One was a quite ordinary affair designed in what used to be contemptuously referred to as 'heritors' gothic', while the other was the only church the great Rennie Mackintosh ever designed. The Council were happy to pay us £9500 for the former, the latter they would on no account accept from us for nothing. In circumstances like these it's not wholly to be wondered at if folk become a little cynical.

Let's not beat about the bush. In the last resort it all boils down to a question of money, and the problem will never be resolved until money is made available in cases where it is obviously needed. An admirable scheme was worked out in great detail whereby the YMCA were prepared to take over and develop Trinity College as a residential and conference centre. Everyone concerned was not merely agreeable but positively enthusiastic about the project, and from every angle. A massive grant was, of course, required, and this was to be met in equal shares by the Historic Buildings Commission, Strathclyde Regional Council, and Glasgow District Council. At the last minute the Region backed out because their funds were fully committed elsewhere, the whole affair had to be abandoned, and that was that. Manifestly this is ridiculous. If Trinity College must be retained, if the proposed scheme is an admirable one, if after many years of searching it is the only scheme, then the money has got to be forthcoming, and haggling over who is to contribute what is a bit silly, considering that at the end of the day it is all coming out of the one purse, even if on the way it has lingered for a short time in a series of other purses.

Unhappily, in my experience, talk is more readily available than cash. Vividly I remember a meeting I attended in the City Chambers connected with the future of the Rennie Mackintosh church at Queen's Cross. If it is possible to have a simple and straightforward case in this area of many complications, this definitely was it. First, there could be no possible doubt about the need to preserve this building, the only church ever to be designed by one of the greatest-ever geniuses in the field of architecture. Second, there was a user to hand—two in fact, for as well as the Rennie Mackintosh Society who were prepared to take over at once with a view to making the church their head-quarters, 'Museums' had indicated a desire to acquire as soon as they were in funds. And third, the total sum required to put the property into perfect shape was reckoned to lie within the £50,000 limit and could be spread over three years.

The company that had gathered to resolve this apparently rather simple issue included top men from District, Region, Historic Buildings Commission and a number of interested bodies, about a dozen altogether. During the duller moments —and there were quite a few—I found myself trying to work out how much per hour in salaries was represented around that table. After protracted discussion the best that could be devised was that we, the Church, should make over the property to the Rennie Mackintosh Society (who were financially in rather worse shape than ourselves), that some small grants would be made available right away, and that at some future time, when the national economy was restored, it was likely that larger grants would be forthcoming. This conclusion—which to me seemed pitiful in the extreme—was hailed as something of a triumph. Find a new nurse for the squawking child, give him a sweetie, and surely he will weep no more. Just how optimistic can you get!

In the days when I had occasion from time to time to visit authority to discuss the possibility of selling them a redundant listed church, I used to open the proceedings with the gambit that I was not there to sell a broken down church building, but to dispose of a priceless art treasure. This invariably evoked the response that they were glad to hear that it was to be priceless, for even if they were to agree to take it over it would certainly be on the basis that no money would change hands. We spend a lot on other works of art for our museums and art galleries, so why shouldn't substantial sums be set aside, if not to buy then at least to restore, repair and maintain those buildings that form part of a great national heritage?

That the foregoing is very much a minority report, I readily concede. It may, for all that, be a fairly accurate assessment of the cost of conservation, and I think it is worthy of more serious consideration than it has yet received.

Chapter 6
Ecumenical Extravaganza

EVERYONE, I imagine, has his favourite *bête noire*, his pet aversion, some subject the very mention of whose name causes his hackles to rise. Mine, I have to confess, is ecumenism, and its name is mentioned often enough these days to keep my hackles in a permanent at-the-ready position. It is a subject on which, over the past thirty years, I must have advanced more unsuccessful motions than I have done on every other theme put together. Year after year the Assembly have been presented with a recommendation to send down for the study and consideration of Presbyteries, and sometimes also of Kirk Sessions, some new proposals for the achievement of organic unity, some report telling us how the doctrine of the historic episcopate can be integrated into Presbyterianism more or less painlessly, some fresh plan for the cobbling together of the united Church of tomorrow, a Church that is to embrace the infinite variety of all the denominations while remaining one and indivisible.

I like to think that my hostility to these proposals does not arise from sheer blind prejudice, although some, I know, would suggest otherwise. My contention is that it arises from two sources—first from a conviction that with all the good will in the world you cannot reconcile the irreconcilable (black cannot possibly embrace white, nor can you have a cold which at heart is really piping hot) and that any attempt to do so is a waste of time and effort; and second that in this materialistic age when life is ruled by mechanical forces, this age when the Kirk has in hand so hard a task if it is to win and to hold the hearts of men and women, there are better ways in which its Presbyteries and Kirk Sessions could spend their winter evenings than in studying the latest plans of the ecumenists to get us all—as many of us as are left, that is—into one big happy family. The record shows us that in the end all of these motions have either been firmly defeated in a later Assembly or they have died from exhaustion, but they have always at the time attracted a considerable following, for ecumenism has been a popular bandwagon, and there are those for whom bandwagons represent an attractive form of transport. I am sure many of those who voted in favour of keeping the proposals alive did so because they felt it would be politic to let the issues go to Presbyteries so that they might be turned down there. In any case they didn't want the Church of Scotland to appear as the niggers in the kirkpile. Of one thing at least I feel quite certain: if the issue were to be put to a referendum of the membership as a whole, the answer would be a resounding 'No'.

Let me make my own position clear. I am wholeheartedly in favour of friendly relations between Christian denominations; I am happy that the members of all the Churches in a neighbour-hood should work together for the achievement of the Christian good of the community as a whole. In so far as this is what ecumenism means, I am all for it. The years of my ministry have seen great strides taken in this direction, for all of which I am grateful. From my boyhood I can remember when every Roman Catholic place of worship was called a 'chapel', the word being uttered in tones contemptuous as well as slightly awed, and the building was hurried past with averted gaze by all good Presbyterians. My first parish was Linwood, a small industrial village three miles west of Paisley, and our manse was the first house by the roadside as you arrived in the village. The next house, only a few yards farther on, was the residence of the local priest, who had a very large following here dating from an earlier day when the cotton mill had attracted a large Irish workforce. I know it is hard to believe this, but, for all our proximity, during the five years I spent there, my neighbour and I did not exchange a solitary word. Nor did that strike anyone as strange. The situation in my other parish of Houston was very similar. Oddly enough, the priest was still my nearest neighbour although we were separated this time by almost of a quarter of a mile. We were no nearer, however, so far as friendly relations were concerned. I did call on him once, though, and I clearly recall the event. It was quite soon after the end of the war, when we had added names to the war memorial of 1914-18 and were making arrangements for a service of dedication. One of the lads who had not returned belonged to the priest's flock and I felt that, for the sake of his parents, it was most important that the priest should be present and take part in the service. So I took the unprecedented step of calling on my neighbour and inviting him to participate. He expressed general agreement with my views, but was a bit evasive as to whether he would be 'able' to be there, and in the event was not—which I felt was very sad.

Until fairly recently that was the typical situation across the Reformation divide. As between Reformed denominations, relations were of a closer and friendlier nature, particularly among the ministers who generally met regularly in one another's manses in a district fraternal, and embracing exchanges of pulpits and the like. Today we attend one another's services, have joint ventures at Advent and Easter seasons and, on national occasions, are welcome at the Lord's Table, and are invited to our neighbours' anniversaries, induction services, and so on. And I imagine any minister today, planning a large-scale evangelistic attack on his parish, would not dream of doing so without inviting congregations of other Christian denominations within the parish to be involved in the venture.

As I have said, if this is ecumenism then include me in. But in my experience the word is now inextricably associated with the endeavour to devise a plan whereby all Christian denominations may be brought together into one single organisational unity. (It is invariably described as an 'organic' unity, but I find the term utterly misleading.) To me this is not an objective to be earnestly desired and sought after, even as a long-term goal, and certainly not as a priority to be pursued at the expense of the more urgent challenge of evangelism. Yet in the past twenty years it has come to figure largely before each succeeding Assembly, scarce a year passing without some fresh report being sent down to Presbyteries for prayerful consideration. If this is ecumenism then include me out. To me the whole thing seems to start from a false presupposition and to proceed by way of much woolly thinking—hardly the recipe for a successful journey! Let me try to enlarge on these two points.

The proof text from which the whole affair proceeds, and which it never wearies of quoting, is that verse found in the tenth chapter of St John's Gospel when our Lord, speaking of himself as the Good Shepherd, tells of the time yet to come when there shall be 'one flock and one Shepherd'. It seems rather a flimsy foundation. For one thing it is dangerous to found quite literal conclusions upon pictorial language. But even accepting the image as it stands, a distinction is clearly being drawn between the words 'fold' and 'flock', and the picture which our Lord presents seems, to me at least, to envisage a variety of folds which are all to be bound together into one flock because of their common dependence upon Himself as the Good Shepherd. In a commentary predating the Age of Ecumenism, the late Professor G H C Macgregor writes, 'The ideas of the fold and the flock are deliberately contrasted. The bond is not in a common organisation, but in a common relationship to one Lord. There may be various folds, though but one flock and one Shepherd'.

To me, then, this passage seems capable of supporting a view of Christian unity totally different from that which the popular ecumenical movement would ascribe to it. A parallel which instantly springs to my mind is that of the British Commonwealth of Nations, peoples as different from one another in every aspect as it would be possible to conceive, yet bound together by a common loyalty to the one Sovereign. No one, so far as I am aware, has ever suggested that the Commonwealth would be a better, a stronger, or a healthier thing were all the nations who compose it to adopt one common constitution and enter into an organic unity; and certainly it has never been suggested that they are all falling sadly short of their duty by failing to do so. Yet that is in effect what is being said about the Christian denominations by those who would have them 'one'. For myself I cannot believe that the text from St John will carry the implications that some would lay upon it. And yet it represents the only Scripture authority I have heard quoted in support.

It is a dangerous thing to found too much upon one proof text—as with the case of quoting a proverb, it is so easy for the other fellow to come up with an adage clearly bearing an entirely contrary message. Rolling stones may gather no moss, but a gangin' foot's ay gettin'. Or, to take the present case, it is tempting to ask what the ecumenical enthusiasts make of the vision of St John the Divine, when he sees the City of God furnished not with one gate to admit a united body, not of strangers but of pilgrims, but with no fewer than twelve gates thrown wide to welcome pilgrims—ay and strangers—frae a' the airts, singing different praises, marching in different formations, clad in a multiplicity of uniforms and in none, with no common bond except their determination to reach the City and their devotion to the Lamb which is in the midst of the throne. We do not need to establish unity to find Christ, for it is in Christ that our unity is to be found.

The famous Bishops Report of 1957 puts the ecumenical point of view in regard to unity both clearly and emphatically, when it says:

'Unity is not a contingent feature of the Christian life, but is of the essence of it. One God, one people of God; one Christ, one Body of Christ; one Holy Spirit, one fellowship of the Spirit—such is the incontrovertible logic of the New Testament teaching. The Church, therefore, cannot but be One, its existence being grounded in that Divine realm where disunity is unthinkable; and of this fundamental unity God has given the separated "Churches" a recovered awareness and experience, most notably in and through the Ecumenical Movement.'

The first thing that must strike the observant reader of this declaration is the absence of any definition of what is meant by the unity which is of the essence of the Church's life. One people of God, one Body of Christ, one fellowship of the Spirit —grand high-sounding phrases, but what in the language of the marketplace do they mean? There is a footnote saying that unity does not mean or involve uniformity, and the reader is directed to a later paragraph where it is explained that, for example, each of the national Churches of England and Scotland is to be free 'under God to continue and develop its own full inheritance of life and worship throughout its parishes and congregations. What is envisaged in these modifications is a fulness of sacramental communion between these two Churches, involving fully authorised interchange of communicants and mutual recognition of ministries'. We can, then, it would seem, have as many differences as we care in the realms of organisation, worship, and even doctrine, so long as we can come to the Lord's Table together. Which sounds very good; until, that is, we read on and discover that, unless we can all be agreed on a common acceptance of a doctrine of Apostolic Succession (if it's easier to swallow, we may call it 'the Historic Episcopate'), there can be no 'interchange of communicants nor mutual recognition of ministries'. So we find ourselves right back in the fields of organisation and doctrine, and no matter how far the three-fold ministry of bishop, priest, and deacon may go in Church history, I for one cannot accept it as part of 'the incontrovertible logic of New Testament teaching'.

It is my contention that the basic assumption regarding unity is one demanding much more detailed scrutiny than it has so far received, and that as a first step we need a clear and specific definition of what that unity is—that is the will of Christ for his Church—and preferably in plain straightforward terms that even the simplest believer can understand.

A further preliminary point on which I should wish to join issue is the suggestion frequently made that we are seeking to 'rediscover' the secret of unity. The impression often given is that the Church had begun as a single unified structure, but that over the years, due to human sinfulness, this has been fractured and divided until it has come to be the present multiplicity of sects and denominations each claiming to be 'the Church'. I am no Church historian, but I am sure this is a completely false picture. I am satisfied too that in all the circumstances it was quite inevitable that the Church should develop as it has done. In its early stages the Church grew in an occasional and piecemeal fashion, and in the absence of any common pattern a number of little groups of deeply dedicated and committed people, living in widely separated communities, each worked out its own structure and discipline, and I feel sure that organisation-wise it developed as many distinctive forms as there were separate groups. Another thing, of course, about which I feel sure, is that a member of one such group, moving to a new neighbourhood, would be instantly and warmly welcomed into the local fellowship. I feel sure too, though, that he would find strange and even incomprehensible many of the things his new friends were accepting as commonplace. And when there was any considerable movement and coming together of different groups, problems were bound to arise.

Is that not the background against which Paul writes the third chapter of his first letter to the Corinthians? In that city, it would seem, factions had arisen claiming to follow particular leaders and no doubt characterised by different theological positions—a Paul party, an Apollos party, a Cephas party, a Christ party. Before them all, Paul sets forth their dependence on Christ crucified, that common basis of unity far outstripping in importance their petty differences. Whatever it may be, this is surely not the picture of a Church characterised by the kind of unity which the ecumenicals are in search of today. It would indeed have been strange had a Church which developed, as did the Christian Church of those days, been anything other than a collection of groups, each of which worked out in its own way and according to its own light and very limited knowledge and experience, the detail of the organisation and practice in which to find expression for its allegiance to its Lord and Master, Christ. I am sure it is no blasphemy to say that if it were Christ's will that his Church should be one in the ecumenical sense of today, he went a mighty strange way about achieving that result.

An old farmer in my country parish had been ailing and bedfast for a long time. He had a notion that it must be within the power of modern medicine to get him on to his feet again, and he had developed a feeling of ill-will towards his own doctor for his failure to contrive this. On the occasion of one visit he had been expressing his feelings on the subject in that forthright way in which countrymen, if they put their minds to it, can so excel. 'I hope,' said his doctor, 'this does not mean you are losing faith in me.' 'Na, na, doctor,' responded the patient, 'naethin' like that.' Then, after a pause—'Ye canna loss what ye never had!' By the same process of reasoning, I do not see how we can 'rediscover' or 'recapture' a unity which has never at any time been a feature of the Christian Church. Here is another reason why we so urgently need a clear definition of the 'unity' we are talking about.

A phrase I haven't heard so often lately, a phrase which never fails to annoy me, is 'the sin of our divisions'. For one thing, I am not at all clear what exactly this is trying to say —beyond spurring us on to greater efforts for righteousness. It could mean that we have entered into an evil inheritance through the sins of our fathers, or it could mean simply that we must be sinful people, for otherwise we should long ago have patched up our differences. Let's pause for a moment and consider these two propositions. It is easy—tempting in fact—to lay the blame for our divisions upon the intractability of our fathers, determined men who insisted on having things their own way whatever the cost to the unity of the Church. But, you know, the strange thing is that the times of most acrimonious division were the times of most acute spiritual awareness. The Reformation, looked at from one angle, was a massive split in the unity of the Church, a tearing asunder of the Body of Christ if you will; but looked at from another angle it was the greatest spiritual revival Europe has ever known, it represented the recreation of a Church which had fallen sick even unto death—a revitalising of the Body of Christ, if you will. The breakaway from the Establishment south of the border led by the Wesley brothers, set up a strong new division within the Church; but it also inspired a surge of new religious fervour and Christian service that carried a nation through the dark days of the Industrial Revolution. The Ten Years' Conflict in the Church of Scotland that culminated in the Disruption of 1843 led to nearly half of the ministry, and also of the people, leaving the Kirk of their fathers to create a new denomination; but it represented too a mighty wave of evangelism that lifted the religious life of a whole people out of the bog of Moderatism into which it had been slowly sinking. If then it is true that by their fruits ye shall know them, it could well be argued that we should speak of 'the glory of our divisions' rather than of their 'sin'.

When someone uses in my hearing this phrase about 'the sin of our divisions', I find myself wanting to ask, 'what should Martin Luther have done when he nailed his ninety-five theses to the door of the Castle-Church at Wittenberg? Should he simply have stuffed them into his pocket and gone quietly home to get on with his studies?' History might seem to teach that it was the path of righteousness which he followed—'so help me God I can no other'. It was through his 'sin' that men were released from deadly error and brought into the freedom of the truth as it is in Christ. I find it hard to attribute blame to those heroic giants of a former day.

It may be, of course, as the second possible meaning of the phrase might seem to suggest, that if we were not so steeped in sins we should take steps to resolve our differences. But what steps? You and I have journeyed together in peace and amity along the same road until we come to a fork—without a signpost. You are determined on the high road, and I on the low.

We discuss the problem, but agreement eludes us. If separating and going our separate ways is sinful, there must have been another course, the course of righteousness, open to us—what was it? At a recent Lambeth Conference the Anglican communion found itself in just such a position as it agonised over the implications of the resolution that autonomous Anglican provinces around the world might appoint women bishops if they so desired. The Bishop of London is recorded as having said, 'If you are in communion with someone, you are saying that you share the same faith and the same understanding of the Christian faith and that neither involves wrong beliefs. We are trying to stick together as much as we can, but you don't preserve unity by agreeing with what you believe to be contrary to the Gospel'. The 'sin of our divisions' just won't do in circumstances like these—and the circumstances are always like these, or so at least they always appear to the participants. Might it be that 'the sin of our accommodations' would be the term most appropriate to describe the kind of compromise based upon ambiguity and doublethink to which we tend to have recourse in our anxiety to show the world that we are united —'all one body we'. To pretend to agree could be a bigger sin than to agree to differ.

Neither can I work up any enthusiasm for the claim so often advanced that 'the mission of the Church is grievously hampered by our disunity'. This at least raises a simple issue that all can understand, and, better still, an issue that can be submitted to pragmatic test as to its accuracy. So let's look more closely at the matter with a view to discovering how our lack of visible unity is hampering the cause of evangelism, and let's try to identify those aspects of our disunity that are the cause of the trouble.

According to a report submitted to the Assembly of 1977 by the Multilateral Church Conversation group, the mission of the Church is so hampered. The relevant section of the report opens with the assertion that 'the unity of the Church must become visible in order ourselves to embody the Christ who makes us one'. That, I have to confess, has me completely baffled. I am prepared to believe it means something, but what I know not. Pressing on, however, we come to matters which I can understand. First of all, the claim that our disunity results in our missionary effort being 'spasmodic and unco-ordinated'. If what is referred to here is the kind of parish mission frequently organised by congregations and groups of congregations, then it is bound to be for that very reason and to that extent 'spasmodic'. And if it is mounted in different areas without adhering to any kind of pattern, it could, I suppose, be called 'unco-ordinated'. But need it be markedly less effective because of this? If it is, then the fault, surely, is to be traced to a lack of adequate organisation by the people concerned and not to the want of visible unity within the Church. This objection appears to me quite irrelevant.

The next paragraph finds that our missionary effort is further prejudiced because, due to our lack of visible unity, 'we are not seen reaching out as one people in love to God's world'. Imagine yourself as part of God's world standing in desperate need of the Christian outreach in love and compassion, and ask whether, when that response reached you, you would be likely to be critical because it came from someone within a denomination and not from someone representing a visibly united Church. Does the drowning man ask searching questions about the affiliation of the lifeboat whose crew are dragging him aboard their vessel? Show me that our divisions prevent us from reaching out in love and compassion to God's world and I'll be seriously worried. But don't expect me to be alarmed if your only complaint is that we are not being seen reaching out as one people. To me this criticism is unrealistic.

It does not appear in the 1977 report, but the other argument in support of the view that the work of mission is prejudiced in a divided Church is that the outsider is confused and bewildered, and continues an outsider, because while he (or she) is prepared—anxious even—to become a Christian, he is not willing to become an Episcopalian or a Baptist or a Methodist—in short he is turned off by our divisions. I have never been impressed by this argument. For one thing, after a long ministry, I have still to meet such a frustrated convert to the faith. For another thing, I wonder whether a man hesitates to buy a motor car because, although he's tremendously keen to drive, he's not prepared to commit himself to a Ford or an Austin or a BMW. Or whether old Mrs Brown, living on her own and longing for the companionship of a dog, feels she has to await the emergence of a standard breed. Or for that matter, do you know any young man keen to marry, but completely put off because girls come in so many shapes and sizes? A fanciful rejoinder, you may say. In my view it is no more fanciful than the argument itself. Is it not the case that so far from the number of our denominations being an obstacle, they would, by the very diversity they offer compared with the much restricted choice a united Church would purvey, prove an advantage in seeking to win the uncommitted? I am told that in Sweden, where the ideal of a one-and-one-only Church is virtually a reality, there has been established the lowest level of Church attendance anywhere in Christendom.

While staunchly standing by the view that no grievous harm is done to the mission of the Church by our disunity, I should readily agree that there are spheres of Christian activity where savings could be effected in effort, thought, and money, and where doubtless the end product could be improved, were we able to achieve a real measure of co-operation—call it unity if you will—among all the Churches. Immediately there springs to mind the work of our own Departments of Education and of Social Responsibility and the pronouncements of our Church and Nation Committee. Social work in the way of providing and running homes for the elderly and other groups, of caring for the alcoholic and the drug addict, of providing support for many classes of the underprivileged—these are things that need know no denominational boundaries. The important business of education, with its attendant question of the connection between church and school in a land which owed its schools to the Church, and which is still, nominally at least, a Christian land, is a far bigger and wider affair than that dealt with in the 1918 Act that guaranteed the Roman Catholic Church its own schools. In this day of the multi-racial, multi-religious, extensively non-religious, society this is a question that has gained extra and urgent significance—and it applies to all our Churches. Then there are the national issues such as housing, health, licensing laws, gambling, armaments and war—all problems that touch the Christian conscience of the nation as a whole and do not merely affect some narrow sectional interest.

It seems perfectly clear that the social work could be carried out more economically and probably more efficiently

were it administered at a national and not at a denominational
level; it seems likely that more attention would be paid by Her
Majesty's Government and by other policy-making bodies to a
Church which spoke out loud and clear with one voice, than to a
collection of whispers—even if all happen to be whispering the
same message. Behind that last aside, of course, lies the secret
of part of our trouble. There are many matters on which there is
not one simple clear conviction to declare—divorce, abortion,
nuclear disarmament, to mention obvious examples. I do not
imagine that, in any single denomination, there is one clear
mind on issues such as these, so how could there be across the
board. We in the Kirk debate them in the General Assembly, and
the media put us on the air at such times, so that the whole
world may see us performing a volte-face from last year's
position on abortion. In the Church of Rome, of course, this
doesn't happen. The Pope issues his declaration and that is that.
Or does it just seem to be that? Even in these areas where
Christian teaching allows for different interpretations of man's
duty, it would be no bad thing were all the Churches able to
debate the problems together rather than take their own separate
votes and present the world with a series of separate and often
contradictory conclusions.

How would we go about achieving this limited degree of
unity that would enable us to work together in these areas of
common concern? The answer seems to lie in some form of
Federation, and the birth-throes of the European Parliament that
we are presently witnessing would seem to me to provide a
model of the kind of structure that would be required, as well as
a foretaste of the kind of difficulties that would be encountered.
The idea of federation is summarily rejected in the 1977
report—it would be a mere face-saver allowing us to preserve
unnecessary traditions. 'Federation, if it is thought of as a final
goal, is a means of running away from the costliness of union.'
The hostility seems to arise from equating the term (foedus)
with a 'treaty'. This, I think, is misleading. I prefer to follow the
Oxford English Dictionary which defines the term as 'bonding
together in league for some common object'. That is to say,
there is no complete merging of identity as in union, but within
a limited sphere of action differences are submerged in the
interest of a common purpose. Under such an agreement each

party would retain its individuality and would continue to function as an independent entity except within a clearly defined and agreed sphere, or spheres, of activity. Within that limited area each party would deliberately renounce its sovereignty and would accept dictation and direction therein from a body on which it was fully and fairly represented. A federal government would have to be given power to act and to speak for all the contracting parties. There could be no question of resolutions being sent down for the approval of all the denominations, nor could there be any suggestion that single denominations would be free to contract out on some issue or to exercise a veto. Within the limited area of common interest and action, sovereignty would have to be completely surrendered. There would, of course, be a great deal of detail to be worked out ere such a formula could be found. In particular, the character, composition, remit and powers of the Federal Government would present problems as wide as they were acute; but given good will all round and a determination to find a way, none that need prove insurmountable. There is nothing here of a self-contradictory nature like the idea of Bishop-in-Presbytery that some are still so keen to pursue.

The 1977 report will, as I have indicated, have nothing to do with federation. For one thing, it says, it 'would cramp the witness of the Church as painfully as our present positions now do'. This is sheer unsupported assertion. If federation allowed all the Churches in Britain to pursue one single united scheme of social and relief work among all the country's needy, it is difficult to see how this would cramp the Church's witness. It is advanced, further, that 'a treaty which dictated terms to each sister-Church would not deceive the world'. So what? Do we want to deceive the world? In any case, talk of dictating terms is nonsense, for the terms of the federation would have to be accepted by all the sister-Churches before it could get off the ground. The report goes on finally to condemn federation on the plea that 'it would be a face-saver, allowing us to preserve unnecessary traditions'. The trouble, as the ecumenists must surely have learned by now, is that one man's God-given revelation of the truth is another man's unnecessary tradition. Could anything be more precious to certain Episcopalians than the unbroken line of laid-on hands, could anything be more meaningless to others? It is just possible that as we worked together in some kind of federation, more and more of us might come to see certain things through the other man's eyes, might come to understand more clearly the reason behind our differences and, who knows, some of the barriers might begin to yield. In so far as our differences were found to be getting in the way of the fulfilment of our common task, there would at least be an incentive to get rid of them that is completely lacking as we discuss them around a conference table.

Further, the report declares, federation would be found 'acting as an obstacle to the growth of a united Church'. So far as that growth has manifested itself over the past twenty years, it can ill afford to have any obstacle put in its way! Federation is sometimes likened to a courtship, and the suggestion is that the denominations could become so contented with that inter-mediate state of affairs that they would have no inclination to go on and get a formal knot tied. I have known of courtships that did not lead to marriage, but that was generally because the courtship revealed the essential incompatibility of the partners, and the fact that it led no further was a good thing. If we are to stick by the marriage analogy, my own view would be that the courtship has lasted far too long already and that federation might be seen as a kind of betrothal, a move to show that we really are courting and not just philandering.

I was myself a member of the Multilateral Conversation group at the time of the report, and I was on one occasion asked to read a paper to our Church of Scotland people on the possib-ilities of federation. I was amazed at the hostility which was engendered, on the ground that federation would be bound to require a relinquishing of sovereignty in the areas affected by it, and that this would never do, the Kirk would never agree to it. They were appalled at the very suggestion. All this from a group of people who are not only willing, but keen, to enter into an incorporating union and sacrifice the individuality and freedom of the Kirk in every department of its life. I have to admit, though, that I think the question of sovereignty is the rock upon which federation would be bound to perish. This need not be from the side of the Kirk, for we really enjoy full sovereign powers in every department of our church life and are therefore at liberty to divest ourselves of these in some limited sphere should the General Assembly be so determined. I cannot see it as being so simple in the case of the Roman Catholic Church with its allegiance to Rome, or of the Episcopal Church with its commitment within Anglicanism as represented by Lambeth. Suppose we were in a position to establish a federation of British Churches that had pronouncing on public questions as its remit. Let it be that after due process the federation resolved to express itself as being in favour of abortion in certain circumstances—then where would the Romans be? Or if it were in favour of the admission of women to the ministry, where would the Anglicans be? These Churches are not autonomous in the way that would enable them to relinquish their sovereignty—like my sick farmer friend, 'they couldna lose what they never had'!

Some time around 1970 I got myself into even deeper disfavour than usual with the ecumenical camp because of an article I wrote for *Life and Work* on the implications of the impasse that had been reached in the Church unity negotiations. Close on forty years had passed since the beginning of the Episcopal-Presbyterian talks without anything concrete having been achieved, the Anglican-Methodist attempt at reconciliation that had seemed quite promising had just broken down: from an ecumenical get-together in the town of Corby (of which more hereunder) we in the Kirk had just dissociated ourselves. Having briefly sketched in the position I went on to say:

'Even if these years of effort have seen little tangible result they must have taught us some lessons. They must have put us in a better position to form a sound strategy for the future.

'One fact seems to stand out very clearly indeed—that the doctrine of apostolic succession (call it by what name you please) is the chasm which at the present time separates Churches of the episcopal and the non-episcopal traditions.

'It is not simply a question of Bishop versus Presbytery as a method of Church government. Or a question whether we could take bishops into our system. Or a question whether the existence of some individual vested with pastoral authority over ministers would be a good thing for all concerned.

'It is not even that while one side insists that the institution of bishop is a good thing, the others say they can get on fine without them. However strenuously these views were held, there could be some hope of reconciliation

'The trouble is that those who adhere to the episcopal tradition hold the view that in the absence of bishops in the historic episcopate (and they would recognise no other) there just cannot be a Church. The logical outcome of such a position is that there can be no other "Church" with which they could hope to enter into organic union, only a number of benighted people needing to be converted to the faith.

'In so far as this view is conscientiously and sincerely held, we who no less devoutly stand at the opposite extreme, can do no other than respect it. But we are foolish surely if we do not take it into account in thinking about future possibilities in the ecumenical field. We are blind if we do not see that the things which wrecked the Methodist union and the Corby experiment will continue consistently and inevitably to arise because of this fundamental cleavage. We are very simple if we imagine that two sides separated by so deep a division will, given enough Christian charity, find themselves organically united.'

I rather imagine that what gave so much offence was that I went on to suggest that we should abandon, at least for the time being, our efforts to bridge the apparently unbridgeable chasm and concentrate our efforts on getting together with the various branches of Presbyterianism, with our cousins of Methodism and our near relatives of Congregationalism.

It was about the same time that, writing under a pen-name in *The British Weekly*, I went so far as to say:

'What is to prevent the Kirk taking the lead here and effecting the kind of breakthrough that could mean so much and achieve so mightily?

'Let the Church of Scotland invite the Methodist Church (north and south of the Border), the Congregational Church (also in both countries), the English Presbyterians, and any others willing to be involved, to enter into a Solemn Alliance for the furtherance of the work of God's Kingdom?

'The first objective of such an alliance would be to bring the message of the Church to the people of the space-age, to clean up the national life, to give a new urge and impetus to living the good life, which all of us know is so different a thing from just having a good time.

'As a secondary aim we might undertake to try to come

more closely together—but we would write in no absolute conditions as to what was to be the shape of things to come.

'As a first step and as a symbol and seal of our good faith we would publicly acknowledge one another as members of the one great family in Christ, and, as befits brethren, we would welcome one another into our respective households.

'It would be a beginning.

'Compared with some of the grandiose schemes for organic union prepared on paper it might not seem very much. But it would be real and actual and not just a vision. It would, in a way that not all the ambitious blueprints have done, bring men of goodwill together on a project about which they were all agreed. And when that has happened anything may be expected to follow.

'Now it is true that in later years approaches along that kind of line were made, but in a piecemeal and half-hearted fashion and always with over-much emphasis on the production of a Basis of Union and always with a signal lack of success. If we cannot achieve results in these negotiations where only a very little pontoon kind of bridge is required, what hope have we of spanning the chasm that sets episcopacy in a place apart?'

The Corby Catastrophe, to which reference has been made above, is a tale as interesting as it is instructive. No history of ecumenism is complete which does not contain a reference to it. Corby is a town in Northamptonshire with which Scotland has very close ties. Until they closed down in fairly recent times, the tube-making firm of Stewarts and Lloyds, whose home town had been Coatbridge, operated a large works in the English town. A vast number of Scots families had moved south, particularly in the thirties, and two Church of Scotland congregations had been established with, between them, a roll of, at that time, more than two thousand members. In the late sixties a new housing area, Danesholme, was in the process of being developed, and Anglicans, Baptists, Congregationalists and Methodists set up a Provisional Sponsoring Body to discuss a document called 'Planning the Ecumenical Parish' with a view to conducting an experiment in ecumenism in the new area. This looked like the real thing. At last we're going to get away from the conference table and the fruitless bickering around hypothetical problems and get down to the real nitty-gritty of making ecumenism work in the service of a real community of real people of varied traditions; now we can lay aside the theological jigsaws and the constitutional conundrums and give our minds to a good solid practical problem that everybody can understand. Not included at the outset, the Church of Scotland was quick to appreciate the possibilities and to seek representation on the Sponsoring Body. Yet in the end, the Kirk, through its Presbytery of England and with consent of its Home Board, resolved that on grounds of conscience it could no longer continue in the experiment. As was to be expected, the trouble centred on recognition of ministries—the unbridgeable chasm.

It was accepted that the ministry at Danesholme should be supplied by a team of at least two ministers, to be appointed in the first place by the Sponsoring Body—men 'from different traditions, one episcopally and one non-episcopally ordained'. The first duties of the team would be to build up a corporate prayer-life, to work out a programme of teaching and of preparation of new members, and to devise an order of service which would at once embody customary practice from the participating traditions and yet be flexible enough to be modified in the light of experience. All highly commendable: nobody could find fault with anything there. The programme becomes a little more open to question when it moves on to the admission to full communion. Initiation is to be by baptism, public profession of faith, and 'the laying on of hands with a prayer for the gift of the Holy Spirit'. The Bishop of the diocese is to participate along with the team at every service of admission—so that whatever hands may be involved, his will certainly be there. Not much room for 'flexibility' here. And even in spite of this it is still only 'to be hoped' that members so admitted will, on moving to a new area, be automatically accepted into the denomination of their choice. It is, as might be expected, when the document turns to the 'weekly Eucharist/ Communion' that the heart of the problem is reached. Here there is to be 'a form in which an episcopally and a non-episcopally ordained celebrant join together in the thanksgiving and the words of institution, the manual acts and the administration of the elements, using traditional words. In the absence of either celebrant the Sponsoring Body is to arrange for his place to be taken by another minister of the same tradition'.

This is what can only be called 'concurrent celebration'. Two ministers stand side-by-side, say the same words and perform the identical acts, but if one of them—the episcopally ordained one—is not there, then for some members of the congregation the sacrament will be meaningless and invalid. This is because the other minister involved, although he has said every word and done every single thing that is required, has not had laid on his head the hands of a bishop in the Apostolic Succession. Which means simply and only too clearly that one of the ministers set apart to serve the Danesholme congregation is for some of his members not a minister at all. It is understood that the representatives of the Presbytery of England were prepared to accept everything else provided that at the Communion an antiphonal form took the place of the concurrent, the two ministers taking separate parts and alternating from week to week. But this was not acceptable. Too serious a matter this for flexibility. So long as a properly ordained minister says and does everything, there has been a celebration of the eucharist, and the presence and vocal interference of the other chap can be overlooked.

If as a Presbyterian you show signs of getting a bit hot under the collar over this kind of thing, you will be assured that the attitude represented here is adopted by only a handful of people within the Church of England, and, it may be added, only a handful of cranks at that. The alarming thing is that the wishes of this handful seem to determine Anglican policy to the extent at least that the Bishop of Peterborough was not prepared to deviate by a hairsbreadth from this pattern because, presumably, while the withdrawal of the Church of Scotland from the experiment was regrettable, to offend the susceptibilities of the handful would be unthinkable. And so a great opportunity was lost for showing to the world a truly united effort in ecumenism as well as of learning a great deal from the experience of working together within a real community. Was I not right in declaring that the doctrine of the historic episcopate is the chasm that persistently keeps us apart? The 'cranks' have a lot to answer for.

I had occasion to visit Corby recently and was interested to learn that the experiment had been abandoned and that the area is now served by a congregation embracing the Baptist Union, the Methodist Church, the United Reformed Church and the Church of Scotland, and that the minister belongs to the last-named body. Until we can bridge the chasm created by Apostolic Succession, it seems to me there is no hope of achieving any union that will include Anglicans—unless on their terms.

It may be thought that Corby was an extreme, even an extravagant and extraordinary case. I do not think so. Let me strengthen the evidence by mentioning two other significant incidents, the first of which occurred within my own experience. Away back in 1963 a minister of what was then, I think, the United Church of Pakistan, was invited over to Glasgow to initiate work among his own people, of whom there was a steadily increasing number in the south side of the city. While he was working here, a further Church union was effected in Pakistan out of which emerged the Church of North India. True to form there was a service of recognition of ministries—a service which, for obvious reasons, our man in Glasgow was unable to attend. Following upon a new Act of our Scottish Assembly governing membership of Presbyteries, I persuaded our people that the Pakistan minister in question was now entitled to a seat in our court, and this was happily agreed. For purposes of the record I had to have a Certificate of Status from the Church from which he came, and so I wrote to India to the bishop concerned asking for such a document—a simple enough request, it seemed to me. It would appear, though, that simple or not it put the ecumenical cat among the episcopal pigeons, for, apparently, since he had not been physically present at the service to have his ministry 'recognised' (that is to say, regularised by having the appropriate hand placed on his head), his ministry had not been so recognised, and was now in some kind of limbo. How then could the bishop give a certificate to say that he was a minister—he didn't seem to be any too clear precisely what he was. Luckily for the peace of the pigeons (if not of Jerusalem) our minister was due to go home on holiday and, I understand—I was careful not to enquire too narrowly—steps were taken to make good whatever was missing in his ministry and he returned triumphantly waving a Certificate of Status duly signed and sealed. A silly, meaningless kind of exercise it seemed to me.

The other instance appeals to me as peculiarly sad as well as silly. In 1984 the bishops of the Church of England brought to their Synod a proposal that the Church of South India should at long last be declared to be in full communion with the Church of England, because only four of their presbyters still survived who had not been episcopally ordained, and these were all old men unlikely ever to set foot on these shores. In the Synod the proposal was thrown out by the Anglo-Catholic party. Until the last vestige of tainted ministry is gone, fellowship at the Lord's Table cannot be complete.

How right the late Professor Ian Henderson was—even if his presentation was blunt to the point of brutality—when he wrote in Power Without Glory: 'The last thing the Anglicans want to do is to unite with Protestant ministers in the way, for example, that the ministers of the Church of Scotland united with the ministers of the United Free Church in 1929. Anglicans do not want to unite with Protestant ministers, they wish Protestant ministers to die off so that they can replace them with Anglican ones. These alternatives give rise to the two Anglican diplomatic techniques of the Dying-off Period and the Covert Ordination. In ecumenical language these techniques are referred to as the South India method and the North India method'.

My two cases above provide us with an example of each of the methods in question.

What, in my experience, Anglicans seem to be quite incapable of either understanding or accepting, is that there can be people like myself to whom Apostolic Succession is not merely something which I do not approve—it is something which, with the whole force of my being, I am obliged to reject—that, in a word, there are those to whom, on grounds of conscience, Apostolic Succession is utterly repugnant and unacceptable. The fact that this is so, and that it is more than just a Scottish idiosyncrasy, was vividly brought out in 1969 when, over the names of Kingsley Barrett and Lesley Newman, there was issued a 'Letter to the Methodist People' in which the authors declared that if a major part of the Methodist Church 'determinatively submits to the historic episcopate', there would be a substantial minority prepared to form a new church rather than participate in the submission. It is sad—sad beyond words

—to see people who have happily journeyed together over many miles, coming to a point where their ways must part for they cannot in good conscience journey any longer in fellowship. At the same time—and don't let us lose sight of the fact —there is something grand and heroic in the sight of people prepared to make the greatest sacrifices for the sake of principles which they believe to be true. Sad to say, 'truth' is a word rarely heard around the ecumenical table. Many things will have to be sacrificed if unity is to be achieved, but truth, surely, must never be one of them.

The trouble within Methodism centred, of course, around the Service of Reconciliation which was to mark the launching of the new united Church. No doubt it is good that when two bodies which had been separate decide to come together there should be some overt act to mark and to publicise the occasion, and to provide an opportunity for an expression of thanksgiving and gladness. But it should be a spontaneous outburst—it shouldn't be set about with mean, calculated undertones. In this case the Service of Reconciliation was just another name for the service of recognition of ministries earlier rejected, and it didn't smell any sweeter for the change. As everyone knew, that had merely been a device whereby the non-episcopally ordained ministers would be brought within the historic episcopate, whereby their defective ordination would be made good—Ian Henderson's Overt Ordination, the North India method—and in the most discreet fashion. You are not, of course, meant to think of the service in that way. So long as you can construe it as something you personally can accept, then you should confine yourself to that interpretation and not allow your mind to wander at large puzzling over what the other fellow may be thinking it means. Yes, but what if you do not need to do any puzzling, what if it is crystal clear what the other fellow is thinking and his idea is utterly repugnant to you? Are you to pretend you don't know, to clap the telescope to your blind eye? Always bearing in mind that God doesn't enjoy the advantage of a blind eye and is bound to see just what you are up to. As it happened, as we all know, the problem did not arise to confront the Methodists since the Anglicans did not achieve the majority necessary to allow the proposals to be taken further.

It was in 1985 that the report of the Multilateral Conversations, 'Christian Unity—Now is the Time', was presented to our General Assembly. This round of talks involving the Congregational Union, the Scottish Episcopal Church, the Methodist Synod, the United Free Church, and the United Reformed Church, along with ourselves, had been going on since 1967. I had myself been one of our representatives on the conferring body in the first few years of its activity, and while I found the fellowship enriching and the discussion often stimulating, I did not see us travelling either fast or far and was quite happy when my time came to an end. My principal worry was that we always seemed to be having a happy time agreeing about things on the perimeter while studiously avoiding so much as touching upon the central issues which we must all have known would have to be faced—and resolved—ere any real progress could be achieved. In 1969 they had got around to producing a report on 'Controlling Principles for a Basis of Union', followed by a series of reports culminating in 1978 in the production of 'The Faith of the Church', a document prepared in the light of comments that had come from the constituent bodies. But now in 1985 they brought forward a proposal that they should be authorised to draw up a Basis of Union. Here, it would seem, was real progress at long last. At considerable length and in great detail the subjects of Baptism, Eucharist, and Ministry are dealt with, leading to the view that there now exists sufficient doctrinal agreement to enable us to enter into Church union. In a closing paragraph, however, the report turns its attention to 'Relations between Church and State', affirming that, in the peculiar status of the Church of Scotland *vis-à-vis* the State, some of the conferring Churches found a significant obstacle to Church union. For my own part, I did not find this the least surprising, but I should have found it helpful had they indicated precisely what the difficulties were and how it was proposed to get around them. The report concludes:

'Two steps, each attended by considerable legal complexities, but in themselves basically simple, would be required in order to pave the way towards union. First, in the context of a firm commitment by the Churches concerned to unite on an agreed date, the Church of Scotland would be asked to interpret and modify her Declaratory Articles in such a way that they can be accepted by the other conferring Churches and become the

Declaratory Articles of the united Church. The changes would be minimal, designed only to make them inclusive of all the uniting Churches and serviceable for the united Church. Second, the united Church would adopt as its own the Declaratory Articles, as amended, of the Church of Scotland.'

The whole thing has been made to sound like simplicity itself, and, we are assured, the changes will be 'minimal'. If it is known that the changes will be minimal, then it must be known with some precision what these changes are, and the question arises sharply why this information was not made available. If, to take the other horn of the dilemma, the changes are not known and so cannot be disclosed, how can we be so sure they will be minimal? No satisfactory answer was received. A cursory inspection of the Declaratory Articles shows that No II declares, 'Its government is Presbyterian, exercised through Kirk Sessions, Presbyteries, Provincial Synods, and General Assemblies'. Are we to take it that some minimal change is going to render this acceptable to, for example, the Scottish Episcopal Church? From their point of view the changes required will be far from minimal. Some of us felt strongly that we were entitled to much more detailed information on the nature of the necessary changes before we were asked to commit ourselves to moving forward towards organic unity —preparing a Basis of Union and even fixing a date.

The recommendation of the Committee was that the Assembly should welcome the report as a statement of guidelines along which the conferring Churches might move towards organic unity, and that Presbyteries should be instructed to consider the report and forward their comments to the Committee. As a counter-motion I proposed that instead of 'welcoming' we should 'receive with interest', and that instead of sending the report down to Presbyteries we should 'delay all consideration of the report until the Committee is in a position to present full and specific information regarding the minimal changes in the Declaratory Articles referred to in the report as being essential if the unity envisaged in the Conversations is to be achieved'. Some other motions were advanced, but in the end the vote was on a straight choice between the Committee's motion and my own. I lost quite heavily by 321 to 247. If, however, I had lost in the Assembly, a different picture emerged when the matter went to Presbyteries, for they very generally took the view that more detailed information was essential, with the result that the Assembly of 1986 instructed that the Multilateral Conversations be requested to revise its guidelines for a Basis and Plan of Union, taking note *inter alia* of the necessity of a precise statement of any proposed changes to the Church of Scotland's Articles Declaratory in advance of any further steps towards union. Since which the Assembly have heard nothing more of the matter.

An interesting commentary on the ecumenical situation in the practical field was to be found in the Glasgow Garden Festival of 1988, when no fewer than fourteen denominations joined forces to plant a garden and to erect a church building in the grounds. The garden was very beautifully done, but the church was a plain building of glass with but one single article of ecclesiastical furniture—a collection plate! There couldn't be a communion table unless there was also (or it was also) an altar; a font would have seemed a denial of believers' baptism; a pulpit in the absence of a table would clearly have been to exalt the Word at the expense of the Sacraments. A reminder, surely, of just how precarious our togetherness is, but a reminder too of the fact that when life presents us with a choice between irreconcilables, we have to go for one or the other, we just cannot have both. It is all very nice to talk about preserving the infinite riches of our diversity within a unity, but the simple fact of the matter is that you have to take your choice, for example, between a Bishop and a Presbytery —bishop-in-presbytery is a contradiction in terms, an unattainable ecclesiastical monstrosity. You pays your money and you takes your choice, and not even by paying a little extra, not even with a large infusion of Christian charity, can you escape the choice. Were we honest enough to face up to this simple truth we would, it seems to me, get a better, more realistic point from which to start off in our negotiations, and we might even end up with better, more realistic, conclusions.

In the meantime, let us press on with united efforts in evangelism, and let them be increasingly united, for I believe it is in evangelistic effort and enterprise that we shall find the unity we are seeking. On the other hand, I am not convinced that in any contrived organic union are we going to find the inspiration for evangelism.

So I end as I began. I earnestly believe that I should live on terms of friendship and 'guid neibourliness' with the widow across the landing, but I see no compelling reason why I should marry the lady and move in.

Chapter 7
Let's Have the Ladies Join Us

'RECOGNISING liberty of opinion on such points of doctrine as do not enter into the substance of the Faith'—this, often referred to as 'the conscience clause', is a much treasured element in our constitution, a guarantee of spiritual freedom to all ordained servants of the Church. The phrase occurs in the preamble read on all occasions of ordination within the Kirk. Having declared the Church's acceptance of the Scriptures of the Old and New Testaments, the supreme rule of faith and life, the preamble reads on, 'The Church of Scotland holds as its subordinate standard the Westminster Confession of Faith, recognising liberty of opinion on such points of doctrine as do not enter into the substance of the Faith, and claiming the right in dependence on the promised guidance of the Holy Spirit to formulate, interpret or modify its subordinate standards, always in agreement with the Word of God and the fundamental doctrines of the Christian faith contained in the said Confession—of which agreement the Church itself shall be sole judge'. The ordinand has then to give an affirmative answer to a number of questions, including one in these terms: 'Do you acknowledge the Presbyterian government of this Church to be agreeable to the Word of God; and do you promise to be subject in the Lord to this Presbytery, or any Presbytery within whose bounds you may reside, and to the superior courts of the Church?' He then signs the Formula and the ordination proceeds.

All of this seems eminently reasonable and proper. It appears to secure to the individual a meaningful degree of freedom to be guided by his own wisdom and governed by his own conscience, and to secure to the Church a proper measure of adherence and conformity. But even the most superficial study of the matter will reveal how heavily loaded it is in favour of the Church and of conformity. Three points are worthy of notice. First, that the liberty of opinion applies only to the interpretation of the Westminster Confession and not at all to the interpretation of Holy Scripture, for there the voice of the Church is to be beyond challenge. Second, that it is only in respect of issues which do not enter into the substance of the faith that the 'liberty clause' applies, that is to say if not to the trivia at least to the things that are on the perimeter, and it is hard to believe that it would be about such things that anyone would feel so strongly, so conscientiously, as to claim the right to deviate from the path of conformity. It might even seem that those issues on which we feel so intensely as to have conscientious convictions are *ipso facto* of the substance of the faith and by definition excluded from the freedom to differ. And in the third place, there is the general claim that in all matters of interpretation the Church itself is to be sole judge. It is to be presumed that the question of what does and what does not enter into the substance of the faith is one of the questions falling within the provenance of the Church courts and not at all to be resolved on the basis of individual conscientious scruples. The person with the scruples is in fact bound by his oath to be obedient to the Presbytery and the superior courts of the Church. In all the circumstances it would seem that the liberty of opinion referred to in the preamble is of very restricted application and not the charter of freedom some would represent it.

But what has all this got to do, you may be itching to ask, with our purported theme of having the ladies join us? What I have been saying about liberty of opinion, as I shall hope to show, is not at all irrelevant to our theme. Questions arising from the proposal to confer ordination on women, which at the moment seem pathetically likely to split the Church of England, have with us north of the Border been resolved at the legal level without leading to secession, or even any threat of it, but they have left unresolved a number of interesting problems about the right to differ. That was why it seemed wise to begin by sketching in a kind of legal background against which much of what follows should be viewed. But let us begin by tracing the history of the issue that acquired the title 'The Place of Women in the Church' from its early beginnings through to its culmination in our acceptance of the ordination of women to the eldership (in 1966) and to the ministry (two years later).

The question of the Place of Women in the Church must

have arisen many times and with varying degrees of urgency and intensity from the earliest days of the Christian Church, but it was in the early sixties that, in the form of raising the ban on their ordination, it began to loom large and to appear frequently on the agenda of Church courts. Prior to that it had been generally accepted—with us at least—that woman's peculiar gifts could find a satisfying outlet, that woman's desire to serve her Lord could find adequate expression, through, officially, the office of Deaconess or Church Sister, unofficially as Sunday School teacher, choir member, magazine distributor, member of the Woman's Guild or what have you. The odd voice had been raised in protest that the ministry should continue a male preserve and that women who felt a call to such service must learn to accept that it was not for them; and indeed Mary Levison (Mary Lusk at that time) had unsucessfully petitioned to be received for such a ministry. Others like Vera Kenmure (née Findlay) left us to find acceptance in the Congregational Union in whose service she exercised a long and distinguished ministry.

It must have been in the late fifties that a questionnaire of sorts was sent down for consideration and comment by Presbyteries on the question of the admission of women to the eldership. I particularly remember this because I was still at that time Clerk to the Presbytery of Paisley and we passed the matter down to Kirk Sessions and got from them some most interesting and a few quite remarkable returns. The one fixed indelibly in my mind came from an important charge, being written by the Session Clerk, a well-known and highly respected solicitor in town. They were (not surprisingly) 'agin' the proposal and they summarised their whole case as follows: 'Those with experience of working with women on public bodies were unanimous in their testimony that either the women never open their mouths and so contribute nothing to the discussion, or else they are continually keeping the business back with their interminable interventions'. A kind of 'no-win' situation one might think. Yet it was solemnly and seriously advanced by a man whose sanity I had never had reason to doubt. It was completely in line, though, with the reasoning of a minister who, in all seriousness, told me that he never visited his congregation—those who didn't come to Church didn't deserve a visit, and those who did come didn't need one. We got a lot of helpful and constructive comments from our approach to Kirk Sessions, but as I have indicated, not all of them were of that quality.

Another outcome of this early reference to Presbyteries was a suggestion, from the side of the 'anti-s', that the matter should be resolved by a referendum to congregations. This arose, rather obviously, because it seemed likely that the opposition to change would be much stronger in the pew than in the session-house. To me it appeared that to have any major issue determined on the strength of a referendum, represented a change in the constitutional procedure of the Kirk much more serious and far-reaching than the addition of a few women to Kirk Sessions. In any case we had no proper machinery for conducting such an exercise. I was glad the issue was not pressed, and all that in fact happened was that the whole affair was passed to the newly-created Panel on Doctrine which was already engaged on a full-scale study of the eldership.

The General Assembly of 1960 remitted to the General Administration Committee, 'for such action as was deemed appropriate', the question of the ordination of women to the Ministry of Word and Sacraments. In that same year the Assembly had agreed to the creation of a Panel on Doctrine to be available to guide the Church on doctrinal matters arising in a variety of contexts. It was felt that the practice followed over many years when any particular issue with doctrinal undertones arose of appointing an *ad hoc* committee was not wholly satisfactory. For one thing, the result of a number of such groups functioning simultaneously and independently could well be a situation where mutually contradictory positions were advanced. The new Panel was to be available to have remitted to it all matters with a doctrinal dimension. The opportunity was too good for the General Administration Committee to miss; they immediately passed to the Panel their remit concerning ordination of women to the ministry—which seemed reasonable enough considering that the Panel was already engaged on a full-scale study of ministry in general. At the same time I think it was scarcely fair, for while undoubtedly the matter has an important doctrinal dimension, there is also—and no less important—a pragmatic angle to the question, and to the assessment of this the General Administration Committee might have been expected to have had something worthwhile to contribute.

The new Panel thus found itself with two separate remits involving women—in the eldership and in the ministry—and suggested that it might bring these together under the general heading of 'The Place of Women in the Church'. The report goes on to say: 'It was the intention of the Panel to wait until it had dealt with the two related questions of the Ministry and of Ordination before taking up this remit. When Miss Mary Lusk presented her Petition for Ordination, the General Assembly resolved in the following terms, "The General Assembly note with interest the crave of the Petition, and are anxious that it, along with all its implications, should be carefully considered before a reply is given. They therefore instruct the Panel on Doctrine to give consideration to the Petition and its crave when it is dealing with The Place of Women in the Church, and to report to next General Assembly"'. The delaying tactics of the Panel had thus been frustrated and the nettle was going to have to be firmly grasped—both leaves of it.

Mary Lusk's petition having thus given an additional impetus to the matter, the Panel submitted to the Assembly of 1964 a very full report in which they listed a number of 'Agreed Theological Considerations'—(1) the Church is Apostolic; (2) all members of the Church have a ministry to discharge; (3) within the general *diakonia* of the Church, a special ministry was instituted by the Apostles; (4) in creation, God's eternal purpose for man is revealed, and in redemption it is brought to fulfilment; and (5) the basic unit of humanity is not the individual human being, male or female, but man-and-woman as one. From all of this, two conclusions are drawn (and apparently agreed)—first, that the place and opportunity granted to women in ministry has traditionally been unjustifiably restricted; and second, that through the exclusion of women the traditional ministry itself has been distorted. One could have been forgiven for expecting that all this agreement on preliminaries was going to lead to some kind of agreement on how the contribution that women have to offer to the work of ministry could most profitably be channelled. Instead, however, it leads us merely to 'The Parting of the Ways'. We are confronted with two utterly contradictory views as to the right of women to be involved in the 'special ministry'—on the one hand, that which asserts that the reasons which, over the centuries, have barred women are based on sound theological considerations valid in both Old and New Testament times and still valid today; and, on the other, that which holds that the traditional pattern owed its existence not so much to theological as to sociological considerations, and that since these no longer obtain, the Church is being called upon to rethink its whole position and practice in this matter.

In regard to the admission to the ministry, the report went on, it had not been possible to reach a common mind. 'Some felt bound to hold that the Holy Ministry was not the form of *diakonia* proper to women; others felt bound to hold that there was no bar to the admission of women to the Holy Ministry.' On the other question, of women and the eldership, although no unanimity had been reached, it was recommended that the ban be removed and thereby women given a place in the courts of the Church. It was argued that, as baptized persons, women have equal membership with men in the Body of Christ and are therefore entitled to take counsel along with them in the government of the Church, and this they can do sitting as elders in Kirk Sessions and in the superior courts. No attempt is made to reconcile this decision with the various Pauline objections to women bearing rule which had always played a large part in ensuring the maintenance of the *status quo*. There is, for example, the passage in I Corinthians 14, 'As in all congregations of God's people, women should not address the meeting. They have no licence to speak but should keep their place as the law directs. If there is something they want to know they can ask their husbands at home. It is a shocking thing that a woman should address the congregation'.

The Assembly directed that the entire report should be sent to Presbyteries for discussion and comment, the Panel to present a further report to next Assembly in light of the returns received. It was further resolved that since the principles involved in Mary Lusk's petition were those involved in the report to be presented to next Assembly, her petition should at this juncture be dismissed.

Presbyteries had a lively time that winter wrestling with the report, and in particular with that part of it which recommended acceptance of the principle that women should be available on identical terms with men for ordination to the eldership. The Panel had in its report, as was proper, confined itself to a consideration of the doctrinal implications, but, as indicated earlier, there are practical or pragmatic considerations to be taken into account. This part of the field was virgin territory for Presbyteries to explore, and, to mix metaphors, some had a ball! One heard the queerest, the most unconvincing, the most irrelevant arguments advanced. On the positive side, for example, it was suggested that many congregations were, on present showing, going to find it increasingly difficult to maintain a Kirk Session at all if confined to men only. On the other side it was pleaded that once vacancies in the Session could be filled from the female ranks, the men would lose what little interest they had had, and ere long some Sessions would be a hundred per cent female. I was amused to hear it said that women were such inveterate gossips they could not safely be entrusted with the confidential material that forms part of the business of all Sessions. The objector obviously did not know some of my farmers who, for all their passion to know everything that was afoot in the parish, yet made good faithful caring elders. The questionnaire that had come down did not specifically ask for a vote to be taken, but in most cases Presbyteries did divide and count heads.

Fifty-three Presbyteries made returns, all of them, it was said, helpful and illuminating. Although not required to vote, 42 had in fact voted on the Eldership issue and 37 on that of Ministry. In the case of the Eldership, the result was 31 For to 11 Against (773 votes to 496), while in the case of Women and the Ministry, 19 had been For and 18 Against (740 votes as opposed to 622).

In view of the very substantial preponderance of opinion in favour of the proposal that women should be declared eligible for the eldership, it was recommended that Barrier Act procedure should be set in motion in favour of an Act decreeing that 'women members of a congregation shall be eligible for election and admission as Elders on the same terms and conditions as men members of a congregation'. An Overture was accordingly prepared and sent down, and it was reported to the Assembly of 1966 that there had voted—Approve, 45 Presbyteries (1783 votes); Disapprove, 17 Presbyteries (931 votes)—and an Act in the above terms was duly passed. Very

properly there is no breakdown in the statistics annually returned as between the sexes on Kirk Sessions, but I imagine that in
most cases today there is a fairly high proportion (say 35-55 per
cent) of women; in some, although not, I think, in very many,
the ladies are in a clear majority; and the number of Sessions on
which there are no women at all, although small, is certainly not
negligible. The subject of the all-male Kirk Session is one to
which I shall have occasion to return.

On the other matter of Women and the Ministry, the report
stated that, in view of the nature of the replies received, further
time should be given for clarification of the mind of the Church.
The Panel therefore asked to be given time to prepare a report
on the theological issues involved, a report it hoped to be in a
position to present to next Assembly. This naturally was agreed.
As it transpired, the Panel was unable to implement this programme and we had to wait until the Assembly of 1967 for the
full report, in which the Panel expresses indebtedness to
scholars from both the parish ministry and the faculties for
background material, although itself claiming full responsibility
for all that is in the report.

After a very full exegetical examination of all the relevant
New Testament passages, the report goes on to set out the two
opposing positions found in the Kirk today. In regard to these
the report is, I think, worth quoting at length.

View A—Some hold that the traditional practice of
excluding women from the Ministry of Word and Sacraments
arose in earlier ages from the influence of non-theological
factors. They argue that the patriarchalism of Biblical and
Apostolic times made it inappropriate to appoint women to
positions of authority in the Church or anywhere else, but that in
the changed social climate of today these old non-theological
factors no longer have any relevance. (They go on to attempt a
resolution of some of the apparent clashes between this view
and many of the New Testament passages cited earlier.)

View B—They recognise that in changing social attitudes
in the modern world, there is to be found evidence of the influence of the Spirit of Christ. But the Church cannot accept
uncritically the social assumptions of the twentieth century any
more than those of the first century. It is quite intelligible to
claim that something should be latent in Scripture awaiting, for

its recognition, the stimulus of the Holy Spirit in new historical situations. Yet whatever claims to be such must itself be judged by the mind of Christ as we know it, in and through the apostolic writings contained in the New Testament. We must be on our guard against the danger of rewriting Scripture in the light of present-day prejudices; all that we may legitimately do is to reinterpret Scripture in the light of such fuller under-standing of the mind of Christ as we have been given. The traditional exclusion of women from the Ministry of Word and Sacraments is not merely the result of social circumstances, but derives from theological principles which pertain to the substance of the faith.

Having thus set forth the two opposing positions at considerable length, the Panel goes on to say it is not going to attempt to adjudicate between them. Reaching a decision on an issue of such significance, it was felt, must rest with the courts of the Church which will no doubt want to take into their purview non-doctrinal matters which do not fall within the province of the Panel. Accordingly the Assembly was asked to transmit the report to Presbyteries in order to help them towards a careful and considered judgment when the time for decision came. Feeling in the Assembly, however, was all against this cautious approach, and a motion from the floor was approved instructing the Principal Clerk and the Procurator to draft an Overture to be sent down under the Barrier Act, to have the effect of enabling women to be ordained to the ministry on the same terms and conditions as men, the said Draft Overture to be submitted to a later sederunt of that Assembly. This was done, and a report made to the following Assembly (of 1968) that, on the question, two Presbyteries had been equally divided, 42 had Approved (1817 votes), and 17 had Disapproved (1030 votes). And so the Assembly put on the statute book Act XXV 1968, ordaining substantially that 'women shall be eligible for ord-ination to the Holy Ministry of Word and Sacraments on the same terms and conditions as are at present applicable to men'.

I have to put on record that on these two questions aff-ecting the place of women in the Church, I was from the outset very much with the minority, even if, as has not always happened to me, that minority finally came to be the majority view. In the case of women and the eldership, I had no difficulties whatever, whereas in the case of women and the ministry I had certain reservations—indeed I still have some —but these were wholly on the plane of the pragmatic, as I will explain in a moment.

On the theological side I had no difficulties. I have never been able to work up any enthusiasm for the theological position that would continue the exclusion. Supremely it seems to me odd beyond understanding that we should claim, as surely we are entitled to do, that woman was able to break out of her position of bondage and subservience due largely to the influence of the teaching of Jesus Christ, and at the same time continue within the Church of Jesus Christ the practice of denying her that equality of status we helped to win for her. Further—and I may be a heretic here—it has always seemed to me that St Paul was very much a creature of his time. And I think that, in some matters at least, we are all prepared to see him as hampered in this way. To take an obvious—and incontrovertible—example. Some of the passages quoted in defence of exclusion are bound up with imperatives about women being 'covered' in Church, which in its day was seen as very definitely a piece of theological teaching. I remember an occasion many years ago when, on a beautiful summer's week day, I was one of a small party of hikers who had found our way into a lovely little Norman church in the Yorkshire Dales. One of the girls was bareheaded. We were admiring the church when suddenly a verger came rushing towards us, demanding that the girl get her head 'covered', or get herself out of building inst- antly. The poor man was in a pitiful state. He seemed to be trying to make up his mind whether the church would need rededicating or whether fumigating would do. His beloved building had been desecrated. Nor was his attitude in any way exceptional. When Mrs Mopp came around with her pail, she might forget to don her apron, she would never think to omit her headsquare. After all, St Paul had said it, what more could you ask. It was of the substance of the faith. That was sixty years ago. If today you were to eject the bareheaded women from the average English congregation on a bright summer Sunday, you'd be lucky to be left with a quorum. Yet no amending epistle has proceeded from the hand of Paul. So far as I can see, the only distinction betweeen the one Pauline imperative and the other is that we are prepared to let the one go, but are equally determined to hang on to the other. For myself I should have thought the salient question was not what Paul wrote to the Churches, but whether in the light of our best understanding of his teaching, our Lord would wish women to be for ever excluded from the Ministry of his Word and Sacraments. I cannot believe it to be so.

I was not quite so happy on the practical side, however, for I felt that women would suffer from handicaps that do not so seriously affect their opposite numbers. While I accept completely the equality of the sexes, I do not at all believe in their identity. For one thing, I am convinced that the ministry is a particularly lonely occupation. You are a confidant and there is no way you can share the burden of that office. For a girl returning alone to a big traditional country manse on a dreich winter's night, I felt this could be indeed a heavy burden to bear. And if it is not to be a celibate ministry—and no one has ever suggested it should—then there is the question of children, or rather two questions: first, about maternity leave, something that cannot be conveniently arranged in the calendar of a parish ministry; and second, the question of being available in the years when children are most in need of a mother's care and attention, and during the very hours when she has to be out and about on parish duties. It's an unhappy story they tell, that of the children who said their father, minister of a busy city parish, was a man they saw daily at breakfast and most nights during the evening meal. Would it not be infinitely worse if they were to say that of their mother? Also in my experience, women seem to prefer a man for a 'boss' rather than someone of their own sex—I do not explain the phenomenon, I merely state the fact. I wondered how far the attitude which this represents would militate against a good relationship being formed between a woman minister and the female section of her flock. It seemed not without significance that the bitterest opposition to woman either as elder or as minister had come from the distaff side. For these and other like reasons I had my reservations, but I certainly did not see these as important enough to lead to my voting Against.

To return to the theological side, I am reminded of an incident in which I was involved fairly early on in the public debate. I had been interviewed on the subject one evening on an STV current affairs type programme, by Lynn M'Donald. A month or two later I was surprised to receive a phone call from the same girl asking whether I would be interested to go down to Manchester where she was now working, to take part in a discussion programme on the subject under the chairmanship of Ludovic Kennedy. I do not remember the names of the part-icipants, but there were two ladies, one a well-known member of the Methodist Church, and there was a priest of the Scottish Episcopal Church. In the course of some preliminary chatter over coffee, this gentleman indicated that he had the perfect, complete and irrefutable answer to the question why we could not have women priests—it was all really ridiculously simple. I could see our questionmaster was most intrigued, and when we got on to the air he took an early opportunity of calling on our Episcopal friend to reveal his secret to the audience. 'You ask why women should not be ordained to the priesthood?' he replied. 'The answer is simply this: that God didn't mean them to be. You might as well ask why men should not have babies.' By a massive exercise in self-control I prevented myself from saying that, in the latter case, the Almighty had made his intention more apparent than in the former!

At a later point in the discussion the Methodist lady said, as I remember it, that in Hong Kong at one point during the war, there was not a man available, and that two women had been, if not ordained, at least set apart and empowered to dispense the Sacrament. Our friend conceded that this had been so. Then, persisted the lady, was it his contention that these celebrations had been worthless? O no, he said, he was sure that God would in all the circumstances have adorned them with his divine blessing. At this point my self-control gave way, and I said, 'You mean that God recognised the ministrations of these women, but that your Church is a bit more particular!' I am not sure which of us was guilty of blasphemy. I have always felt that the Episcopal Church, because of the position it insists on adopting in relation to the historic episcopate has, strictly speaking, excluded itself from inter-Church relations. If yours is the only Church, there is, after all, no other with which you can confer. If pressed on the point the answer is usually the one we got at Manchester—that God in his infinite mercy has blessed these ministries of other denominations in spite of their obvious inadequacies. And I think the answer I gave at Manchester is still valid. It was an interesting experience, that visit to Manchester—it convinced me of a lot of things, but not of the validity of the theological objections to the ordination of women to the ministry.

The fears expressed by some, that we would soon be swamped with women ministers, have not materialised—I had never imagined they would. What did worry me was whether all those women attracted to the ministry would be successful in securing calls to parishes, for the last thing we needed in the Kirk was a situation where specialised jobs were having to be found, or worse still created, if the women who had qualified were to be kept in employment. I was very conscious of the fact that many of those who had voted For in the final count had done so because they felt it wrong that women should be barred because of their sex—but they themselves didn't want a woman minister—because of her sex! From what I could sense of feeling generally throughout the Church, there would be no immediate rush by congregations to avail themselves of the services of a woman so long as a man was available; and I think it is only now, twenty years on, that that attitude is beginning to break down. And even yet, only beginning. A quick run through the Year-Book shows that fewer than 80 of our 1374 churches are filled by women, whereas out of 64 persons licensed last year, 16 were women—that is to say, with an intake at roughly 25 per cent women, there are still only about 6 per cent of charges filled by them. In fairness it has to be said that a few years must still elapse before a fair comparison at this level can be made, but I still think the figure is low. What disturbs me most from my quick glance through the Year-Book is that, out of nine ministers working in charges in the Presbytery of Shetland, no fewer than five are women. I cannot believe that this is attributable to an insatiable demand for women ministers on the part of these northern islanders, any more than that the harsh conditions inevitably attaching to such charges are ideally suited to the fair sex. I incline to think that from the point of view of being chosen by a congregation as its minister, the ladies are still liable to get less than a 'fair do'.

I well know how easily a claim for a 'fair do' can become

a demand for preferential treatment. I would go so far as to say that some of the complaints concerning racial discrimination that we hear about these days arise from a failure to recognise this distinction. For example, I remember a newspaper-man phoning me at the time when the Moderator of Assembly was being chosen away back about 1975, highly incensed that apparently no woman had been considered for the office. I pointed out to him that up until then no Moderator had ever been appointed who had given less than twenty years' service in the ministry, and that the longest-serving woman had at that time given five, so that for her to be considered would mean departing from the rules and treating her as a special case. It had apparently never occurred to him.

Someone recently put me on the spot with the awkward question, 'From your fairly intimate knowledge of their track records, what would you say about the quality of our women ministers?' To this I gave the guarded, but honest, answer: 'We have some women ministers of quite outstanding quality, we have a few pretty dismal failures, and we have a lot in between'. And lest he should have missed the point, I added, 'If you can supply me with a more accurate evaluation of our male ministers I'll be interested to hear it!' By and large I should say the ladies are acquitting themselves exceedingly well and I am not aware of any difficulties that have arisen—or that have been raised—on either doctrinal or practical grounds. There has, I understand, been the odd case where a Moderator of Presbytery, being one bitterly opposed on conscientious grounds to the ordination of women, when one of the charges chose a lady licentiate, has arranged for his predecessor to deputise for him at the service of ordination. That apart I think it may be said that we ministers did well when we agreed that the ladies should join us.

The cases of difficulty that have arisen have all had to do with the ordination of women elders. There have been a few, and I fear there will be more. The pattern is a fairly standard one. Mr A goes to be minister of the parish of St B's, and soon thereafter it is decided to add to the number of the Session. Of the six persons elected at a congregational meeting, one is Miss C, a devoted and dedicated member, of unimpeachable character, who on being approached indicates that she will be proud to accept office. Mr A, however, has other ideas; he objects on conscientious grounds to the ordination of women and declares that he will have no part in such an offensive operation. He puts his case to Miss C who is quite unsympathetic; she claims that according to the law of the Kirk, her sex is no barrier to her becoming an elder, that both congregation and Kirk Session support her 'to a man', and that she is keen to serve. Mr A remains obdurate. His objection is on grounds of conscience and the Kirk recognises liberty of opinion on matters that do not enter into the substance of the faith. He claims the liberty which the conditions of his induction afford. Deadlock having been arrived at, the Session appeals the case to the Presbytery. Where do we go from here?

For myself I cannot see Mr A as having any valid defence. He will argue freedom of conscience, but that applies only to matters that do not enter into the substance of the faith, and the case advanced by the 'anti' group in 1964, as quoted above, included the affirmation that this position 'derives from theological principles which pertain to the substance of the faith.' If, then, the issue lies so near to the heart of the faith and is no kind of frill, no sort of optional extra, it is difficult to see how it can attract the degree of freedom claimed for it by Mr A—freedom to impose his interpretation. In that connection it has to be noted that what is guaranteed is freedom of opinion, not liberty of action and the two are manifestly different. A further substantial argument arises from the question, 'whose conscience?' Mr A argues that he has on this issue a tender conscience that would be offended were he to ordain Miss C to the eldership. Miss C argues that she too is equipped with a conscience from which there springs a desire to serve the Kirk in every way that is open to her—to do other would be a cowardly betrayal of what she conscientiously believes to be her 'call'—the congregation have indicated their wish that she should so act, and this has been unanimously ratified by the Kirk Session. Surely any court of the Church would be bound to adjudicate in favour of the conscience which conforms to established law and practice. Which would, it seems to me, lead a Presbytery to ordain that Mr A make arrangements for the ordination of Miss C. I imagine a Presbytery would put its judgment in that form, rather than as a direct command that Mr A actually ordain—thus offering him a way out. But if he feels strongly enough about the matter, he may well take no action, thus laying himself open to a charge of contempt with all the grim consequences that must follow.

Presumably the issue would be appealed until it reached the bar of the Assembly, where we should have on our hands what amounted to a heresy trial (even if the charge was contempt). And that is something unknown for many a long day, for heresy trials necessarily belonged to a day when orthodoxy was much more clearly defined than it is today. The contemporary position is that it would be very difficult indeed to prove that someone, say in a sermon, had been guilty of heretical teaching. Long, weary and unprofitable hours could be spent arguing the precise meaning of terms, the correct exegesis of a passage of Scripture, the exact implications of a doctrine; and at the end of the day—if it ever reached an end—there would be a Not Proven verdict of the most unsatisfactory kind. Not so with the question of whether or not Miss C is to be ordained. Here the issue is clear-cut, the facts are not in dispute, there are no fine shades of interpretation, and the conclusion is inescapable. A court cannot have its explicit orders set at naught. Suspension, if not actually deposition, is sure to follow. To anyone with a legal mind this is obvious if regrettable. But to the man in the pew, and even more vividly to the man in the newspaper office, the message is clear—if you are a minister today you can with impunity declare to your heart's content that you don't believe in the Resurrection of our Lord; but try saying that you don't believe in women elders and you're out on your ear. I can picture the headlines.

I should be more than happy if some way could be found to have the question of the applicability of the 'conscience clause' argued out in the Assembly on purely theoretical grounds and without any personalities involved, without anybody being at the bar. I should want the end product to be a statement of principle, not a verdict. At the moment I cannot but feel it is only a question of time until we have a 'case' with all its unhappy concommitants.

While I am wholly against Mr A above, I regret to find myself no less at variance with the Principal Clerk in regard to the purport of a communication he sent to Kirk Sessions a couple of years ago 'clarifying' the law in regard to women and

Kirk Sessions, and stating *inter alia* that any decision by a Kirk Session to the effect that women will not be considered for the eldership, is a denial of the eligibility conferred by the General Assembly, and is therefore in breach of the law of the Church. He goes on to speak of breach of ordination vows. This whole affair has an odd history. The Board of World Mission and Unity a few years earlier had appointed a sub-committee on the Community of Women and Men 'because this is integral to both mission and unity'. The reasoning seems as facile as it is specious, but let's not pursue that. In the course of its report to the Assembly of 1986 this group presented a series of figures showing the percentage on Presbyteries and their Committees of women ministers and of women elders and pleading for a wider representation. Apart from the general observation that 'by its failure to be truly representative of both women and men in the places where decisions are made, the Church is depriving itself of resources and experience and knowledge, and of insight and perspective, which it can ill afford to be without', there is not a word said in the report about Kirk Sessions. Yet in the Deliverance, a clause appears instructing Presbyteries to seek consultation with those congregations where there are no women elders, to draw their attention to the 1966 Act and to urge that consideration be given to the appointment of women to the eldership. Since it is for the Kirk Session to decide who are to be added to its numbers, and since the Kirk Session does not take direction from the congregation on this (or any other) matter, one would have expected the consultation to be with them rather than with the congregation. It was arising out of this instruction that there appeared the directive from the Principal Clerk, including the 'clarification' referred to.

If Presbyteries wish to meet with all-male Kirk Sessions and point out to them how they are weakening their witness by not including some of what we used to call 'the fair sex', that seems to me to be perfectly in order. But for the Presbytery to go on and tell them that if they resolve to continue without women they are in breach of ordination vows, is to me false and unacceptable. It seems to be based upon equating 'eligible for' with 'must be included in'—which is quite wrong. Some years ago the minimum age for elders was reduced to 18. If a Kirk Session in its wisdom decides it is going to stick by the old rule and have nobody under 21, is it to be regarded as in breach of ordination vows? The parallel seems perfect. And what of the Vacancy Committee that decides not to entertain any applicant over 45, when the law of the Church says he may continue as a minister to the age of 70? The law of the Kirk as I read it is perfectly clear in laying three responsibilities upon Kirk Sessions: (1) to determine when it wants to add to its number; (2) to resolve how many it wants to add; and (3) to decide who these are to be. The fact that women are now eligible means that they may, but not that they must, be so chosen.

There is a point which I feel I must make in defence of my own integrity. Away back in the middle sixties, when people were hotly debating the possibility of removing the barrier, I used to say to those who were hostile, 'You may not want women on your Kirk Session, but there are those Sessions that are desperately keen to recruit women members; there are cases where, unless women can be brought in, it will be necessary to appoint assessor elders from neighbouring Sessions—do you want to stand in the way of these things being done? Vote for the barrier to be lifted and let those that want women elders have them—it doesn't mean that you've got to have them'. The legislation, I went on, is permissive, not compulsory. I am sure I was right in this. But maybe I was in breach of my own ordination vows. Aggravated by inciting others!

I am quite clear that the whole life of the Kirk has been enriched by our having the ladies join us. I am sure that in any institution, especially one that digests change as slowly as the Kirk does, time—a good deal of time—has to be allowed for the full implications of so radical a change to be worked out, and that to try to hurry on the process can be more harmful than helpful. What will do most to ensure a fair deal for the fair sex is when it is seen just what excellent ministers of parishes, what valuable members of Sessions, the ladies are proving themselves to be. I have no fears for the future.

It is tempting to say something about the situation among our neighbours south of the border who are making such heavy weather of this issue—but I propose to resist the temptation. I feel sure that one way and another devices will be found for delaying the moment of decision for a long time yet. Equally I feel sure the change will come, and while I believe our neighbours will find it a change much harder to accept than we did, I feel confident that in the end of the day it will prove much to their advantage to have done so.

'Why didn't we think of this long ago?' is a question often asked in every walk of life.

Chapter 8
Going Global

WHILE PRESBYTERY CLERK at Glasgow I received one day
a letter from a minister in California. He had at one time held a
charge in the Presbytery but had relinquished it some years
before to take up teaching in a college on the Pacific Coast, and
he was writing to ask about the possibility of getting a
commission to the General Assembly because, he explained, 'I
am to be spending the next few months in New York and I
thought it was a pity to be so near Glasgow and not to come
across'. I had to read the sentence a second time. It made good
enough sense, I'm sure, for it takes less time to get from New
York to London than it took to get from Glasgow to London a
few years ago. The trouble was, I still had in my mind a picture
of the scenes so often re-enacted at Princes Dock during the
'hungry thirties,' when the Canadian Pacific Line was taking
out boatloads of young people to begin a new life in Canada and
tearful farewells were being taken on the quayside; for it was
well accepted that, for ordinary folk at least, you did not cross
the Atlantic more than once in one lifetime. And here was a
man who thought it a pity, having crossed the American
continent, not to finish the journey by crossing the Atlantic. It
reminds me of the tale of the Glasgow man writing to his son in
Los Angeles to let him know that his young sister was going out
to the States and suggesting it would be a nice thing if he were
to meet her at Kennedy Airport. To which he got the reply,
'Come out and meet her yourself—you're nearer'.

Whether or not we appreciate it, let alone realise all the
implications, the plain fact is that all the old physical barriers
that used to separate peoples and enable them to enjoy a
comparatively self-contained existence, have been relentlessly
swept away thanks to man's technical ingenuity. The whole
world now constitutes one single neighbourhood. It inevitably
follows from this that we are all of us neighbours of one

another. All that remains is for us to learn how to live together as 'guid neibours'. And that is where our technical ingenuity is of little help.

These same forces that have brought peoples together have not been without their influence on the Church, and it is being driven home to us increasingly that while we may, and I think should—indeed must—have a Church of Scotland, a Church of England (although in both cases I think 'in' would be better than 'of'), a Roman Catholic Church, a Greek Orthodox Church, a United Church of Canada and so on, there should be some bond to hold them all together in virtue of their common allegiance to the one Lord and Saviour of all. Just what form that bond should take is an intensely interesting, if also a quite baffling, question. One feature of this quest which emerges very early, and which should not take us wholly by surprise, is that the ease with which any degree of fellowship is achieved varies in inverse ratio to the proximity, geographical and traditional, of the denominations concerned. Thus we in the Kirk find it easier to engage in meaningful dialogue with, say, our erstwhile adversaries of the Roman Catholic persuasion than we do with our close relatives in the smaller groupings within the household of Presbyterianism. As I say, this shouldn't wholly surprise us, for it has always been easier to be sympathetically disposed towards the Chinese or the American Indians, than to that aggravating Scottish family that has moved in to the house across the landing!

In this connection one cannot but admire the consummate skill and brilliant statesmanship—for I am sure it must have demanded both in large measure—that has held the Roman Catholic Church together as one throughout the whole of the world during so many centuries. If rumour is to be believed, this principle may be under greater threat today than ever before, and, oddly enough, for the very reasons that are bringing other Churches into closer integration. And just as the conception of the Pope has been a focal point around which a common loyalty could be built, so the idea of 'Lambeth' has provided Anglicanism with a rallying-ground. Even while I write, the question of the ordination of women priests is putting that common loyalty under intense strain from which one can but wait to see what emerges.

While, then, there may well be a tendency towards division in the one-Church structures, there can be no denying that in recent years there has been a steady progression towards closer links among Christian denominations through the emergence of inter-Church organisations, of which there are many. It would seem reasonable to expect that the inter-Church organisations themselves would form closer links with each other with a view to the emergence of the one Super-Church, and signs of this seem already apparent. In the meantime, however, let us look in some detail at the emergence and development of some of these organisations, and let us then consider the intensely interesting stage that has presently been reached in this field.

One such organisation with which we in the Kirk have the closest links is the World Alliance of Reformed Churches (WARC) which, dating from 1875, is far and away the oldest of all such bodies. It was founded when twenty-one Reformed and Presbyterian Churches sent delegates to London where they constituted themselves 'The Alliance of the Reformed Churches Throughout the World Holding the Presbyterian System'. Two years later the first General Council of the Alliance met in Edinburgh, where it also established its headquarters, although later these were removed to Geneva. Twenty years ago it consisted of a General Council comprising 400 delegates from 104 Churches; it met once every five years; and it had as its avowed aims (1) the creation of a bond of unity among denominations of the Reformed tradition; and (2) the provision of a forum for discussion of programmes and doctrines of special interest to Presbyterian Churches. It will be noted that there was no talk of 'uniting', but merely of 'bonding', the constituent bodies together, and that their wider agenda extended only to embrace subjects of interest to Presbyterian Churches. They had, apparently, no ambition to unite all the Churches, nor did they see themselves with a duty to set the world to rights. Their aim, in fact, appeared to be the limited one of giving to world-wide Presbyterianism a meeting-place, something akin to what Lambeth supplied for Episcopacy.

In 1891 representatives of a number of Congregational Churches met in London and in consequence of their deliberations the International Congregational Council was formed. This body worked very closely in harmony with the

WARC. This it was easy for them to do since they had common roots in the Reformation tradition associated with the names of Calvin and Zwingli, and it was not surprising that at Nairobi in 1970 when the WARC held its twentieth, and the ICC its eleventh, Assembly, the two organisations should simultaneously have voted themselves out of existence and have united to form (and for the next ten days to sit as) 'The World Alliance of Reformed Churches (Presbyterian and Congregational)'. It is reckoned that with 150 Churches in 76 different countries, the total number of people belonging to this family could be as high as 70 million. The objectives which the new body set itself were those of liaison and enabling, while coordinated theological studies and the creation of caring relationships within the family stand high on its list of priorities. Clearly its business was still to bond, not to unite. In 1977 the Centennial Consultation of the Assembly was held at St Andrews, attended by 250 people from every corner of the globe, the theme of the consultation being 'The Glory of God and the Future of Man'. The Kirk took pride in the fact that its eleven representatives included four women and two students, but the relevant deliverance of the Assembly of 1978 regretted that no representative of the Church of Scotland had been appointed to the Executive Committee. Considering the historical position of the Kirk in the world-wide Presbyterian family this omission was indeed both surprising and regrettable and the deficiency has long since been made good. Whether the same considerations would apply today is questionable in light of what follows.

The General Assembly of 1988 received an interesting report in the following terms:

'In August 1989 the World Alliance of Reformed Churches will hold its General Council in Seoul, Korea. This will be the first time in its 145 years' history that a General Council will be held in Asia. This is slightly surprising since there are more Reformed Churches in Asia than in any other continent—49. Next comes Africa with 39; then Europe with 37; Latin America with 21; North America with 11; and finally Oceania with 7. In other words, over two-thirds of the 164 member churches are in the 'two-thirds' world of Asia, Africa and Latin America. The most spectacular growth of Reformed Churches has been in

Korea, Indonesia, Taiwan, and in many parts of Africa. This is the large international community into which the Church of Scotland delegates to the 22nd General Assembly in Seoul will enter; one in which European and North American influence is no longer predominant. In this regard the Alliance has changed as dramatically as the World Council of Churches.'

The Report continues as follows:

'The Churches in the Alliance differ greatly in size, ethos, and organisation. Sadly, many of them share an unhappy relationship with the state in their respective countries. Their witness to the Gospel brings them into conflict with their governments; this is specially so in Korea, Taiwan, South Africa, Latin America and Islamic countries. The Alliance is a source of support to them in their sufferings, and for Churches in countries where there is no such repression it is a constant reminder that their loyalty is higher than national.'

It was at Amsterdam as recently as 1948 that the Faith and Order Movement (which had come into being in 1927) and the Life and Work Movement (established in 1925) representing between them some 147 Churches on an international basis, declared their intention 'to stay together' and so constituted the World Council of Churches (WCC). Thirteen years later, at the Assembly of the Council, 198 member Churches approved a Basis in the following terms—'The World Council of Churches is a fellowship of Christians who confess the Lord Jesus Christ as God and Saviour according to the Scriptures and therefore seek to fulfil together their common calling to the glory of one God, Father, Son and Holy Spirit'. For myself I have never found this Statement fully satisfactory because for one thing I have never understood the justification for the use of the word 'therefore'. To me it seems that its replacement with the word 'which' would give us a perfectly adequate description of what I imagine to be the aim of the Council. The use of 'therefore' seems meant to give the whole thing a force of logical inescapability which I do not believe it to possess, for I am sure that before the uniting Churches took steps towards becoming a World Council, they were already, each in their own way and their own sphere, being true to their calling of glorifying God. What I should have found much more helpful, and what I think I was entitled to look for in such a declaration, was a clear definition of what this 'common calling' was. As it stands, the Statement merely begs the question. This is surely an area where greater clarity of definition is urgently called for.

Since its inception in 1948 the rise to prominence, importance and indeed dominance, of the WCC has been nothing short of meteoric. Today they employ a large staff in what our American friends describe as prestigious buildings in Geneva, and their annual allocation for the travelling expenses of the staff must alone be very high indeed. In 1972 I was on my European tour as Moderator of Assembly and I spent a few days with our congregations in Geneva and Lausanne. Naturally, I visited the offices of the Council where a lunch was given in my honour by the American Secretary of the Council, Dr Eugene Carson Blake, who was shortly to retire. The impression I formed as a result of my—admittedly fleeting—glimpse of the whole affair was that it was a kind of cross between United Nations and the Vatican—if on a much reduced scale. A distinguished visitor of an earlier day expressed surprise that there was not somewhere in the grounds a statue of Parkinson holding the Table of his Laws!

The power and influence of the WCC has grown relentlessly since its early days, so that it is now very much a force to be reckoned with in the affairs of its constituent Churches, and, it likes to think, of the nations in general. About the former there can be no doubt, the latter must be difficult to assess. The Council now embraces over 300 Churches in all parts of the world. It works through various Commissions and Programme Units, and Working Parties locally based. In 1989 it held in San Antonio, Texas a world conference on Mission and Evangelism which lasted eleven days, the theme being 'Your Will be Done: Mission in Christ's Way'. That an enormous amount of work went into this exercise, and that those who attended found it of great significance, is quite certain, but I find myself wondering what will be its long-term effect in the realm of the evangelistic outreach of its component Churches. Next summer it is to bring the worldwide Christian process on 'Justice, Peace, and the Integrity of Creation' to a climax with a 'global convocation' in Seoul, South Korea. In February 1991 the Seventh Assembly is to be held, this time in Canberra, Australia. From all of which it must be apparent that its range is wide both geographically and thematically. It is also to be noted that, as hinted in its Statement referred to above, its aim is not merely to be a bond, it is an ecumenical instrument committed to achieving union within its constituent bodies. For a Church like our own, membership of the WCC is an expensive affair. Not that the 'membership fee' is high—indeed it is surprisingly modest—but the expense involved in sending delegates hither and yonder cannot but be high. Sometimes in the train returning from a Committee meeting in Edinburgh, I find myself asking just what I had contributed to the discussion that could justify the cost of my fare—and sometimes the answer is far from reassuring. And that is going to Edinburgh, not to Seoul or Canberra! At the very least it might be worthwhile ensuring that if we are to send representatives so far at so great a cost—and I don't see how we can avoid it—we should be at pains to satisfy ourselves that they are truly 'representative' of that vast amalgam that we call the Church of Scotland, and not merely ecclesiastical globe-trotters often lamentably out of touch with opinion within the Kirk's membership.

Then there is the Conference of European Churches, a body with a very significant role to play at this time when, as a consequence of the 'Single European Act', 1992 will be the year when Europe really becomes one in a way our fathers could never have conceived possible, a day when there will be free movement both of people and of goods, when customs barriers will go, when there will be a single common passport, when each country will recognise the laws of the other as valid and binding; a totally new conception of inter-State relation-ships demanding a comparable new conception of inter-Church relationships. The Conference of European Churches was established during the period of the Cold War to assist in the business of reconciliation, and it now consists of 118 Churches from all sectors in Europe—Orthodox, Reformed, Anglican, Baptist, and so on, representing in fact a far wider membership than the WCC. In its latest arrangements for a Conference at Basel in 1989 on 'Peace with Justice', it had the full support and co-operation of the Roman Catholic Bishops' Conferences in Europe. In 1986 its Ninth Assembly was held in Stirling and, although the event did not attract much coverage on the media, an important programme was undertaken involving, we are told, the study of peace, justice, human rights, as well as in the fields of theological study and evangelism. Is it not strange, though, that theological and evangelical studies come in at the end of the programme as a post-lude to peace, justice and human rights. One could be forgiven for thinking that the theology should have been dealt with first so that a true Christian standpoint might be found from which to examine and pass judgment on events in these other spheres.

Coming nearer home we must say something about the British Council of Churches (BCC), although in view of recent events stemming from Swanwick its days are numbered. This body came into being in 1942 when 16 denominations, including the Kirk, agreed to form themselves into a British Council. This was to be composed of representatives of all the constituent bodies in an agreed proportion, it was to meet twice a year in Assembly, it was to operate through various divisions —on Ecumenical Affairs, on International Affairs, on Community Affairs, on World Mission, and on Christian Aid. Its declared intention was to be the official instrument of the Churches for facilitating common action, for promoting the study of matters of common Christian interest, and for furthering the cause of Christian unity. There is a great deal of truth in the claim that 'while the Council is consultative, not legislative, its statements and plans receive widespread endorsement by its component Churches whose thought and action are increasingly guided by them'. There are now 29 British Churches representing almost every denomination in the membership of the Council, as well as a number of associate members, while the Roman Catholic Church in England and Wales and the Roman Catholic Church in Scotland are represented by consultant observers.

I was myself for a time a member of the Council and more particularly of its Executive Committee. James Longmuir, who was then Principal Clerk of Assembly, had been pressed to fill this post, but did not feel equal to the added burden (and frankly I do not think he was madly enthusiastic in any case) and he suggested that I should attend in his stead. So for quite a few years I attended meetings in London with some regularity; but while I got quite a bit of satisfaction out of the work of the Executive, it being largely of the legal and constitutional character that appeals to me, I cannot say the same about the meetings of the Assembly itself, which I always felt to be characterised by a certain air of unreality. It came as little surprise to me when a change in the constitution requiring the size of the Executive Committee to be reduced by the members re-electing themselves, resulted in my ceasing to be of their number!

From my experience and observation of it, I should say that while the BCC was officially committed to advancing the cause of Church union among its members, it did little directly in this connection, for it principally saw itself as the brain and the voice of the Churches of Britain, studying from a Christian point of view all national affairs characterised by a spiritual, moral or social dimension, as well as matters of wider inter-national, economic and industrial concern, and speaking to the nation thereanent in the name of the Christian people of the land—a kind of British Church and Nation Committee. Writing to the Home Secretary, our own Church and Nation Convener is on record as describing the British Council as 'acting on behalf of all the Churches in Britain'. Over the years, as well as pron-ouncing on many subjects, it has produced a great deal of literature in a variety of fields, and this, it has to be said in fairness, has been directed to the study of, and for action if thought appropriate by, its constituent Churches.

The BCC is voluntarily bowing itself out in order that it may be replaced by a new 'instrument', following upon the enthusiasm recently generated by the 'Not Strangers but Pilgrims' movement. We are to have a Council of Churches for Britain and Ireland. How far this new instrument will be genuinely new, and how far it will be the same people with an added Roman Catholic participation doing substantially the same things under new names (and at greater expense), is an interesting speculation which only time will resolve. For the moment, though, it is interesting to see how all this has come about—as we shall try to do in a moment.

For the present let us come still nearer home with a quick glance at the Scottish Churches Council. Prior to 1964 a body known as the Scottish Churches Ecumenical Association had been functioning in Scotland organising inter-Church end-eavours of one sort and another. Their most notable contribution had been the establishing and running of Scottish Churches House, a conference centre created most imaginatively out of a row of old dwelling-houses situated just opposite the Cathedral in the heart of Dunblane. In 1964 this Association was dissolved to be replaced by a new body, the Scottish Churches Council, which was to include all Scottish denominations that were members of the BCC (and which now takes in also the Roman Catholic Church on an observer basis). The Council had four avowed aims—(1) to interpret the ecumenical movement as a whole, and to promote its interests, serving the WCC and the BCC in the furtherance in Scotland of their plans and policies; (2) to initiate and promote inter-Church co-operation in prayer, mission, study and practical action; (3) to provide opportunities for the discussion of Faith and Order issues by ordained and lay representatives of all the Churches; and (4) to give expression to united Christian opinion on important issues. The Council was to meet normally twice a year for a full day and there was to be an Executive Committee as well as Committees on Churches House, on Inter-Church Aid, on Mission, on the Witness of the Laity, on Ecumenical Education, and on Local Co-operation. Apart from the staff attached to the House, there has been a full-time General Secretary.

In its maintenance of Churches House at Dunblane, the SCC is providing a valuable service, but as a Council it seems to be at best a mild echo of its British counterpart. Zealots for Scottish Nationalism would be quick to point to the incongruity of a 'British' Council which is self-sufficient south of the border but needs a back-up organisation in Scotland. It is emphatically not an official voice of the Scottish Churches. I remember an occasion when a Government Department sent to Dunblane for comment some proposal for change in the law when it should quite definitely have been directed to the Church of Scotland which, so far as was appropriate, would have taken other denominations into consultation. Inevitably the maintenance of the work of the Council costs quite a bit (the Kirk's share is more than two-thirds of that for the BCC) and there are those who view it as a luxury which in the present financial crisis we can ill afford. Like its London equivalent the SCC has a limited future, due to be replaced with a new 'ecumenical instrument' following upon Swanwick. That, however, will not resolve and may well accentuate the financial problem.

A completely fresh impetus was given to the ecumenical drive as a result of a conference held at Swanwick in Derbyshire in 1985. This conference had followed on a resolution of the BCC in the previous March and was attended by a much larger than usual lay element, which probably explains why there was a mighty upsurge from 'the ranks' that they should 'cut the cackle and get on with the business of getting themselves united'. One can well understand the conviction of the ordinary member, once charged with ecumenical fervour, that the rate of progress in this field is ridiculously slow. So often a process is begun that holds out high hopes of great things to be achieved (described probably in extravagant terms), but that peters out a few years later having come up against insuperable difficulties. On this occasion it would seem *vox populi* took over with one almighty shout, saying, 'We are all friends together, we have a common purpose, let's close our ears to those propounding difficulties and let's close our ranks and press on with our task as one united body. All one body we!' A most admirable and commendable thing, you might incline to think. But is it? I can picture the scene on a building site with the architect and the surveyor standing, blueprints in hand, listening to the site engineer discoursing on the results of his test-borings and explaining why the house planned for this particular plot just cannot go up here. They are all looking very glum when along comes the prospective householder wreathed in smiles, demanding that they stop all this idle chatter and dismal stories and get on and put up his house on his chosen site. In this harsh world, cheering assurances and ignoring of difficulties do not produce worthwhile results. In the ecumenical realm I seem to remember an absolute undertaking given (and I'm sure accepted by many) that we would have achieved unity by Easter 1980. Here we are ten years later and all we have achieved has been frustration, disillusion, lots of talk and reams of reports.

The trouble, as I see it, is that for all our talk we are not so utterly convinced of the need for 'organic unity' as to be prepared to pay the price which it is bound to demand. The benefits to be achieved would be peripheral and ornamental while the coin to be paid would be basic and precious. It is not just a measure of goodwill and Christian forbearance that are required but a readiness to sacrifice elements in our practice of the faith that, over the years, have become to us enormously precious, indeed essential to the faith as we have come to understand it. A round peg fits into a square hole only after one or other has sacrificed its identity—or with the aid of a chisel a compromise has been effected—so that now neither is recognisable as such. And all for what? These, however, were most emphatically not the thoughts in the minds of the company at Swanwick as they hastened on to plan the Inter-Church Process.

The Swanwick position was presented to our Assembly in 1985 in a report which read:

'Possibly the most significant action of the BCC in 1984 was its decision to invite all British churches, including those not in membership of it, to share in "a process of prayer, reflection and debate together, centred on the nature of the church in the light of its calling in and for the world". This invitation is based upon the conviction that the churches in this country will only fulfil their mission if they are renewed and reformed, and that their reformation and renewal will be greatly assisted if they listen reflectively and prayerfully to one another and to what one another believes about the nature and task of the Church. There has been an eager response to this invitation, with the Roman Catholic Church and "Holiness" churches joining the BCC's member churches in welcoming it and agreeing to participate in it. It is accompanied by a readiness on the part of the BCC to reform or reconstitute itself to meet the new situation of the 1980s, and to widen its ecumenical spread to do justice to the full range of traditions, "evangelical", "catholic", "pentecostal", or however described.'

The Kirk agreed to throw in its lot subject to certain reservations about 'the best way of promoting the process in Scotland'.

At Swanwick in the September of 1987 a further conference was held, described as the most significant gathering in Britain since the Reformation (how's that for hyperbole?) when the Churches were called upon to move closer together in the search for unity. This meeting marked the culmination of the Inter-Church Process, 'Not Strangers but Pilgrims', begun three years earlier, and was attended by 300 delegates, forty of them from the Kirk, although I cannot find any record of the Assembly having appointed them. Their task was to discover 'new instruments'—new structures that would enable Churches to do more together and to include the 'grass-roots' elements in the denominations to be involved in decision-making and planning. 'This is a new beginning,' we are told, 'we now declare together our readiness to commit ourselves to each other under God. Our earnest desire is to become more fully, in His own time, the one Church of Christ, united in faith, communion, pastoral care and mission.' Encouragement was derived from a call by the Roman Catholic Cardinal Basil Hume to his delegates that they should recommend to their people 'that we now move quite deliberately from a situation of co-operation to one of commitment to each other. I mean that we commit ourselves by praying and working together for Christian unity and to acting together, both nationally and locally, for evangelism and mission'. The conference went on to frame a Declaration which they hoped would be read in all Churches.

The General Assembly of 1988 found itself with the Swanwick Declaration on its hands. The catchword of the movement had now been adjusted to read 'No Longer Strangers —Pilgrims!', and for the benefit of those who 'do not have the English', it is repeated in what I take to be Welsh and Erse. The Declaration having been adopted with acclaim had been personally signed by all those present at the Hayes Conference Centre, Swanwick on Friday 4th September 1987. It reads:

'Appointed by our churches and under guidance of the Holy Spirit we declare that this, the broadest Assembly of British and Irish churches ever to meet in these islands, has reached a common mind. We are aware that not all Chistians are represented amongst us, but we look forward to the time when they will share fully with us. We came with different experiences and traditions, some with long ecumenical service, some for whom this is a new adventure. We are one band of pilgrims. We are old and young, women and men, black and white, lay and ordained, and we travelled from the four corners of these islands to meet at Swanwick in Derbyshire. There we met, we listened, we talked, we worshipped, we prayed, we sat in silence deeper than words . . . . Driven on by a Gospel imperative to seek unity that the world may believe, we rejoiced that we are pilgrims together and strangers no longer. We now declare our readiness to commit ourselves to each other under God. Our earnest desire is to become more fully, in His own time, the one church of Christ, united in faith, communion, pastoral care and mission. Such unity is the gift of God. With gratitude we have truly experienced this gift growing amongst us these days. We affirm our openness to this growing unity in obedience to the Word of God, so that we may fully share, hold in common and offer to the world those gifts which we have received and still hold in separation. In the unity we seek we recognise that there will not be uniformity but legitimate diversity . . . . It is our conviction that as a matter of policy at all levels and at all places, our churches must now move from co-operation to clear commitment to each other, in search of the unity for which Christ prayed, and in common evangelism and service of the world. This is a new beginning. We set out on our further pilgrimage ready to take risks and determined not to be put off by "dismal stories".'

If all that is proclaimed in the Declaration is true, then we have indeed reached something new. However much the other inter-Church organisations may be dedicated to the search for One Church, their primary purpose is to forge a bond between churches, to provide the machinery that will enable them to study together, to make common pronouncements, to mount common enterprises, to work together in ever closer harmony. The Declaration turns its back upon all these as things of the past—'we must move from co-operation to clear commitment'—and our objective must be the establishment of 'one Christian Church of Great Britain and Ireland'. It is easy to see why, in such a context, great encouragement must have stemmed from the fact that Cardinal Hume had indicated that the Roman Catholic Church was now wholeheartedly in as part of the enterprise. 'No Longer Observers—but Participants' was to be their slogan.

Following upon so specific and so emphatic a declaration of intent, it might seem strange that the conference went on, not to arrange a basis of union nor to discuss the doctrinal differences lying in the way of unity, but to plan the creation of new instruments that would encourage and simplify closer co-operation among denominations, one for the north called

'Scottish Churches Together' and another for the whole country, probably to be called 'The Council of British and Irish Churches'.

So far as the particular Scottish scene was concerned, the outcome of all this was that the SCC would be wound up, its place to be taken by a body to be called Scottish Churches Together which was to 'continue in Scotland the process in Britain and Ireland under the title Not Strangers but Pilgrims'. It was proposed that all the work carried on hitherto under the auspices of the SCC should now become part of Scottish Churches Together. (The title of this body, incidentally, is now the rather odd one, 'Action of Churches Together in Scotland'.) On examining the proposed constitution and so on, it looks rather like what doctors used to put on prescriptions—'the mixture as before'. In any case the matter does not appear of supreme importance since the real guiding force is going to be the 'Ecumenical Instrument for Britain and Ireland', in which, of course, we in the Kirk will play a considerable part, having a representation of 30 out of a total membership of 284. This Council of British and Irish Churches is to take the place of the BCC which has agreed to dissolve, and it will meet in plenary session every second year. Then there will be 'the Church Representatives Meeting' which will take place two or three times a year and which will provide 'an opportunity for senior representatives of the member Churches to meet together regularly for prayer, discussion and study. It will have as its major concern the growth of visible unity and common mission in the life of the churches of Britain and Ireland'. So we have returned to the business of promoting unity rather than organising co-operation. And we have also fallen into the hands of 'senior representatives of the member churches', and these sound uncommonly like the 'Church Leaders' whom we hear so much about these days. The Kirk ofcourse doesn't have any. The subjects about which the Council is to concern itself are to 'include issues concerning public services (eg, education and health); areas of deprivation; race relations; the place of women and young people in society and the church; and other social and moral/ethical issues'. It is interesting, isn't it, that a movement that began with an uprising from the grass roots has so quickly fallen into the hands of the Church leaders, and that a drive declared to be aimed at achieving union should so quickly find itself embroiled in race relations and other suchlike social issues.

When this whole package was presented to the General Assembly of 1988 there was a great wave of enthusiasm—I heard it described as 'ecuphoria'. The next step was the usual one that the proposals went to Presbyteries for consideration and comment. So far as I can discover, the reception there has not manifested anything like the same degree of enthusiasm. I remember a colleague telling me once of how he had conveyed to his Kirk Session some proposal come down from the General Assembly. 'As I was getting the message across,' he said, 'I could feel a distinct wave of no-enthusiasm sweep through the meeting.' I could not put as strongly my own impression of what happened in our Presbytery of Glasgow, but it required all the best efforts of an able Convener to win approval for a recommendation that we agree that the proposals were 'adventurous and commendable and that every encouragement should be given towards their implementation'. There was much more hearty support for a motion from the floor which 'urged the Church of Scotland to continue discussion, giving priority to doctrinal issues rather than issues of co-operation national and local'. For myself I have never been able to engender any zeal for the ambition to create a kind of Super-Church, be it for Scotland, for Britain and Ireland, or for the world. The project seems to me to be beset with difficulties, and to be a thing, in any case, not worth the effort.

Many years ago I was sitting at a meeting of the Synod of Clydesdale when a speaker made reference to the World Presbyterian Alliance. My neighbour on the right whispered to me, 'Now that's a really worthwhile affair—that actually ministers to over sixty million people'. My neighbour on the left, who had overheard the comment, whispered in my other ear, 'Don't believe him—it doesn't minister to a solitary human being'. I'm sure that the latter speaker, though he had my left ear, had the right end of the stick. When it comes to the business of bringing people to Christ, or ministering to the spiritual needs of those who have committed themselves to Him, it is the denomination and the congregation that are involved. The inter-Church bodies may play a useful part in providing a service, in making a resource available (in modern jargon), but the actual ministering is done on a completely different plane. I think it is possible to ascribe far too much importance to the work undertaken (usually under floodlighting) at the inter-Church level, often to the detriment of the far more important contribution in the winning of souls undertaken in the obscurity of our parishes. However prestigious the Super-Church may be made to appear on paper, it can never take the place of the Parish Kirk.

I feel too that in these inter-Church bodies decisions on important issues are reached by people who are out of touch with the people in the pews, and in a day when we never tire of proclaiming how dependent we are upon the ministry of the laity. I was much impressed with this aspect of things during the time I served on the Executive of the British Council. I don't think there was one of us on that body who was still functioning as what might be called an ordinary parish minister, not one of us who was in direct daily touch with the membership of his denomination. I was probably as near as any, but I was clearly conscious of a gap. For such people it is easy to forget the persons-in-the-pews, or at least to think that they can know little of such highly complicated issues—they need to be told what is best for them. It is so easy to forget that it is the persons-in-the-pews with whom the whole business is concerned and that, what's more, they are providing the wherewithal to make all the efforts of the inter-Church councils possible. The danger of creating an ecclesiastical jet-set flying regularly to London and from time to time to Texas, to Seoul, to Canberra, and wherever, is a very real one. I cannot imagine that lonely impoverished souls faithfully filling their FWO envelopes week by week, envisage themselves as subsidising this kind of exercise. Theirs is a simpler idea of how the Lord's work is to be accomplished— and, who knows, it may well be a more accurate idea.

One has to agree that it would be good if the Christian Church in these islands could speak loud and clear with one common voice on some of the burning moral and spiritual issues of the day. It might well be that government, industry, education and the other great entrenched powers in the land would pay heed to such a unanimous shout when they can afford to ignore a succession of whispers coming from this body and that. But does anyone honestly believe that we are going to be able to create any Council that will be invested with that degree of authority? Suppose every major denomination in these islands throws in its lot with the proposed new British and Irish Council, they are not thereby empowering that body to speak on their behalf. At best what will happen is that the Council will study some problem (say the position of refugees) and will then communicate its findings to all the member churches which will then be free to adopt, adjust, amend these findings at will and then take whatever action thereanent they consider appropriate.

So we will still not have one loud voice, we will still have a collection of whispers, and not all whispering precisely the same thing. The tone of the present report might seem to suggest that in fact the new Council would have power to speak for us all, but I cannot believe that this will ever—or indeed can ever—be the case. There is a sharp distinction between, for example, the Church of Scotland and the Roman Catholic Church in Scotland in that the former could, if its General Assembly so resolved, resign its sovereignty to the extent of handing over power to some central body to determine and speak on its account in certain fields, whereas the Roman Catholic Church in Scotland does not have that kind of sovereignty that it could relinquish even if it wanted to. To take the obvious illustration: let it be that Action of Churches Together in Scotland took up the very thorny, but very urgent, question of abortion, and let it be that by a very large majority it approved a report declaring abortion acceptable in certain clearly prescribed circumstances. The Roman Catholic Church would then require in some way to dissociate itself from the resolution, for it is not for the Roman Catholic Church in Scotland to determine its position on such an issue—it takes its orders from a higher plane. I imagine a similar (although not identical) kind of situation would arise for the Episcopal Church in Scotland were the Council, after due doctrinal deliberation, to determine that women should be eligible for ordination to the priesthood. The loyalty of Scottish Episcopals to Lambeth takes precedence over that to Dunblane.

I believe there is a place, a quite significant place, for inter-Church councils today. As I see it, they enjoy opportunities for studying subjects of contemporary interest at a depth never easy and often quite impossible for the separate denominations, particularly the smaller ones. On these and such-like subjects, they are in an admirable position to speak *to* the churches, although they must never presume to speak *for* the churches. They have no mandate entitling them to do so, and given the various constitutions of the constituent bodies they can never be given such a mandate. In any case I believe that all material coming from such Councils should, before acceptance by the Kirk, be subjected to the most careful scrutiny, particularly at the 'lower' levels within the system. There is a real danger in placing too much trust in the judgment of the so-called Church Leaders—it has always been a contention of mine that a leader can get so far separated from the main body of the troops as to have become a deserter.

If we feel there must be a Super-Church, then let's try to convert our own denomination into just that!

Chapter 9
Keeping the Nation On Course

ONE FEATURE of the Assembly, in my attitude to which I must be one of a fairly small minority, is the annual report of the Church and Nation Committee, for I have never seen that event as one of the highlights of the week, as the day not to be missed on any account. The subjects discussed are generally of considerable interest and frequently of great importance, level of debate often reaches a quite remarkably high standard, comparing more than favourably with what is fed to us from party political conferences (and, even worse, from the House of Lords), we can count on a packed, expectant Assembly and an Order Paper bristling with Notices of Motion, and it has been found that nothing short of a guillotine will bring it all to an end. All of these things I readily concede. However, for me the whole tone of the proceedings has an air of unreality in the context of the business of the supreme court of the Kirk. Over and over again, I have found myself asking about some item in the Report the following three questions: what concern is this of ours? how far are we qualified to pass judgment on an issue of this complexity? and, what conceivable good is going to come out of all this argument and counting of heads?

To be more specific let's look at a typical year's agenda, and take the most recent at the time of writing—1988. We begin with 'Poverty in Scotland', and here the efforts of the Committee are given a very significant slant by being described as a consideration of 'the cultural, social, and economic gap between the life of the Scottish poor and the life of the Church', but which travels as far afield as Nicaragua in search of evidence, and which has little if anything to say about the relation between Scottish poverty and the life of the Kirk, being primarily concerned to trace it to the inadequacies of government policy. We then move to Northern Ireland, and here I prick up my ears, for here there is both a sectarian and a religious interest involved, here supremely is a theme on which the Church has a right, indeed a duty, to speak, and to do so emphatically. It may be not without significance that the subject is summarily disposed of in eleven lines. Next we pass to Scottish Prisons and the Sentencing Policy of the Courts; then to Scotland's Travelling People and the Kirk's responsibilities towards them 'through pastoral and other involvement and generally by calling upon the Secretary of State to extend the availability of capital grants'; then to the Funding of the National Health Service, where we advance a specific point of view, not on the ground that it represents the Christian standpoint, but because 'we believe the vast majority of the people in the country want it'; and from there to The Christian Use of Sunday. Moving to a new section on Economic and Industrial Interests, we deal with the Community Charge, with the privatisation of the Scottish Steel Industry, with the significance for Scotland of Multi-National Enterprises, with Trade Union Legislation. The section on International Interests includes references to Refugees and Asylum-seekers, to South Africa, to the Peace-Making Process. And a closing section on The Media deals with The Changing Scene, with the Independence of the Media, and with The Need for the Expansion of Gaelic Broadcasting. Adding all that together you have quite a menu for a five-hour session, and, since each dish has at the very least to be tasted, quite a meal!

That may well have been your thoughts when reading through your papers in advance! But not everyone in the Assembly shared your view of it as a full enough or a varied enough or a wide-ranging enough programme to occupy the whole of a five-hour debate, for no fewer than fifteen Notices of Motion were tabled, almost all of them raising new matters such as poverty among older people, the rising tide of lawlessness, criminality and violence in society, Scotland's falling population, the promotion of a maritime policy for our island nation, whether it was right that timber-growing should have been taken out of the normal tax system, the need for the P&O Shipping Company to depart from its insistence on ships' watches being of more than twelve hours' duration, the Government's plan to abandon the Community Programme coupled with the morality of the proposed new Employment Training Scheme, the plight of 'tug-of-love children', and the democratic control of Scottish affairs—the creation of a Scottish Assembly and means by which a national referendum on devolution may be effected. Quite a menu, as I say, and not one from which you could select—every single dish had to be consumed.

Long and varied as the 1988 list of topics discussed indisputably was, it was, in fact, one of the most restricted reports for some years past. In the previous year, for example, although there were only 34 paragraphs to the Deliverance, no fewer than 38 amendments were advanced from the floor once the commissioners had got their teeth into the stuff of the Report. The year before that saw a Committee Report running to 54 items and producing 29 counter-motions, et cetera. As I have suggested, the Committee in 1988 deliberately restricted itself, making no mention of hardy annuals like war, the use of nuclear weapons, the restriction of manufacture of the materials of war, subjects which in varying forms have appeared year after year. Other themes which have engendered lively debates on this report have been the need for the introduction of legal restrictions on transactions in, and on the ownership of, land in Scotland, the long-term effects of large-scale coniferous afforestation, the adoption of the Trident missile system, violence and vandalism on the media, refusal to buy South African goods, the imposition of sanctions on South Africa, Scottish housing. And, of course, over the years, the Falklands War, the Cod War, the Israeli conflict—all have had their turn of appearing in the pages of the Church and Nation Report and of being hotly debated on the floor of the General Assembly. On one occasion, I remember, Mrs Thatcher was an overnight guest of the Lord High Commissioner and was present for a while in his gallery the following morning. She had been told great things about the way in which the Assembly tackled (not to say solved) some of the intractable problems confronting the nation. As it transpired, most of the time while she was present was occupied in discussing the effects on old ladies living alone of a proposed rise in the cost of a dog licence! No one can say we are not thorough when it comes to keeping the nation right!

It is important to understand how it all began. From the theoretical point of view, the Church and Nation Committee report has its roots in the doctrine that religion is not an affair concerned wholly with individual salvation, not something to be confined within a dedicated building on one day of the week, that the Christian faith must affect our behaviour and our attitudes in every department of life. Our faith must exert its influence on all aspects of our living. It is our duty to apply Christian principles to all our thinking and all our doing. There is no use talking piously about justice for all if we are going to sit passively by and see injustice suffered on every hand, no point making prim pronouncements about the need for houses for all, while happily accepting that a million people are homeless. Doubtless the priest and the Levite were inspired by the highest religious principles, they were good men, so good that they had to avert their eyes as they passed by on the other side, for the mere sight of such suffering caused them grievous pain; but the victim owed his life to the Samaritan who was prepared to translate his doctrine into action. If in this hard-bitten twentieth century the Church of Christ wishes itself to be taken seriously, it must do more than preach pie-in-the-sky-when-you-die, it must be seen to be taking a very active interest in the conditions affecting God's creatures in the years before they qualify for their share of the 'pie'. Of all this I shall have more to say hereafter. For the moment I advance it as the reason why the Kirk has come to be interested in subjects so varied in their content and so far-flung in their geographical incidence as those which characterise the typical Church and Nation Report of today.

It can further be argued that Government takes a great deal to do with the life of contemporary man, setting out for him all kinds of imperatives, instructions which may well conflict with the Christian imperatives to which he owes obedience. What, for instance, if his Christian allegiance commits him to pacif-icism and his Queen causes to be served on him a notice calling him to military service? In a perfectly understandable way, the Church and Nation Committee sees itself as having a duty to represent the cause of the Christian when the demands of God and of Caesar conflict—and indeed to move in with guidance for the government if possible, even before the conflict has arisen.

It is instructive, in the second place, to follow the historical development of the position as it has become today. It was as comparatively recently as 1920 that the Church and Nation Committee was created as a vehicle for the formulation and expression of the Church's concern, on moral and social grounds, about current trends in the life of the nation. A fairly wide remit, certainly, but at least confined within 'the life of the nation'. That year was a significant point in world history. The war to end war, the so-called Great War, had just ended, a conflict that had taken such a terrible toll of the nation's manhood. Surely it had not been sheer waste, surely we were about to see the dawn of a new world. It was not long ere it became apparent that the tendency was all towards getting back to life as it had always been—only more so. Now supremely was the moment when the Church should be speaking out loud and clear, passing moral and spiritual judgments upon the trends of the time, leading the nation forward and upward. The Kirk had, surely, a major role to play in helping the nation to win the peace. In those early days the Committee was content to deal with large public issues in a general way, by stating Christian principles without going on to suggest specific remedies. It dealt with such themes as gambling, mixed marriages, rural depopulation, Irish immigration, and unemployment in the mining industry. Even after the Second World War, the tendency of the Committee was still to confine itself to matters that were truly domestic to the people of the specific areas of trouble, with a view to recommending the right remedy. Some might have said we did our own job and left the politicians to get on with theirs. The inclination to roam wide and to seek to ally the Kirk with specific policies is a fairly recent phenomenon and may, I think, be traced to a great extent to the influence of our increasingly close connection with, and allegiance to, ecumenical bodies, and in particular with the World Council of Churches.

The precise terms of the Committee's remit today is 'to watch over developments of the nation's life in which moral and spiritual considerations specially arise, and to consider what action the Church may, from time to time, be advised to take to further the highest interests of the people'. The new Convener, who took over in 1988, is on record as saying, 'With this remit we must be prepared to discern and comment upon social, moral and spiritual trends, and we cannot run away from controversial topics. Our approach is based on the conviction that our

Christian faith is relevant to the whole of our lives and that we have therefore a responsibility, not only as individuals but also as a Church, to seek to interpret the will and word of God in relation to social, economic and political circumstances'. This sounds quite unexceptionable, indeed quite admirable. It is when the attempt is made to put it into practice that the problems arise.

Right at the outset we are confronted with two practical problems: first, how a remit of such extensive proportions can be fulfilled by a comparatively small group of people, each one of whom has lots of other things demanding attention; and second, how the whole thing can be encompassed within an Assembly report of restricted size and disposed of in a debate of limited duration. About the former of these difficulties, I am in no position to speak, but one is sometimes tempted to wonder whether a particular theme appears because it is a hobby-horse of a single member who welcomes the opportunity of giving an equestrian display, and one is also sometimes tempted to wonder how much is accepted—and none too critically—from one or other of the ecumenical bodies who employ people specifically to study such themes and to work in such areas, and who are therefore accepted as specialist witnesses.

About the latter difficulty—that of timing—I can speak with some knowledge. People talk loosely about 'Church and Nation day' at the annual Assembly—which seems now to be permanently fixed for the Wednesday—but it is by no means a 'day', being at most around five hours. For the affair is now governed by a 'guillotine'—ie, when a certain moment is reached, the whole matter is departed from, never to be resumed. Assembly Standing Orders ordain that when an Order of the Day is reached for taking an item on the agenda at a specific hour, although the earlier business is still in progress the Assembly will pass to that item, returning at a later time to take up and conclude the interrupted earlier business. Some years ago, however, Standing Orders were amended by the introduction of the ominous words, 'provided that in the case of an Order of the Day following the report of the Church and Nation Committee such unfinished business shall not be taken up'. Thus, inevitably, the shadow of the guillotine hangs over the whole debate, and generally the discussion of the last few items is shamefully scamped.

It was not always so. My own early recollection of the Church and Nation report saw it invariably taken on the Monday of the second week, the Assembly having convened on the previous Tuesday. Monday was the day of the Garden Party at Holyroodhouse, and the anxiety of the commissioners to foregather with spouses suitably bedecked, and stroll around the lovely gardens below Arthur's Seat, ensured that the business would be completed at worst not later than 3.30, and since in those days we took no lunch break this meant roughly six hours of debate. There were times, though, when we had quite a rush to make it. I remember in the year when a group of doughty young Scottish Nationalists had removed the Stone of Destiny (alias the Stone of Scone) from the place in Westminster Abbey it had occupied for many a day, this subject produced a heated Assembly debate in which one distinguished divine, who in his mind was obviously already in the tea-tent at Holyroodhouse, referred to the relic as 'the scone of Stoone'!

The new system works—anything as drastic as a guillotine is bound to work—but it is not entirely satisfactory, and to those in particular who feel very strongly that the deliberations of this Committee are of vital importance for the well-being of the nation, it must surely appear that they are undertaken under very restricted conditions so far as time is concerned. Since the guillotine is not likely to yield, the answer might lie in the Committee itself drastically curtailing the number of subjects presented in any one year, and in the Assembly refusing to accept any new theme unless a strong case could be made out for its urgency. Even at that, the final items would likely be rushed and someone would feel cheated!

Even though the debate has to be confined within five hours, for many commissioners it is time exceedingly well spent. It is here precisely that I should wish to take issue, and to do so, for one thing, on the ground that so much of the time is invariably devoted to telling other people how to solve their problems, one of the simplest and most unrewarding exercises known to man. To take the year 1987 as a random sample, we find that on seven particular issues the Assembly 'called upon' HM Government to do something or another, on six other issues they 'urged' HM Government to take certain action, in another case they 'encouraged' them, in yet another they more modestly 'requested' the Government to take a particular course, while in one matter which was already beyond the stage where exhortation counted, they 'deplored' the action that had been taken. What in simple terms does all this amount to?

To take a case in point, the Assembly called upon HM Government 'to take independent disarmament initiatives and especially to give support to moves towards a comprehensive international multilateral test ban treaty'. Manifestly to take independent disarmament initiatives is one of the most serious steps any government could contemplate, one beset with the gravest dangers, a step to be taken only with the most profound sense of responsibility. There are countless factors to be taken into consideration, many of them, I'm sure, quite unknown to the fathers and brethren who were being asked to do the 'calling'. The government which is going seriously to answer the Church's call in this matter has a heavy and responsible job on its hands. But having issued our 'call' to HM Government to take steps, we can all go home to our parishes feeling we have done a good job in advancing the cause of world peace, and satisfied that if disarmament does not follow, the fault is not ours. It is a totally different matter if we are debating a report on, for instance, evangelism, a 'call' to get people back into our pews, for then we have to return to our parishes and try to do something about it, to find for ourselves just how intractable the problem can be—and unhappily there is no one else we can 'call' to solve *our* problem for us. Good advice for resolving other people's problems is one of the cheapest commodities—I hate to see the Church peddling it. In any case, it is worth noting that the terms of the Committee's remit are 'to tell the Assembly what action the Church ought to take' on these tremendous issues, not to tell HM Government what action it ought to take, or to have taken.

The Convener has reminded us that there is good Scriptural authority for the Church to be heard speaking out on the social issues of the time. How often do we read of the prophets of the Old Testament confronting the King with his evil and unjust dealings, no less than with his acts of apostasy. And nearer our own time, did not our Presbyterian forefathers insist on their duty to 'preach up the times', to apply the Christian Gospel to the problems of their day. True enough. But for my own part I cannot get away from the fact that our Lord himself was so remarkably silent on the social injustices of his day. What had he to say about slavery? Or about the place of women in Jewish society, and more especially in the worship of the Temple and of the synagogue? Or of Jewish national aspirations under Roman domination? Not a word is recorded as having been uttered. Indeed, when confronted with the nationalism issue—should we pay tribute to Caesar, should we pay the poll tax? Our Lord neatly sidestepped the issue by turning the horns of the dilemma on his tormentors with the injunction that they render unto Caesar the things that are Caesar's and to God the things that are God's, and leaving it to them to determine where the boundary lay. Or again, I am reminded of the time when the suppliant asked him to have a word with his brother about the division of the inheritance, and instead of discussing the rights and wrongs of the law of succession, our Lord's word was simply to 'beware of covetousness', advice which he backed up with the tale of the prosperous farmer taking the most elaborate precautions for a future which was not to be his to enjoy.

In this example of our Lord and the question of the inheritance, we see quite vividly the nature of His approach to such questions, namely that of going straight home to the real root of the man's trouble, identifying the spiritual sickness. The Scottish Law Commission is presently engaged on a study of the Scots law of inheritance with a view to recommending changes therein. I am sure they will do a very sound job, but of one thing I am even more certain—that no matter what they do with the law of succession, there will never be any peace within the family of the deceased so long as the life of each one of them is ruled by the desire for possessions—even he who gets most will be convinced he has been cruelly cheated. One is reminded of Thomas Carlyle and his picture of the Edinburgh shoe-polisher, his 'Infinite Shoeblack', who, given half a universe, half an omnipotence, would immediately start quarrelling with the owner of the other half and declare himself the most scurvily treated of mortals. What the disgruntled brother needed was not a larger share of the estate, but a reassessment of what value property had for a man created in the likeness of God, a man with eternity in his soul, a man whose soul might that night be required of him. What better advice could the man have been given than to beware of covetousness.

Our trouble arises because we cannot rest content with putting our finger on the heart of the spiritual problem, we feel under obligation to come up with a solution of the whole issue down to the last detail. Not enough for us to say, 'beware of covetousness'—in fact we are unlikely to say that at all, for we will be so busy propounding new and better proposals for the disposition of the inheritance. And this inevitably, as I see it, is where we are bound to get into water far beyond our depth. Solicitors who have spent the whole of their working lives dealing with this aspect of the law, confronting the discontented relatives, listening to the hard-luck stories of those who feel themselves ill done by—such men would be the first to confess themselves unable to come up with proposals that would be utterly fair. For this is one of those areas where, as soon as you have found a way of ironing out an injustice here, you have thereby created an inequality somewhere else along the line. What chance then have we, with no specialist training, no matter how devoted Christians we may be, of solving so complex a problem? And if we are not able to come up with a solution, are not we better to hold our tongues. In this whole field, we are at best well-meaning amateurs, and there can be few more exasperating, more useless—or indeed dangerous —species known to man. Are not we wise, as our Lord did, to confine ourselves to declaring clearly the Christian principle, and leaving it to those who know what they are about to work out how that principle should be applied in the far from simple particularities of the practical situation.

To take an obvious example from the 1988 Report, what do we, in virtue of being dedicated Christians, know about the intricacies of running a national health service? The answer, I'm sure, must be, 'mighty little'. In common with all other citizens, of every religion and of none, we are entitled to draw attention to the inadequacies, the inequalities, the frustrations, and the failures of the system as we find it, and, as a Christian Church, it is right that we should particularly emphasise the respects in which it is working to the disadvantage of the aged and the underprivileged. Nothing could be easier than to plead that more funding should be made available for the service. But that represents a judgment about how the nation's finance should be used, and as that has limits, it must mean that something else gets less. In the absence of complete knowledge of the demands on the funds, that is a judgment we are in no position to make. But even if much more money was poured into the service, there is still no guarantee that any of it would reach the areas that are the subject of our concern, for in such an enterprise the possibilities of spending are limitless. For us as a Church to go into detail about steps that should be taken, is only to lay ourselves open to being shown to be utterly wrong—with a consequent weakening of our position in relation to the main guiding Christian principles, on which emphatically we are not wrong.

The same kind of considerations must apply to the quest-ions surrounding the privatisation of the steel industry, or about multi-national enterprises as a feature of modern commercial life, about trade union legislation, and about the community charge, and no less also in the matters of refugees and of asyl-um-seekers—all subjects on which the Assembly of 1988 was asked to pass judgment, sometimes highly critical and always highly specific judgment, as, for example, when we 'call upon HM Government to reconfirm its support for the 1951 UN Con-vention on the Status of Refugees; to review its present restrictive legislation in respect of genuine asylum-seekers; and to persuade our European partners to reintroduce more liberal policies in respect of such persons'. I would like to think that all who voted knew precisely what all that meant.

To look for a moment in more detail at the Ravenscraig case. Here we were, among other things, asked to urge HM Government to rethink their plans for privatisation and to consider alternatives: '(a) the merits of continuing in public ownership with a renewed commitment to Scottish and regional interests; or (b) reversing their privatisation plans so as to break the British monopoly of the British Steel Corporation (BSC) as presently constituted by selling off Ravenscraig, Dalzell and Shotton as a separate complete unit; or (c) prior to privatisation, instructing the Board of BSC to install a finishing plant at Ravenscraig in order to privatise a Scottish steel company as an independent unit'. Even after the most careful scrutiny of the four closely-packed pages of reasoning which the Report carries in defence of this conclusion, I must confess myself still very much at sea in waters where I have neither chart, compass, nor even much sense of direction. Keen that the tragedy of unemployment should not be further imposed upon Lanarkshire, I voted in favour of the motion, believing that at worst no harm could come of HM Government looking again at alternative solutions to what I am sure is a highly complicated problem. But, believe me, I did not do so from any deep sense of Christian conviction. And I don't imagine I was alone in that!

In presenting the Report of the Church and Nation Committee to the Assembly of 1988, the Convener proposed an amendment to the opening item of his deliverance to the effect that the Assembly Council should 'give priority to funding a research facility in consultation with the Church and Nation Committee'. No reference had been made to this in the Report, nor had notice of it even been given in the order-paper for the day. Had it been otherwise, someone might well have asked what subject or subjects of research were here envisaged. I imagine that what is in view is the kind of research involved in giving detailed answers to the questions of what is to be done in particular circumstances in giving effect to a Christian principle —the kind of thing represented in the example I have just quoted of advancing alternatives to the Government's plans for Ravenscraig. What we have there is a highly specialised field where we sorely need the guidance of experts. But that, on my contention, is the area we should leave alone, for we as Christians have no skill to judge therein (that's why we need experts), and for us to become a chorus of Yes-men to the research wallahs is not only an expensive but a peculiarly useless exercise. If, as I would maintain, our job is clearly to define Christian principles involved in national trends and contemporary problems, then that is a field in which it is we ourselves who are—or at least ought to be—the experts.

There are questions of public policy where clearly issues of deep spiritual concern arise and where the Church might be expected to have a word to say, to have a lead to offer. One thinks immediately of the Christian's response to war and to the related subject of armaments and especially the so-called 'nuclear deterrent'. The trouble is that in most of these areas of concern, the Church itself does not have a clear mind. I quoted the new Convener as saying that we cannot run away from controversial topics. In many cases the controversy is not with the secular forces outside, but occurs within our own ranks. For many years during the fifties, successive Assemblies were entranced to listen to George MacLeod preaching the cause of pacifism, and to Professor Pitt Watson responding with the doctrine of the 'just war'. It was oratory at its ultimate pitch. Just how many 'converts' were made by either side as a consequence of the speechifying, I would not care to guess, but the debate was certainly appreciated, enjoyed and cheered to the echo. In that connection I am reminded of an occasion when I was sitting beside an elder from a country parish attending his first Assembly and was trying to unravel for him some of the mysteries of the procedure. At one point a brilliant speech was made by an orator who shall be nameless and was received with tumultuous applause to which my neighbour contributed heartily. As the noise was subsidising, he turned to me and said, 'That was great! Really great! When do we get voting *against* that?' As I say, I do not know how many were converted in these debates. The voting, as I remember, generally revealed a majority, not necessarily a great majority, on the side of the just war. What kind of conclusion are you justified in drawing from such an exercise? Are you entitled to say at the end of a debate of keen interest and a vote so close as to require the services of the tellers, that the will of God has been discovered? Would it not be, rather, a true reflection of the case to say simply that, in a representative gathering of roughly a thousand Scottish churchmen, the view was held by a small majority that it was consistent with Christian principles to resort to arms in defence of truth and freedom. And in so saying, one is not passing any judgment upon the pacifist whose Christian conviction leads him to a different conclusion. In arguing the case we may not be running away from controversy, but we are certainly not resolving it.

The activities of the Assembly in the matter of the recent hostilities in the Falklands is interesting as an example of how opinions can change. It was on 2nd April 1982 that Argentine armed forces occupied the Falkland Islands in an act of sheer unprovoked aggression. A few days later, local 'Christian' opinion was given expression at a Good Friday procession in

Buenos Aires, when Cardinal Juan Carlos Arumburo declared they were living in a historic moment, their boys in the Falklands were heroes and they were reclaiming their nation's land. Britain despatched a strong task force and at the same time appealed to the United Nations Security Council, Britain's declared aim being to restore her legal sovereignty over the Falkland Islands. At the UN the illegality of the Argentinian action was quickly confirmed, she was called upon to withdraw her forces, and all parties were urged to seek a peaceful settlement of the dispute. On 25th April, British forces reoccupied South Georgia. The tragedy of the whole affair was greatly intensified by the sinking of an Argentine cruiser and of a British destroyer, involving in each case considerable loss of life. This was pretty much the situation when the Church and Nation Committee reported to the Assembly in May, asking the court to 'express deep concern at the dangerous implications and possibilities arising from the Falklands events and commending all measures towards a lasting and peaceful solution'. It required a motion from the floor of the Assembly for it to be agreed to add to this, 'while at the same time emphasising the Kirk's support for HM Government in its handling of the Falklands crisis'. To 'commend' HM Government for any activity was something of a novelty in the history of Church and Nation.

By the following May (1983) the Committee had fully recovered from any feeling of pride in HM Government foisted upon them from the floor of the Assembly—very fully recovered. They pointed out, in terms of the Franks report, that even if our Government was not itself to blame for the whole thing because it had failed to foresee or prevent the invasion of 2nd April, it was still clear that the responsibilities of good government had not been adequately discharged in recent years, and that even if there were no identifiable sins of commission, there had been many very serious omissions. It was not surprising therefore, the indictment went on, that the morale of the islanders was low and that Argentina also concluded that Britain had little interest in the islands. On the other hand, Argentina wooed the islanders with offers of money, scholarships, Boy Scout exchanges and tourism, and provided essential oil and medical facilities and an air link to the mainland. It may not have been surprising that the islanders' morale was low, but it was surprising in the extreme that in all these circumstances the islanders were still so utterly determined to remain British, and so bitterly hostile to their apparently most considerate and generous neighbours on the South American mainland.

The report concludes with the statements that 'the military victory has exacerbated, rather than removed, the cause of the conflict', and that 'any tendency towards triumphalism will inflame matters still further'. The relevant deliverance was in these terms: 'Urge HM Government to act upon the UN Resolution 37/9 of 14th November 1982, and to consider as a matter of the highest priority how a long-term internationally acceptable political settlement can be achieved in relation to the Falkland Islands with due regard for the interests of the Falklanders'. Two things here are worth noting. First, that not a word is said in acknowledgment of the fact that the military victory effectively put paid to a quite unjustifiable act of aggression and aggrandisement, doing so at great cost and at no obvious advantage to the British nation. And second, that the 'internationally acceptable political settlement' is to pay regard to the interests, but not apparently to the wishes of the Falkland Islanders. Once again it required an intervention from the floor to secure that the final Deliverance would include an expression of appreciation of the restraint, courage, devotion to duty and compassion displayed by members of HM Armed Forces during the Falklands conflict.

To all of this there was an interesting sequel three years later, by which time, apparently, the British Council of Churches had sent a delegation, including representatives of the Kirk, to visit the Falklands. There they had had an opportunity to discover at first hand some of the facts of the situation, and in particular to learn something of the intensity of the determination of the islanders to remain British. The Church and Nation Committee had advanced a deliverance calling upon HM Government 'to resume negotiations with the Argentine Government on the future of the Falkland Islands, including the question of sovereignty, the cessation of hostilities, and the safeguarding of the interests of the Islanders'. What the Assembly eventually agreed was as follows—'Encourage HM Government to pursue policies both bilaterally with the

Argentine and multilaterally with other interested parties with a view to the settlement of the situation in the South Atlantic, the safeguarding of the long-term interests of the Falkland Islanders, and the solution of the problem of sovereignty'. Since then, I am not aware that any reference whatsoever has been made to the situation in these distant southern waters. Maybe just as well, for I am not, personally, satisfied that any very useful purpose was served by the Kirk's intervention in the earlier stages of the affair.

The whole incident represents an interesting commentary upon the difficulties which confront a Church that conceives itself as having a duty to pass informed judgment upon events occurring at the other end of the world, in circumstances of which it has little or no first-hand knowledge. Maybe the experience of these years should act as a damper upon our enthusiasm for making learned pronouncements about events in South America—and in South Africa.

The mention of South Africa reminds me that I have deliberately said nothing about our attitude there. All I personally would want to say about that unhappy land and its problems is that once we have ourselves resolved the situation in Northern Ireland (disposed of in eleven lines of the Report) we will be in a strong position to offer advice to the people in Pretoria. Until then, we should remember them in our prayers.

In all of the foregoing cases—the 'just war', the health service, the steel industry, the Falklands crisis—there is a quite specific Christian principle at stake, even if it is sometimes a trifle obscure, and even if at other times we are not terribly clear just where we stand in relation to it. The same, however, cannot, in my view, be said in relation to another subject which has sorely exercised the Church and Nation Committee and, through it, the General Assembly over many years, and which has resulted in the production of countless pages of report—the subject of self-government for Scotland in some form and to some degree. That this is a theme which has for long been of consuming interest to Scots (both at home and abroad) is beyond question, that the steps that will have to be taken to achieve any one of the many solutions advanced will have deep and far-reaching effects upon the whole life of the Scottish people must be obvious, that the subject is one which naturally lends itself to debate, a debate that in turn is capable of arousing the greatest ardour and engendering the most intense bitterness, has been proved over and over again. That there are vital economic interests at stake is clear enough, that there are deep cultural, historic and national considerations involved, no one would deny—but what is the Christian principle that lies at the heart of the matter and that entitles the Church to pronounce upon it?

That Christian people can be deeply committed to this view and that, is clear enough. In the following chapter I go to considerable length to explain how even a non-political person like myself got caught up and swept along by the business at one time. But it was not as a Christian that I found myself on the side of Scotland Says No, and I was prepared to concede that others—every bit as good and often better Christians than I—were standard-bearers on the other side. I cannot see why this should be the subject of Assembly debate and for the passing of resolutions by the supreme court of the Kirk. If we want to take a couple of hours off our proper business and have an interesting, enlightening and no doubt edifying debate on Scottish devolution, I should be the last to want to deprive what can often be a dull enough Assembly of so worthwhile a relaxation, but when we have so much business to get through which is properly and inescapably our business, and which no one else is going to undertake for us, such a diversion is an extravagance we can ill afford. I should hate to see the day when, in consequence of some Assembly resolution on the subject of Scottish self-government, it was possible for one group of contestants in this arena to declare their opponents to be less Christian than themselves. It was most interesting that the Church and Nation Report for 1989 came up with what might be called a theology of Scottish Nationalism, but even accepting it as such, I find it remarkable that after 'consistently calling for an effective form of devolution for the past forty years', it has taken us until now to discover we have a good theological foundation for our position—I should have expected the theological foundation to have been laid forty years ago, rather than that we should have erected the structure and then after nearly half-a-century found we had a foundation for it. This is surely justification *ex post facto*.

My own position remains unchanged—as a Scot I emphatically say 'No'; as a Christian I hold my peace.

It may seem late in the chapter to be raising the question as to where we should start from in considering this issue of the nature of the Church's responsibility in national affairs. The question may be worth asking for all that. Our fathers were wise in starting their consideration of man from the proposition that man's chief end is to glorify God and to enjoy him for ever. By a like process we might begin from the proposition that the Church's chief end is to bring men and women to Jesus Christ and to teach them to direct all their words and works in every department of their lives to the glory of God's Holy Name. If as a Kirk we can do that job sufficiently well, then we can leave it to the Christian politicians, the Christian trade unionists, the Christian parents, the Christian schoolteachers, and all the other Christians, to do the right things, and a great many of our national and international problems will vanish from the scene. The hireling fleeth because he is a hireling—the good man does the right things because he is a good man. Could it be that over the years the Churches have tried overmuch to tell people the things they ought to be doing (and even more the things they ought *not* to be doing) in the belief that by observing such teaching they will become good men and women. Rather, we should properly be approaching the problem from quite the other end—concentrating all our powers on making them good men and women, for then we won't need to tell them what not to do; winning them for Christ, for then they will do all the right things.

But then it is so much easier to keep the government of the nation right than to make the people of the nation good. Easier, yes. But what does it achieve? And it is, after all, the latter and not the former to which we as the disciples of Christ are supposed to be committed.

Chapter 10
Scottish Nationalism

WHAT was eventually to become my fairly deep involvement with the 'Scotland Says No' campaign at the time of the Scottish National Referendum in 1979 began, as so many things do in this life, in a quite accidental and completely innocent fashion. Had it been otherwise I should have been at pains to see it did not begin at all.

One guiding principle which, throughout my entire ministry, I have studiously observed has been to keep myself absolutely aloof from politics. Not at any time have I made from the pulpit any observation that could be construed as party-political; never have I discussed openly my own party-political allegiance; no one, so far as I am aware, knows how I have voted at any election; when members have sought to involve me in political discussion, I have invariably taken the conversation in another direction. You may think this is a stupid attitude, and you may well be right. But then I have adopted a lot of stupid attitudes in the course of my life, and for this one I have had a number of, what appeared to me, good and sufficient reasons.

For one thing, I am not at all a political person. I find myself quite incapable of working up any burning enthusiasm over political issues. Often I have marvelled at the amount of heat some people can generate on issues which to me appear either trivial or doctrinaire. I had a member, a grand old man with many admirable qualities, who during a period of Labour administration was in the habit, any time I called, of treating me to a diatribe on the incredible stupidity—not to say criminal lunacy—of the latest measure instigated by Harold Wilson. I found it all utterly boring. For the sheer mischief of the thing, I was often tempted to contradict him, but then I would remember he had a bad heart and I felt the risk was too great. I'm afraid I just got into the way of making my visits brief. For my own part I had a lot more sympathy with one of my farmers who, after one election, told me he 'hadna bothered gaein' to vote'; he was keen to get the turnips in, and in any case 'it didna maitter ower muckle which side got in, for they a' made the same juck o' things in the lang run'.

For another thing, I have a profound distaste for the practice of building up my own case merely by pouring scorn on the proposals of the other side—and that appears to me to characterise almost all political debate, especially at election times, at party conferences, and even on the floor of the Chamber itself. Besides, there was the fact that in my congregation I had people of every shade of political opinion, some of them intensely partisan. Although party lines could be crossed—I recall an occasion when the winner of a very splendid prize at the Conservative Whist Drive had it raffled in aid of party funds at a Labour function the following week! Unhappily politics is a subject about which people rarely agree to differ, it generates not difference of opinion but hostility and ill-will, and that to a terrifying degree.

Finally, and perhaps most important of all, while I believe the citizen has a duty to take full advantage of the suffrage won for him at so great a price, a duty to take a responsible interest in how his country is being governed, a duty to cast his vote at election times, that seems to me to be his private affair, and I am not satisfied that it is for the Church to become involved at any point in the process—beyond perhaps reminding him that he has such a duty. I will be told, no doubt, that this was precisely the attitude adopted by German Christians as Hitler tightened his grip on the nation, but I think that is an over-simplification of a highly complicated situation. On this whole theme I have more to say in another place, so for the moment suffice it to repeat that as a minister it has been my deliberate policy to eschew political involvement.

So far as our General Assembly with its Church and Nation Report is concerned, it is well known that on this issue I stand very much in a minority, and each May a great many subjects which are basically party-political are faithfully, sometimes hotly, sometimes furiously, debated by the fathers and brethren —as often they are still quite inaccurately described. The point is frequently made that our Assembly is the one forum available in Scotland for the airing of these issues which in many cases are of paramount importance for all Scots—and this, of course, is perfectly true. Proposals that have emerged year after year for the introduction of some form of devolution, including the creation of a separate governing body for Scotland, have been discussed and debated over and over again, and have resulted invariably (I at least cannot think of a single exception) in support of the thesis that Scotland should enjoy self-government in some form and to some degree. Apart from getting up at the appropriate moment to be counted—and usually among the 'No-s'—I have never taken any part in these debates.

Then one day sometime around 1975 I was approached by a friend, a leading figure among the Tories, to see if I would go to their Party Conference at Blackpool and give a talk—as one of the smaller sideshows—on what I thought of the idea of a Scottish Assembly. My whole inclination was to decline—I wanted to stick to my rule and keep well away from politics. But having frequently sat spellbound watching on the box excerpts from party conferences, curiosity got the better of me and I thought it might be worthwhile to see one of these affairs at first hand, and to discover whether they were really as entertaining as they had always appeared. I thought too that it might be a good thing to let it be known that not all Scottish churchmen were as madly enthusiastic for devolution as might appear from reading Assembly reports. So I agreed to go. And thereby I took my first step on the downward path. How often have I warned people of how easy it is to take just such a step!

Finding something to say on the subject presented me with no problem—the case was one where the difficulty lay in deciding what to leave out. One thing that had to be said, for example, was that if what was envisaged was a real full-scale separation of the kind that the Scottish Nationalist movement had always insisted on, then that was surely an attempt to turn back the hands of the clock, a process that rarely does the mechanism any good. Time was in the history of these islands when a line could be drawn along the River Tweed or some-where nearby, a line that would meaningfully divide two separate peoples. It is easy to envisage Mary, Queen of Scots setting sail from Dundrennan on that Sunday afternoon in May 1568 to cross the Solway and enter a foreign land. But that day has passed, and there is nothing we can do to bring it back

—even if we wanted to. Man's cleverness has destroyed all these old lines of demarcation, not just a river like the Tweed, but the English Channel—and the Atlantic Ocean—and has brought us all into one single neighbourhood, even if we haven't yet begun to learn how to live as neighbours. To me, the old schoolbook picture of King Canute sitting getting his feet wet in the incoming tide is no more pathetic than the sight of twentieth century man building a Berlin Wall, hanging an Iron Curtain, imposing a system of apartheid. Could a more ridiculous contradiction be envisaged than one little island which, at one and the same time, is seen to be boring a Euro-Tunnel and re-erecting a Hadrian's Wall.

If, on the other hand, what is in view is a modified form of self-government with at its heart a Scottish Assembly at Edinburgh, then a great deal will depend upon the nature and the extent of the responsibilities that are going to devolve upon such a body, and even more upon the precise powers with which it is to be entrusted. And even if you manage with some degree of success to solve that one, you are still at best, as I see it, merely adding another layer of government when the last thing in the world we are needing is to be more governed. If only we could be *better* governed! The general consensus of opinion would seem to be that the result of superimposing regional government upon local government has been to slow down rather than to accelerate the business of getting anything done, to add to the expense and not to the efficiency, to contribute further to the frustration of the man who has ideas and wants to get them put into practice—and it is with such a man, and not with the committee that sits upon his ideas, that the hope for the future lies. Why add yet further to this superstructure of control? We have no want of mechanism; what we are sorely needing is a little dynamism. I recall remarking at the time that my experience in the Presbytery Office was that if I wrote to a District official, I could count on getting a postcard of acknowledgment in five days, whereas if I wrote to an official of the Region it took eleven days. I could not but wonder how long it might take at Assembly level. And that, mind you, was just the postcard of acknowledgment. If, it seemed to me, the power to raise money were to remain at Whitehall, any Scottish Assembly was going to be fitted with the tightest possible curb on what it could achieve—and, by way of compensation, was being provided with the perfect excuse for its every failure.

A further point was that I have always been unhappy about the people who are most prominent in the cause of Scottish Nationalism. That they are each and every one admirable persons in their own way, I have no reason to doubt; but they do not seem to be my kind of people, their interest in Scotland is not my interest, their ambition for Scotland does not correspond with mine, and most emphatically they are not the kind of people by whom I want to be governed. All this, I happily admit, is sheer prejudice—but the right to his own prejudices has always been dear to the heart of the Scot, the most basic of all human rights. Only, for him they are principles!

Finally, and it may be no more than a straw in the wind, but a point that for me has always assumed considerable significance has been the choice of the name 'Assembly' for the proposed new Scottish parliament. From the middle of the sixteenth century, this term has in Scotland had a very specific meaning. It has referred to the supreme governing court within the Kirk—the General Assembly. Why then pick on that title when there are so many to choose from? If this choice does not point to the fact that its authors are not dyed-in-the-wool Scots, it points—beyond a peradventure for me at least—to the fact that they are not dedicated Scottish churchmen, and that is something I should dearly have liked them to be.

It would appear that my talk created quite a bit of interest —it was certainly very well received. And as a bonus I did enormously enjoy seeing at first hand something of the hurly-burly of the Party Conference. That my effort must have been successful up to a point was confirmed for me when a couple of years later I was asked to do a repeat performance. On this occasion I was met off the train at Lancaster by Adam Fergusson, whose father, Sir James Fergusson of Kilkerran, as Keeper of the Registers of Scotland, had had dealings with us in regard to Kirk records, and whose uncle, Bernard Fergusson, of Black Watch and Burmah fame, was a very good friend of mine. Adam wondered whether I would be prepared to act as joint chairman of a special committee that was being formed to take charge of the devolution issue. The other half of the 'joint' was no less an authority than Lord Wilson of Langside who was

House of Lords spokesman for Social Democratic Party (SDP) on Scottish legal affairs. He was the man who would do all the work, make all the public appearances, attend all the meetings; I was to be the sleeping partner—a role for which I felt myself well cast. All that was wanted from me was my name to put on the notepaper. The Kirk had in the public mind got itself so completely committed to self-government that it was thought important to have the name of a recognisable man-of-the-cloth on the other side. He was most persuasive. So much so that by the time we had reached the outskirts of Blackpool, I had succumbed. As I saw it, if they had got down my length they must be pretty desperate, it was a cause with which I was much in sympathy, and in any case the issue was primarily a national and only incidentally a political one. The second step on the slippery slope had been taken. About the ease with which this can be done, I had also frequently spoken in warning!

When in 1978 the Scotland Bill made its appearance with its specific proposal for Scottish devolution, a totally different complexion was put on things. Here was a clear and precise plan for limited self-government worked out in detail, and it was provided that a National Referendum would be held when the Scottish electorate would vote For or Against its adoption. If I hadn't been enamoured of the idea in general, I liked still less the particular proposals of the Bill. And so, in an instant, the job which I had undertaken as a sinecure had turned into one of major significance and considerable urgency. We at once got busy, we set ourselves up under the slogan 'Scotland Says No', we engaged a public relations firm to guide us on strategy, we held press conferences, and we arranged public meetings in every corner of the land. It is true that Lord Wilson, my better half, accepted responsibility for most of the work at the planning level, and at the interviews my part was largely a walking-on one. The task in whose performance I took my full share was that of addressing meetings throughout the country, and this, I have to confess, I rather enjoyed, finding it interesting, enlightening, and very stimulating. Addressing audiences was no new experience for me, of course, but to date mine had always been the captive audience of the pew or the dinner-table—and this was rather different. Although, let it be said, most of my hearers seemed to have been converted in advance! For some reason—I know not what—the hecklers stayed at home. And this I thought a great pity.

It was in the course of these travels that I happened on a coincidence so remarkable that I am tempted to record it. It was the kind of thing that can happen only in real life, no fiction writer would dare report it. I had been speaking at Dumfries and was being entertained overnight at Dalswinton by David Landale (now Secretary to the Duchy of Cornwall). During a blether over a pre-bedtime cup of tea, he casually remarked that he could claim connection with the ministry of the Kirk to the extent that his namesake and forebear had been minister at Applegarth. Nothing remarkable about that. The very next evening my engagement took me to Hamilton, where the meeting was being chaired by Sir Andrew Gilchrist of Arthur's Craig in the Clyde Valley. Before the meeting, we were talking of this and that, when he remarked that he could claim connection with the ministry of the Kirk to the extent that his namesake and forebear had been minister at Applegarth. You could have knocked me over with the proverbial feather—I was sure I was dreaming. When I got the opportunity to check, I found that, sure enough, David Landale went to Applegarth in 1886, to be followed in 1900 by Andrew Gilchrist. My next host, at Plockton, laid no claim to ecclesiastical ancestry, and the spell was broken.

What with contributing articles to the press, being interviewed on radio, making appearances on television, and above all scouring the country addressing meetings, the month of February 1979 was for me an extremely busy time which passed quickly to culminate on Thursday 1st March, the day of the fateful Referendum—and what an anti-climax it was to prove. I imagine most would now agree the whole affair was something of a fiasco, indeed a farce—a complete waste of time, money and effort. And largely because of the introduction of a complete irrelevance. An English MP had been successful in having included in the Bill a condition that unless 40 per cent of the total electorate registered a 'Yes' vote there was to be no devolution. This had been carried by a fairly narrow majority in face of strong opposition from Scottish MPs. As was to be expected, it proved in every respect a most mischievous provision. There was no precedent for it, no excuse for it, no need for it. Those of us on the 'No' side were happy at the prospect of a straight fight and asked for nothing better. Because of the 40 per cent rule, it was widely canvassed that if you were 'Against' it did not matter whether or not you went to the polls, for your 'No' vote would have no effect one way or the other on deciding whether the others had got 40%. True, but far from the whole truth. It is beyond doubt that many of our supporters were encouraged in this way to stay at home. I am sure the point was made with no deliberate intent to mislead, but I am clear that that was its effect, and since the day was one of storms, high winds and snow, many did indeed stay at home. To that extent —and in my view it was a considerable extent—the 'Against' vote was not a true reflection of how many Scots were hostile to the proposals.

When the result was declared at 1,230,917 For and 1,153,502 Against, it was obvious that the requisite 40 per cent had not been achieved. We had won, but we could take little satisfaction in our victory. What was worse, there was little recognition that we had scored a victory. For, not unnaturally, the other side, having achieved the majority, loudly proclaimed that once again it had been clearly demonstrated that most of the Scottish people were in favour of devolution, and it was only as a result of a mean trick devised by 'thae English' that they were being cheated of it. For my own part, I am convinced that it was only the 'trick' that enabled those in favour to register a majority. Otherwise I am confident the majority (not a very large one perhaps) would have been ours. I cannot prove it, of course. From every point of view the whole affair was most unsatisfactory and left a bad taste in everybody's mouth. One thing and one thing only was certain—the demand for some form of self-government for Scotland would not go away in consequence of Scotland's trip to the polls on 1st March 1979.

For me personally, one of the most exhilarating incidents in the whole campaign had occurred just exactly a week before the poll. With a view to making provision for the emergency situation that may arise between Assemblies, one of the last things which each Assembly does is to appoint a Commission consisting of all its own membership, to meet in October and February, conferring upon it certain powers to dispose of matters of urgency. In virtue of this delegated power, the Church and Nation Committee presented to the Commission that met on 22nd February, a week before the poll, a report in regard to the Referendum situation, ending with an invitation to ministers to read from their pulpits on the coming Sunday what purported to be an exhortation to their people to turn out and vote in the Referendum, but which went on to indicate that they should vote in favour of the proposals, because the General Assembly had for many years expressed the support of the Church for some degree of self-government for Scotland.

This I vigorously attacked, and on two grounds. First, that while we were perfectly entitled to remind our people of their obligation to make up their minds on this important issue, and to turn out and vote, we were certainly not justified in telling them how their votes should be cast. In the second place, I argued that while it was true that successive Assemblies had declared in favour of some form of devolution, it was quite untrue that the Assembly had expressed itself in favour of the specific proposals now before the nation—if for no other reason than that these proposals had not been finally framed until after the Assembly had risen. Further, the details of the proposals were utterly at variance with almost every point which the Assembly of 1977, in a closely reasoned paper, had forwarded to the Secretary of State, and which contained nine basic principles which, it was maintained, would have to be adhered to for any scheme of devolution to be adequate. Indeed in a Supplementary Report the previous May, the Committee had asked the Assembly to 'regret the failure of HM Government in the Scotland Bill to make provision for devolving to a Scottish Assembly powers of taxation, adequate arrangements for the provision of finance, and election by the Single Transferable Vote System of proportional representation', and also 'deplore the proposal to hold a referendum of the Scottish electorate on an unsatisfactory and tendentious basis'. It seemed to me, therefore, that the document should not be read in pulpits, and I moved accordingly. When the votes came to be counted, I was a little surprised, but very happy indeed, to discover that I was on the winning side. So our congregations were spared having to listen to the Statement—not that I imagine it would have made any difference to the result. But we Scots being the kind of rebellious (we prefer to call it independent) people we are, it is perhaps not surprising that one minister, having been prevented from reading the document to his people from his pulpit, had copies of it printed and handed to them at the church door on leaving.

Apart altogether from the completely unconvincing and generally unsatisfactory outcome of the Referendum (thanks to the introduction of the 40 per cent rule) there can be no doubt that the demand for some form and measure of self-government will not go away. The present enormous disparity in party allegiance in the two nations is making the problem even more acute. It seemed to me a peculiarly cynical thing that before arrangements for the Referendum had properly begun, vast sums of money were spent on converting the Boys' High School into a beautifully appointed meeting-place for an Assembly which, at that stage, was not known would ever meet. I was asked at the time to contribute a short piece to *The Scottish Field* on the subject of the Assembly Hall, and I remember writing that while 'Scotland's Folly' stood proudly on the crest of Calton Hill, 'Scottish Nationalism's Folly' was going to adorn its eastern flank. I had my tongue in my cheek, I have to confess, for I realised clearly enough that so long as England behaves towards her northern neighbour in the way she does, there will always be a strong case for Scottish Nationalism. It is the English who make Scottish Nationalists.

It was in the summer of 1977 that I accepted an invitation to go on a preaching tour in the United States in connection with the celebration of the bicentenary of their achieving independence—a tour that took us from New Jersey, through some of the southern states, to end up in Texas. In the course of one of the functions given in our honour, the chairman, in introducing me, made the point that it seemed odd to bring someone from our side of the Atlantic to share in a celebration of this nature. I had little difficulty in coping with that one—I said it seemed eminently suitable, for as a Scot I could claim to be a fellow-victim of English ham-fistedness. And I wasn't just being funny. A System Three Opinion Poll recently conducted in these parts showed that only 9 per cent of Scots thought that Mrs Thatcher was 'good for Scotland'. A Downing Street spokesman, when asked to comment on this, expressed surprise that such a poll had been taken at all—they might just as well have asked whether Mrs Thatcher was doing a good job for Birmingham. Could any answer be more irrelevant or more offensive? Will our southern neighbours never learn that Scotland is a nation in partnership with England in virtue of a Treaty of Union, a condition I cannot imagine even Downing Street spokesmen would think applied to Birmingham. The trouble about being consistently slighted is that you become 'touchy', you come to expect slights, to see them when they do not exist, to exalt them into deliberate insults.

I am not qualified to speak on the Welsh situation, but I am clear that so far as we Scots are concerned, we are a nation that of its own free will entered into a union with England to form the larger unit known as Great Britain. We are not just a province of Great Britain, much less an appendage of England. Besides all that, as a people we have characteristics that mark us off as a separate race. I know how dangerous and misleading generalisations can be, but I think the marks here are sufficiently clearly defined, and, greatly daring, I would venture a few observations on some of these.

It is frequently said of the Englishman that he has a genius for compromise, and this, I am sure, is absolutely true. In fact, I am convinced that this particular trait goes a long way towards explaining Britain's enormous success in the past as a world power—this hard-headed ability to grasp what is essential for the immediate purpose and to make all sorts of concessions on things which, however important they may seem, really matter little in the long run. Don't worry too much about the precise meaning of terms, don't allow yourself to get excited about the punctuation marks, don't trouble to put on your reading glasses to decipher the smaller type; so long as we've got something here that both sides can sign, and that in a general way conserves for both of us the conditions each of us see as important, let's get our names down on the paper. Should we run into snags we'll find a way round them, never fear. This is a policy which in theory may not much commend itself, but it is one which in a harsh world seems to work. May it not be, though, that it is a policy which has earned for England the appellation of 'perfidious Albion'?

For me this genius for compromise has been highlighted in the negotiations that have been going on for so long between the

Church of England and other denominations in the ecumenical field. Let's hammer out a formula to which both of us, each of us interpreting it in our own way, can say 'Amen'. If there is a suggestion of *double entendre* then let's thank God for ambiguity. Be a good chap and put your name on the dotted line and don't ask niggling questions about problems that may never arise anyway. I remember at the time of the Anglican-Methodist negotiations, a minister from the latter side—and a Welshman at that—telling me about his conscientious difficulties with the proposed Basis of Union. This among other things made provision for a Service of Recognition of Ministries in which each side would publicly acknowledge the validity of the orders of the other. Since the Methodists had never either doubted or challenged the validity of Anglican orders, the whole exercise was for them a bit pointless. But it was a very necessary exercise since, as it appeared to him and I think to any discerning reader, the service was so designed as to provide the Anglicans with an opportunity not to recognise existing orders (which some of them were not prepared to do), but to confer proper orders on those whose status was by their standards suspect—all, naturally, in the most discreet fashion. If you were one of the 'suspects', it was hoped that, being a reasonable person and a gentleman, you would accept the service at its face value and not go asking awkward questions about how others might be interpreting it, questions that could lead only to unpleasantness and embarrassment. Nothing less than a genius for compromise will enable you to go places in this kind of company. My Methodist friend was deeply exercised. He was keen to see the union achieved. But could he, in good conscience, subscribe to a formula when he knew very well that to other subscribers it meant something which he was not prepared to concede at any cost. The basis of any contract is *consensus in idem*, not *consensus in verba*. As a Christian he felt he had some concern for honesty of intention, a condition that to him mattered more than mere visible unity of denominations.

We Scots know nothing of this genius for compromise; the corresponding quality for us—let's face it—is a genius for controversy. Let there be somewhere in the small type an item of possible ambiguity, the Scot will surely pounce upon it, and until the offending phrase has been rewritten to his dictation, he will have nothing to do with your formula. What's more, he'll enjoy every minute of the debate. Until a comma somewhere has been upgraded to a semi-colon, don't even offer him the pen. It has to be admitted that he can and often does carry this tendency to the most ridiculous extremes. Here again an example from church history springs instantly to mind. In 1733 there occurred a secession from the national church under the leadership of the brothers Erskine, and a new denomination was formed which took the name of the Associate Synod. A short thirteen years later, following upon the Jacobite rebellion of 1745, an Act was passed by Parliament requiring that burgesses take an oath in which *inter alia* the subscriber protested that he 'professed and allowed in his heart the true religion presently professed within the realm and authorised by the laws thereof'. Innocuous enough, you might have thought. Everyone knew perfectly well that what was being struck at was the Roman Catholicism associated with the cause of the Pretender. But within the ranks of the Associate Synod, there arose the most diabolical controversy between those who found the oath compatible with their faith and those for whom it was anathema. Not surprisingly perhaps the fight raged most bitterly in country districts totally unaffected by the Act. A storm in a teacup you might think. Maybe it was, but it was no less fierce a storm for all that. It split the new church in two, creating Burghers and Antiburghers happily engaged in excommunicating one another, and it had effects that ran deep into Scottish history and character.

No genius for compromise here, indeed a complete incapacity for it. And the sad thing, of course, has been that while the Scot has been enjoying a highly interesting, if unprofitable, time arguing about the position of a comma, his English counterpart has got his compromise accepted and has been getting on with the serious business of conquest.

A second point of fundamental difference. I have never subscribed to the doctrine that the Scot is hard-headed, for that is a term I reserve for his southern neighbour. The story is told that a visitor from the States was being shown a bridge in some corner of Scotland where, built into the parapet on one side, is a tablet bearing Walter Scott's famous lines, 'Land of green heath and shaggy wood, land of the mountain and the flood, land of my sires, what mortal hand can e'er untie the filial band that knits me to my native strand', while the corresponding plaque on the other side reads, 'This bridge, opened on such-and-such by Lady So-and-so, was built at a cost of £53,829'. Said the visitor, 'Yes, there's the Scot for you: sentiment on the one side, siller on the other'. Within limits it would seem to me to be a fair judgment. Oddly enough, I think it is no less true of our friends from across the Atlantic who, for all their desperately accurate assessment of just how many bawbees go to make up a dollar, are capable of the most fantastic extravagances of sheer maudlin sentimentality. When the chips are down, though, and the reckoning comes, Uncle Sam's children will go for the dollar, while Rabbie Burns' countrymen will tend to be swayed by the things of the heart.

It cannot be without significance that for so many Scots the two figures from their national history that are most clearly remembered, most deeply admired, and most warmly loved, are Mary, Queen of Scots and Bonnie Prince Charlie—our two most abject and dismal failures. But then, you see, we have a sentimental attachment to failure, provided it is on a sufficiently dramatic scale—we are great losers, magnificent in defeat. For most of us, the name Flodden evokes far more response than Bannockburn. The latter gave us a victory, but the former gave us 'The Flooers o' the Forest'. The axe that had to fall three times on that grey morning at Fotheringay has carved for Mary a lasting place in our affection. And what of that lonely hunted figure, the Young Pretender? We find it easy to forget his weaknesses and to forgive his stupidities—'better lo'ed ye canna be; will ye no' come back again?'

I made reference earlier to an opinion poll recently conducted in relation to Mrs Thatcher's standing in Scottish opinion and to the appallingly low rating it revealed. May it be that, though her policies make a considerable appeal to our heads, she herself has never won our hearts, or even, so far as I am aware, made any effort to do so? Is it not time someone explained to her about the Scots? It could be, of course, that she is not a very good listener.

A third and final point. Thanks largely to his peculiar brand of religion, the Scot has tended to be an individualist. The Kirk has always laid great stress upon the importance of the individual, has emphasised individual responsibility, individual opportunity, individual destiny. It was this which alleviated the baneful influence of the doctrine of predestination, this Reformed insistence on the priesthood of all believers, this conviction that neither priest nor saint can intervene on your behalf, for you are directly answerable for what you make of your life. Everyman matters in the sight of God, and from this it follows that Everyman is directly answerable to God. It is not to be wondered at that such a doctrine should have begotten in the people of Scotland qualities of self-reliance and dependability, that it should have sent them forth as explorers to distant lands, and as pioneers in far realms of human thought and discovery, that it should have made them in fact a peculiar people, exerting in world affairs an influence out of all proportion to their numerical strength or to the significance of their land which, after all, is a mere speck on the hemisphere. It is widely believed that Scotland's principal export is whisky. That is not so. For many generations Scotland's principal export has been her sons and her daughters, and she has sent them forth to the ends of the earth, well equipped because of their individualism to deal with every kind of situation. This quality of the Scot has fitted him remarkably for his role of explorer and globetrotter extraordinary.

Unfortunately, however, this same quality has not had a like beneficial effect when the Scot has stayed at home. Here his tendency to be always the lone individual has unfitted him for the kind of working in harness that can often be essential if progress is to be made, his refusal to compromise has created stalemate situations that need never have arisen, his tendency to ponder and philosophise has held him back from decision when the moment for action came—and passed. I imagine that the greatest single weakness of the official drive towards Scottish Nationalism lies in the fact that for no two people does it mean precisely the same thing, and each supporter is satisfied that his concept, and his alone, represents the one true and practical form, and he'll be hanged if he'll go along with any other. To defeat by dividing is never difficult where the Scot is concerned. For some, Scottish Nationalism is a thing of heather and bagpipes and kilts and the language of the Gael, with an odd haggis thrown in; for some it is a fairly straightforward affair of the diversion of the income from North Sea oil, the retention of steel-rolling at Ravenscraig, the re-establishment of ship-building on the Clyde; for others it is a talking-shop set up in Edinburgh to match the existing one at Whitehall—and so on. And the trouble is that the Scot being the kind of person he is, there can be little hope of pulling together until we are all agreed on the pattern, and little hope that our differences will ever be settled.

As I have indicated, we have this tendency to fracture ill-ustrated only too clearly in the Kirk's divisions of the eighteenth and early nineteenth centuries, people splitting, miscalling and excommunicating one another for what to us seem unessential and even trivial reasons. While we have got over that in the Kirk today, the reason, I'm afraid, is not that we have become any less thrawn, or any more reasonable or tolerant, but just that we no longer feel so strongly as did our fathers about these religious questions.

There, then, for what it is worth, is my very partial and partisan picture of the Scot, this thrawn, sentimental indiv-idualist. How best can he fit into his role as citizen of the United Kingdom? I think the short answer is, by insisting on continuing to be himself. To put it into more personal terms, what are we to do, we who are not merely conscious of being Scottish, as well as British—not to say European—but proud of it into the bargain? What is the distinctive witness we have to bear, what is the unique contribution we have to offer as a minority group, but a not insignificant one? For, as I see it, Britons we now are, for better or for worse, for richer or for poorer. It is understandable that we should resent having our land referred to as 'North Britain', unless England is going to accept a comp-arable description as 'South Britain', but we are part of that larger whole, politically and commercially, and so we will continue to be. This may be attended by disadvantages and loss, but we should be honest enough to admit that over the years, not least in those immediately succeeding 1707, it worked much to our profit. As a native of Glasgow, a seaport that looked towards what were then the English colonies, and that benefited so mightily from the trade established therewith, it would ill befit me to say other. All of that is history, the question is what is the position today? Things having advanced to their present stage, what are the steps we should now be taking?

Two things I think we can do. First, we can let it be seen that we are proud of our Scottish background, culture and traditions. Part of today's problem lies in the fact that while, with a little usquebaugh to inspire us we're ready enough to shout, 'Wha's like us?', behind that brave front lies the stark reality that, for many people north of the border, whatever is English is accepted as superior, the proper thing, while its Scottish equivalent is seen as 'native' (in quotation marks), as 'not quaite quaite', a thing to be deplored among the best people. In his book *Power Without Glory,* my very dear friend the late Professor Ian Henderson went so far as to say that for the bulk of middle-class Scots all English institutions are 'U' while their Scottish equivalents are 'non-U'. The generalisation is sufficiently accurate to be disturbing. Being Scottish should call for no apology. We may hail from the provinces, we may even be the poor relations, but we have nothing of which to be ashamed. A new sense of pride in our Scottishness is a first necessity today.

The second thing which as Scots dedicated to survival we must do, is to take active, positive and urgent steps to secure the continuing existence of our peculiarly Scottish institutions, for at present they stand in the most deadly peril.

Perhaps the most glaring example of this is the Scottish tongue, and even the Scots accent, which, with the possible exception of the night of the Burns Supper, is regarded as *de trop* compared with the emasculated English affected by radio personalities, although what claim to perfection these latter have I know not. Often it has occurred to me that were a weather forecaster 'on the box' to warn us that we might expect 'snaw on the heich grun',' there would be a bonnie to-do, with questions on the floor of the House, I shouldn't wonder. Yet his diction would to me have sounded every whit as good as—and a great deal more authentic than—what we have become accustomed to, namely 'snow (to rhyme with now) on the ha'a gra'an'. I find it won't even transliterate very convincingly, but we've all heard it often enough to reproduce it for ourselves. I'm glad I don't live on the 'east coust' to have to endure all the 'gyles' that they are promised. Quite recently I heard a Scots announcer refer to a man rejoicing in the name of 'Murdoch' as 'Mista Mirdock'. Instantly I had a mental picture of that same announcer's grannie complaining to her butcher that his haugh was cheuch and took a lot o' chowin'! And this is where we have arrived today—Mista Mirdock, forsooth! How low can a Scotsman sink? I suppose everyone knows the tale of the Scots counsel of yesteryear, who was appearing in a southern court in a case having to do with water rights. His pronunciation of the word 'water' had a splatter to it not unlike the sound of the tap being turned on—so much so that his opposite number was moved to remark in an aside to the bench that 'where my learned friend comes from it would appear they spell the word "water" with two T-s'. 'Na,' came the instant rejoinder, 'but we spell the word "manners" wi' twa N-s.'

Personally I like very much to hear someone talking on the media in a good recognisable accent, be it Welsh, Irish, Yorkshire, or whatever. I prefer it enormously to the nondescript stuff to which we are so often subjected. Surely we can be proud of and affect a good Scots accent in all our communications at international level; and why shouldn't we, at least for domestic consumption, keep alive some of the grand expressive words that were the everyday currency of an earlier generation, but which seem to be disappearing so fast. I know, of course, that there is no such thing as a Scottish language, that Gaelic is confined within a limited area, and that Lallans is just a collection of words that are in use in different parts of Scotland, but which are not common to the vocabulary of any single Scot anywhere—it is a vocabulary and not a language. On a personal note, and probably again in a minority, I feel bound to add that however much I may admire the work as an exercise in a neglected field, I do not welcome the publication of the New Testament in braid Scots—for it appears to me as precious and unreal. When the Scot went to worship he laid aside his working clothes and decked himself in his best, as befitted one preparing to keep tryst with his Maker; and by the same token he laid aside the language of the byre and the kitchen ingle and adopted the magnificent English of Shakespeare and the Authorised Version. It is 'the King James' and not braid Scots that is the traditional vehicle of Scottish worship. The man that tended the sheep on the hill might describe himself as 'a hird', but the Lord was his 'shepherd'; in a blether with his buddie he might talk of 'gaein' intae the bucht by some ither gait', but in the Kirk he would 'enter the sheepfold by some other way'; in a moment of exasperation he might describe his friend as a 'muckle gommerel', but he believed his Lord had said 'thou fool'.

In the Scots tongue, it seems to me, we have something in which we are entitled to take considerable pride. Will it not be a tragedy if, by letting it pass out of daily use, we sign its death warrant. For words are kept alive not in dictionaries or encyclopaedias, but on the lips of living people.

What I have just been saying about the Scots tongue you may choose to laugh off as so much drivelling sentimentality, but you most certainly cannot say the same about what is happening to the Scottish legal system. It would, I am confident, be universally conceded by those best qualified to know, that as a judicial system the law of Scotland stands far above that of England. This is attributable to a number of circumstances affecting their origins which we need not enlarge upon here. Accept it as a fact. A simple soul unversed in the peculiar relationship of our two peoples might imagine that when the two nations came together the better legal system would be chosen for adoption throughout the united kingdom, and that things would gradually work around until it became the only system. How very simple that simple soul would have proved himself. In the present commercial set-up, for example, every company has an office, generally its head office, in London, and it has become customary to write into contracts—even into those that are to be operative exclusively north of the border, ay, even a hire-purchase agreement affecting a crofter in Benbecula —that they are to be construed according to the law of England. The next step—obvious and inescapable—is that some of the best legal brains in Scotland elect to study in English universities and proceed to the English bar where the most interesting —and lucrative—cases are to be pleaded.

In this way a distinctive and essentially Scottish institution, admired in the world context, is being slowly but relentlessly pushed from the national scene. Nor is it easy to see how we can stop it—but stop it we must. It is greatly cheering to see that the present Lord Chancellor seems bent on trying to do something about it. More power to his gavel!

The position in relation to religion is even more intriguing—and no less menacing. In the very opening stages of the ecumenical get-together in these islands, it was agreed that the goal towards which we ought to be journeying was not one vast 'Church of Great Britain', but a national church on either side of the border, each in full inter-communion with the other. Which sounds both reasonable and fair. That is, until one wakens up to realise that the Anglican Church will not enter into full inter-communion with any body whose ministry is not within the Apostolic Succession, that is to say whose ministers have not been episcopally ordained. So, if the ultimate goal of full inter-communion is to be achieved, then quite simply we will require to have a full-scale episcopal church both north and south of the border. You may care to call our part the National Church of Scotland, but it will not remotely resemble the Kirk we have known and in which we and our fathers before us have worshipped for the past four centuries. And I can't imagine anyone seeing that as either reasonable or fair. In some departments of life the whole exercise would have earned the description of a massive confidence trick. Certainly it is not a proposition acceptable to Scottish Presbyterians. And yet new devices for getting us channelled into such a structure are being presented every other year to the General Assembly—Bishops in Presbytery and Permanent Moderators of Presbytery being among the more obvious.

Since 1560 we Scots have been Presbyterians. Our Kirk has been marred by many faults and its history tells of frequent failures. But it has shown itself well fitted to satisfy the needs, to hold the allegiance, and to suit the character, of the Scottish people. It is, of course, quite possible that things should be put the other way round and that it is the character of the Scottish people that has been shaped in large measure by the influence of their Presbyterian heritage. It matters little which is the true order. The plain fact is that we have a national church with a distinctive witness which, in its doctrine, its worship and its discipline, suits us well as Scots—why should we abandon it in favour of a foreign system bound to a theological concept of ordination that is utterly repugnant to us? All this merely because Scotland is now part of Britain. We are not asking Anglicans to accept our system—merely to leave us alone.

There, then, are three features of Scottish life—language,

law, and religion—where national institutions are under serious threat. It is imperative that we muster to their defence.

For myself, as I have indicated, I have little sympathy with the aspirations of the Scottish National Party and I take little joy from the prospect of having another talking-shop on the slope of Calton Hill. To me this is chasing shadows, while the things that are really 'Scotland' are slipping (or being deliberately whittled) away. It is clear enough, though, that whatever may have been the position in 1979, the situation today is that my hostility to official Scottish Nationalism and to Scottish self-government generally places me in a minority, and probably a shrinking minority at that.

I am happy to continue in that minority, while at the same time emphatically declaring myself to be a Scot—ay, and proud of it. Wha's like us? It's a good question, and I have still to hear a satisfying answer.

Chapter 11
Dabbling in the Law

RECEIVING the other day a letter about a proposed 're-union weekend of law graduates of Glasgow University of the years 1954-1956', I was reminded that around that time I had actually constituted a minority of one in the Faculty of Law at Glasgow—well into my forties, I had been the only really mature student in these classes. I'm afraid I had little interest in the proposed weekend, or even in the dinner with which it was to be launched, for I have always had a distaste for re-unions. For one thing, I object on principle, for re-union is basically an attempt to go back and recapture something from the past, and not only is that impossible, but to attempt it is unwise. And for another, I object at the pragmatic level, for I find meeting classmates of all these years ago a distinctly humiliating experience. It's not that I mind finding them such a bunch of old fogeys, it's just that my pride is hurt at the realisation that they are probably thinking the same about me. And here I have a twenty year start!

It was for me an intensely interesting spell that time in the early fifties when I returned to Gilmorehill as a spare-time student of law. I was old enough and sufficiently detached to learn a great deal (not exclusively about law), but of necessity I was very much an outsider in a minority position, not just because of my age, but because in view of my many parish commitments I was not able to participate in any way in the corporate life of the student body. Since it is there that you get to know your fellow-students, it wouldn't be much of a re-union for me to meet them now.

But what, you may wonder, led to my being involved in all this at that time? It is an interesting enough story which all began very simply in the early days of 1950.

It was by far the most exciting single event that had disturbed the peace of the community at Houston during the twenty years of my ministry there—maybe indeed during the

229

nine centuries of their history. One day, early in January 1950, to our complete surprise and dismay we found ourselves featuring on the front page of the national press. We were to enjoy the distinction of providing the site of Scotland's latest New Town. Not a whisper had been leaked in advance, although the whole affair must have been well enough known for some time in County Council circles. The ostensible reason for the creation of such a new town was to provide homes for overspill from Greenock, Renfrew and Port Glasgow—thirty thousand of them in all—and the community was to be centred on the existing village of Houston, although it would naturally spread out to include a dozen or so of the surrounding small family-run dairy-farms that were typical of the whole parish.

Country folk are not easily excited, but the ferment that day was intense. Reporters of all sorts, sizes and sexes descended upon us from every quarter. They interviewed the postman, the policeman, the schoolmaster, they photographed the shops, the kirk, the mercat-cross, and inevitably quite a few found their way to the manse. One mildly amusing incident occurred during this barrage from the media. *The Bulletin*, that popular picture paper of an earlier day (produced in conjunction with *The Glasgow Herald*), had sent along a young lady reporter accompanied by a photographer. I was on the point of saying that she was a charming young lady, but it would be more accurate to say that she exuded charm to a degree that was scarcely decent—I know, for I had basked in the radiance of her smiles at the manse. Having exhausted the possibilities of the village, she proceeded to one of the farms on the outskirts where the farmer, a particularly bucolic-looking specimen, admitted in answer to leading quest-ions, that it all came as a bit of a shock, that it would certainly mean the loss of his farm, that he had no other means of livelihood, nor had he any skills in any other line of business. 'Have you given any thought to what you are going to do for a living?' she enquired, pencil expectantly poised. 'I'm juist staun-din' here thinkin',' he responded in his ponderous, deliberate way, 'that I could dae a lot waur than get a job as a Bulleteen reporter.' It was always fatal to imagine that the Houston farmer was even half as stupid as he would have liked you to believe—and was deliberately arranging himself to appear.

Once the first cloud of dust had settled, one or two of us

got together to discuss the situation and to decide what was to be done. It was scarcely to be expected that we would welcome the prospect of being engulfed in a new town. It would mean the end of the Houston we had known, and an end to the way of life that had led some of us to choose Houston as our home and that had kept others of us there. You can't add thirty thousand to a population of a single thousand and hope to retain anything of the identity of the original community. You may keep the name, but that is all. Besides all that, we had no reason to believe that twenty thousand inhabitants of Greenock—or seven thousand from Renfrew for that matter—had any desire to move to Houston. Admittedly building-land around Greenock was at a premium so that new housing was being driven farther and farther up the hill away from the river. Still, we thought, the people of that precipitous town might prefer to climb a mile uphill to a new house rather than cross the hill and go on a further thirteen miles to a new town. More worrying still, it was to be purely a dormitory town with no industry of its own, so the business of getting all these workers to Greenock each day would present a formidable problem. We certainly didn't relish the idea of welcoming none but unemployed and unemployable.

A largely-attended public meeting was called which loudly applauded the suggestion that the proposal should be contested as vigorously as possible. In this effort I found myself pushed into a position of leadership. It is remarkable in these days when so many would assure you the Kirk has lost her influence that, when a situation of this kind emerges, people turn to the manse for guidance and help. 'If the minister'll no' help us whaur can we turn?' It could be, of course, that their reason for looking to the minister is that they see in him the one man in the parish with no better way of filling in his time! It surely proved a time-consuming job. We attacked on many fronts, we wrote articles for the press, we attended and addressed meetings of local councils, we mounted an almost 100 per cent signed petition, we had a meeting with Mr Arthur Woodburn who was then Secretary of State for Scotland. One effort alone involved my calling personally on each of the members of Renfrew County Council—more than fifty of them—in their own homes to present our case, and I have reason to believe that in consequence we gained a fair amount of support in the Council, although the Convener, some leading figures, and the officials, all continued solidly to support the plan.

In the end, I am glad to say, the project was abandoned, and life in and around Houston returned to a more normal pattern. It was quite shortly after this threat that I wrote the article appearing over my name in the Third Statistical Account of Scotland, these events doubtless explaining how I came to conclude the piece—'One of the things that is probably worth saying about Houston is that it is a real community and not just a heterogeneous collection of folk who through some accident happen to live in close proximity. We enjoy a real and vivid communal consciousness, and this leads us to hope that those who plan satellite towns and build industrial estates will look elsewhere, and that we as a community may be allowed to continue on our own way in our own cannie fashion. As a way of life it may not appeal to everyone—we would force it upon none—but as an industrious and God-fearing people we ask the right to work out our own destiny along the lines of our own best traditions'.

We thought we had won a resounding victory when in fact, all we had done was to gain a reprieve.

The reprieve lasted, though, for twenty years, by which time the estate of Craigends came to be sold to a developer who had obtained planning permission to transform it into a housing estate providing 'quality residences'. The estate lies to the east of the village of Houston, the river Gryffe flowing through the centre of it. At one time it lay partly in the parish of Houston and partly (including the 'big house') in that of Kilbarchan, but around 1930 the ecclesiastical boundaries were changed and Craigends was brought wholly into Houston. The 'big house' was well named. It was a massive baronial affair of I know not how many rooms, but its inhabitants could look out, I believe, from any one of 365 windows. If you washed one a day, you would get round them in a year! I never checked the figure but I can well believe it to be accurate. During the war the house and grounds were occupied from time to time by units of the Army, usually awaiting embarkation at Greenock, and I'm sure the property was none the better for the experience. The estate had from ancient times belonged to the family of Cunningham, a branch of the House of Glencairn. In 1940 when I went to

Houston, the house was occupied by Mrs Cunningham, the
widow of the last representative of the line, and she and her
sister Miss Pearson lived what must have been a remarkably
lonely and comfortless life in that vast mausoleum with less
than the bare minimum of staff. And yet they retained a great
dignity and lived in some semblance (it could have been no
more) of the style of a more gracious earlier day.

When Mrs Cunningham's interest ceased, the property
passed, I understand, to a nephew who had little concern for
it—in any case what can one do with 365 windows rotting in
their frames and looking out over acres of untended policies?
So, as I say, he sold for development. Following upon what
proved to be a successful venture, housing of the same type
mushroomed around the village of Crosslee and out towards
Bridge of Weir, so that the population of the parish is now in the
four thousand bracket, with the village still, from what I hear,
inclining to see itself as a little enclave of natives surrounded by
a body of reasonably friendly-disposed 'incomers'. It will break
down in time, I'm sure, and in any case it is much to be pref-
erred to the threatened overspill New Town of 1950. Our
labours, I like to think, had not been wholly in vain.

By one of those odd quirks of fate, of which life seems so
prodigal, the principal result of the New Town controversy of
1950, so far as I personally was concerned, was to strengthen a
long-standing interest in the law and to lead to my taking some
qualification therein. It would not be true to say that it engendered
such an interest, for the law had always been a subject that, so far
as my limited experience went, I had found utterly fascinating. I
hadn't been long engaged in the Battle of the New Town ere I
realised that if I was to be equipped to carry on this kind of
campaign, I stood in need of a vast deal of guidance on some of
the tricky legal questions involved. Even to carry on a correspondence with County officials could, on occasion, be a
complicated legal exercise. Much of the necessary help and advice
I sought and obtained from my friend, John Clyde, a well-known
Paisley solicitor of great acumen and ability. From him too I was
able to borrow the books that contained, for example, 'The Saga of
Stevenage', for that new town on London's northern fringe had
been responsible for 'making' quite a lot of law in this field.

As I thumbed my way through these great tomes I found

that many of the reported cases caught and held my attention, so that whole realms of law of which I had known nothing were opening up before me to my intense interest. The clarity and precision of expression, no less than the closely reasoned logical inescapability with which Their Lordships set forth their judgments, held me entranced. How I envied the ability to set things down like that. At school Euclid had always been a great favourite of mine, and at home of an evening I would work at geometrical problems with the single-minded devotion that others reserve for bridge and crossword puzzles. Here, it seemed to me, was the same basic discipline applied not to cold dead things like isosceles triangles and the square on the hypotenuse, but to the warm, vibrant, interest-packed situations of daily living. This was great stuff.

I decided it would be a good idea to attend a class in Scots Law. It was close on twenty years since last I had seen the inside of a classroom or done any intensive studying, and at that stage I had no intention of taking the business too seriously—it was just that I thought it would be nice to know a little more about the law of Scotland. I made some enquiries and learned that the class met first thing in the morning, which in the light of my parish commitments couldn't have suited me better. I also discovered that for practically the same fee I could enrol for three classes as for one. As a good Scot I found this bargain package quite irresistible and duly enrolled for the three. What happened thereafter in the matter of my University course I discussed at some length in the chapter on 'Alma Mater'. Quite shortly, after having taken the full course in Law, I graduated LLB in 1956, and having served an apprenticeship (of sorts), in due course I 'extracted' and had my name entered on the Roll of the Law Society of Scotland although in fact I never got round to practising.

Had I entertained any serious idea of transferring from the Kirk to the practice of law—and I never had—it would have been in court work that my interest would principally have lain. The firm with which I fulfilled enough of an apprenticeship to allow me to extract was deeply involved in reparation work, and much of this led to the Sheriff Court and not uncommonly to the Court of Session. As an apprentice I could see this only from the sidelines, but I used to appear quite a bit in police courts and juvenile courts, at medical appeal tribunals and the like, and there I both gained some experience of pleading, and saw life in some aspects that are not always visible to the man of the cloth. When finally I did qualify, I conducted one successful case in Stirling Sheriff Court and immediately retired from the scene, for I had just been appointed full-time Clerk to the Presbytery of Glasgow and this inevitably precluded any legal cantrips on the side.

While, then, I have never been able to put to any specific practical use my qualification as a solicitor, I keep my name on the Roll by way of recognition of the fact that I have been greatly assisted in my work as Presbytery Clerk and as intervener in Assembly debate in consequence of the training I underwent in the field of law. In saying this I am thinking not of any specific body of factual knowledge I acquired, but of what, for want of a better term, I should call a 'legal slant' which I developed and which became second nature—an ability to arrange a problem in an orderly kind of way, an insistence on withholding judgment until I hear all the evidence, a recognition that however good the story I am listening to, there is someone somewhere itching to tell me a rather different but no less convincing story, a conviction that finding the right solution is far more important than coming up with the instant answer.

I remember speaking to a group of women in a Paisley congregation on some purely ecclesiastical subject. In the course of the inevitable cup of tea which followed, I was approached by three ladies whose spokeswoman said, 'You're a lawyer. You're the very man we want to see. This congregation was lately left a lot of money. We say . . . . but the Kirk Session say . . . . surely we are right?' 'Well,' I began, 'I would first of all need to have a look at the will.' 'Och,' she responded, 'you're as bad as the rest o' them', and the deputation turned away in exasperated disgust.

A less excusable case was during a Presbytery debate on one occasion. I suggested that in my view the demands of justice indicated a certain line, and I was followed by a distinguished minister who expressed disquiet at the suggestion that we should confine ourselves to being just—'as a court of the Christian Church we have a clear duty to be more than just'. This was received with some cheering. I had to point out that justice is a fine line, and that to transgress it by a hairsbreadth to right or to left is to be guilty of an injustice. I illustrated the point with the tale of the Irish labourer who was putting up a brick wall. 'Paddy,' said the foreman, 'yer wa's no' plumb'. 'Plumb,' retorted the outraged builder, 'I've just had the line on it an' it's two inches more than plumb.'

I like to think that due to what limited knowledge I have of the law, I have been able to steer the Presbytery of Glasgow along courses whose wisdom may have been suspect, but whose legality was beyond all possible challenge. In matters which lie properly within their province, the courts of the Church of Scotland have a jurisdiction parallel with that of the civil courts, and their judgments cannot be made the subject of appeal to these latter bodies. In Church affairs the litigant who has reached the General Assembly has arrived at the end of the road, and not the Court of Session—not even the House of Lords—has any standing in the matter. In recent years it is not unusual to read of a minister of another denomination having appealed to an Industrial Tribunal claiming that he had been wrongfully dismissed. This is a situation that could not arise in the Church of Scotland. Should one of our ministers consider himself to have been deposed by the Presbytery without just cause, his remedy lies in appeal to the Synod, and thence if still dissatisfied to the General Assembly. But civil tribunals are not for him. That is one reason why it is so important that courts of the Church should move in this realm with the utmost circumspection. While I should never claim to have known all the answers, I have generally known where the answers were to be found, and I have invariably known some authority in the legal world who was prepared to help me with advice. My good friend Andrew Ralston, as sound a lawyer as he is a Churchman (even if a Baptist!) has been a constant source of guidance. I hope I may never have been unduly legalistic, but I adhere to a very simple doctrine that there are two ways in which a thing may be done, the legal and the illegal, and I have always had a distinct preference for the former.

The legal procedures of the Kirk contain some peculiarities, some interesting survivals (as might be expected) of customs long since departed from in the civil sphere. One trivial thing, for example, is that a petition ends with the strange phrase, 'and your petitioner will ever pray'. I understand that this was once in universal use, and according to the authorities the words are an expression of deference and represent an attitude of waiting—not inappropriate in such matters! The phrase led in my experience to a quite amusing incident when a solicitor in town, who was involved in preparing a petition for a congregation who were his clients, sought my help with the framing of the document, he himself being unfamiliar with our forms. I told him if he sent me the material I would knock it into some kind of shape. This he did and I returned the stuff in due course—handwritten. Now I am the first to admit that my handwriting bears no resemblance to copper-plate, but I was surprised when scanning the typed draft sent to me for final revision to read, 'And your petitioners will even pay'. Amazing the lengths to which some people will go to win their case.

One particular instance in which it seems to me our Church courts follow a much more logical sequence than their civil counterparts, appears when one of our ministers steps badly out of line and it is necessary to institute the equivalent of a criminal case, to subject him to what is called a 'libel'. This today, with the language suitably modernised, addresses the party by name and then goes on in some such form as this—'Albeit by the Word of God and the laws and discipline of the Church, drunkenness [let us say] is an offence unbecoming your profession and severely punishable by the laws of the Church: Yet true it is and of verity that you are guilty of the said offence in that . . . . . : therefore you ought to be punished according to the rules of the Church'. As can be seen at a glance, this is a perfect syllogism. We start off by setting forth the general proposition in the major premise (All men are mortal): we follow with the minor premise bringing the accused within the ambit of the proposition (Socrates is a man): and we are driven to the inescapable conclusion (Socrates is mortal).

I have a shrewd suspicion that at one time the courts of the land must have followed a similar pattern in a civil suit, but if so they have departed from it quite substantially, doubtless for very good and sufficient reason. Today a Summons in the Court of Session begins with a Conclusion—which on the face of it seems a little odd. In a writ in the Sheriff Court you begin with a 'crave', but this still represents the end product desired and, no less than 'conclusion', might be expected to appear at the other end. Having thus got off its chest what it is asking the court to do, it passes on to a series of Condescendences setting forth the facts which are alleged and which it is averred will, with the aid of the legal principles to be invoked, justify the court in granting its request. And the document ends with a section called Pleas-in-Law which has always seemed to be intended quite specifically to lay down the legal grounds on which the action is founded, but which I feel has inclined to become a kind of stylised formula. At its best this is a syllogism set on its head and to me it doesn't look any the healthier logically for the somersault.

A more significant peculiarity of our ecclesiastical procedure in this kind of case has to do with the verdict that will be pronounced, for this has to be either Proven or Not Proven. Again I should contend that from a logical point of view our position has much to commend it. The man was charged with certain offences and the accuser undertook to prove these by good and sufficient evidence. If at the close of the hearing he has discharged this obligation the case is Proven, if not it is Not Proven. What could be simpler? The difference between not having been proved guilty and having been proved not guilty is a very real one, and not one of those 'nice distinctions' thought to be so dear to the heart of lawyers. It is comparable to the very valid distinction drawn by the mediaeval churchmen between the claim that our Lord was not able to sin and that He was able not to sin.

While I was a member of the Presbytery of Paisley (and long before I became its Clerk) we had a most unhappy and unsavoury case in which a girl in town named her minister as the father of her child. The allegation was such as could neither be hushed up nor brushed aside and an action was instituted. After the fullest possible enquiry, the Committee, to which had been entrusted the conduct of the hearing, returned a unanimous verdict in the minister's favour—a verdict of Not Proven. I recall there was a very bitter outcry on the part of many of our members that this was grossly unfair because in the eyes of the world at large, and of the good folk of Paisley in particular, it conveyed the impression that verdict invariably does in a criminal court—for the run of the mill Paisley buddy it meant simply, 'They knew it was him but they couldna pin it on him'. I am sure this is only too near the truth, but the blame does not lie at the door of the Kirk.

Instead I think the fault lies in our distinctive Scottish practice whereby in a criminal trial the jury is given a choice among three verdicts—Guilty, Not Guilty, and Not Proven. It is a practice that has always attracted a great deal of controversy, and people feel very strongly both for and against. There seems no justification today for its retention. If the case against the accused has not been proved to the satisfaction of judge or jury, then he or she is entitled to continue in the enjoyment of the presumption of innocence, which is our common birthright, and therefore to be declared Not Guilty. It is true that for all practical purposes so far as the prisoner is concerned, the outcome is the same with a Not Proven as with a Not Guilty verdict—he is immediately released and he cannot subsequently be charged on the same count, for he has tholed his assize and that is that. In the days of capital punishment, the Not Proven verdict relieved the jury of the awful responsibility of condemning a man to death if there was the slightest glimmer of doubt regarding his guilt. But that consideration no longer holds and there seems no reason for retaining the triple choice.

That would leave us with the simple alternative of Guilty or Not Guilty. For myself I have still a distinct preference for the Kirk's position of Proven or Not Proven, for that seems to me to describe quite accurately what has been the outcome of the trial. I am, however, only too well aware that we are stuck with Guilty or Not Guilty. This, of course, is the proper choice for the accused when he is pleading—'How plead you, Guilty or Not Guilty?' It is not without significance though that, if he opts for the latter alternative, he is put under no obligation to prove that he was not guilty, but only to rebut the efforts of the Crown to prove that he was.

For those not familiar with the law it should be explained that there is an exception to this, and that is the case of the so-called special defence of, say, alibi when the man claims that he was somewhere else at the material time, or of impeachment when he maintains that someone else whom he names struck the fatal blow. In these cases the *onus probandi* falls upon the accused, and if he is successful in discharging this to the satisfaction of the jury then it can genuinely be said that he has been found Not Guilty, not merely that his guilt has not been proven. The fact that the Crown failed to prove that the accused was in Glasgow's Renfield Street at the time when the man was murdered, does not prove him Not Guilty, although it may lead to his release; but if he has been successful in proving that he was in Edinburgh at the time, that does prove him Not Guilty. This clearly would be a case where my alternative of Proven and Not Proven would be inadequate. My complaint is that there can be circumstances where the choice between Guilty and Not Guilty is no less inadequate.

The kind of thing I have in mind is clearly illustrated in the case of a murder trial of some years ago. The accused was a youth who had recently started his first job in a local iron foundry. In the absence of the friendly bank manager so convincingly portrayed on the telly screen (if not always in his private room at the bank), there was in this firm a 'friendly usurer' who for a consideration was only too ready to help his mates out of financial stringencies. He was found murdered and money was missing. Suspicion pointed to a youth who was taken in to 'assist the police with their enquiries' and subjected to a pretty thorough grilling. As a result, he not only provided a confession, but for good measure took the police to a field and pointed out the precise spot where the money and the weapon were buried. Obviously while the confession could have been 'rigged', the other evidence was genuine and convincing enough in all conscience. Conviction and sentence followed. The verdict was appealed on the ground that, because of his tender years, the youth should have had the comfort of his father's presence throughout the grilling, and since this was not done the evidence obtained thereat should not have been allowed to be put to the jury. The Appeal Court had no difficulty in upholding this plea and quashing the conviction—with which I have no quarrel. My point here is simply this, that while the Appeal Court could quite properly recall the verdict of Guilty, they could not, given all the circumstances, possibly restore the presumption of innocence, for that had been well and truly rebutted. Given our laws of evidence, the case was clearly not proven; given the meaning of words in the English language, I cannot see how the boy could be described as not guilty. You may think I am just arguing about words. Of course I am, but this, as I see it, is a case where words are of the greatest significance.

The courts themselves are, as we all know, very fussy about the meaning of words. A quite entertaining, to me, episode has recently been reported in a case involving the Royal Prerogative of Mercy. This centred on the meaning of the word 'Pardon', a subject, incidentally, which has exercised my own mind on occasion, for I have always wondered how it was possible for the Queen to pardon someone for something which it has been shown he did not do. In the course of his opinion, Lord Robertson expressed the view that 'in the ordinary use of language . . . if you pardon someone you pardon them for something that they have done and not for something they haven't done'. This seems clear enough to banish any confusion one might have on the subject. But listen to the Note which has been appended: 'His Lordship may well be right with regard to the "ordinary use of language" but it is clear that in several instances the Royal Pardon has been used to remedy clear miscarriages of justice, including wrongful conviction. As regards the effect of the pardon, it appears that much of the confusion arises from the archaic language of the Free Pardon as presently expressed, and from the assumption that the term, as used in English law, has the same meaning as in Scots law. In English law a "free pardon" is recognised as not only removing the consequence of conviction, but of removing the conviction itself. In Scotland the term has no greater significance than the distinction between an unconditional ("free") pardon, and a conditional pardon. Even then, the pardon probably only extends to the consequences of conviction, unless by its terms it expressly states otherwise'. I am glad to have this opportunity of clearing up, and so vividly, a confusion that doubtless exists in the minds of many of my readers!

As I mentioned earlier, the Paisley firm where I gained my little legal experience had an extensive practice in reparation cases of every description, and I was not very long with them before I was brought into close touch with a legal question which for long had given me, as a layman, cause for concern—the way in which alone compensation can be recovered in certain types of cases. Some time before this we had been consulted by the widow of a railway surfaceman who had been struck by a train and killed when on fog duty near North Johnstone station. Twice the elements of a case had been put together, but each time it had been rejected by the Legal Aid people as being without hope of success. My friend John Clyde had just dropped the papers into the waste-paper basket—and when he abandoned a case, it was not just a forlorn hope, it was a lost cause. I happened to come into his room at that very moment and, seeing me, he recovered the papers and handed them to me. 'You're greatly interested in the railway,' he said, 'see whether you can make anything of that'. It was true that I was interested in the railway, not least in that corner of it where the tragedy had occurred, for it was near there that my father had been yard-foreman for many years and I knew the locus like the proverbial back of my hand.

To be able to sustain a successful claim against a body such as British Rail, one has to prove negligence on their part, and this, naturally, will be a kind of vicarious negligence of which some of their servants had been guilty. The facts of this case constituted literally a 'grey area', for it all happened on a night of keen frost and thick fog. Our man, Campbell, was on emer-gency duty clearing points and suchlike, all under the orders of the signalman at Cart Junction signal cabin, a young man with little experience in 'the box'. A goods train from Greenock to Glasgow had been stopped at a signal some two or three hundred yards short of the cabin. When the line was clear for him to let this train through, the signalman couldn't get the signal to move, the frost having taken control; it was at red and at red it stayed. He tried flashing a green hand-lamp out of the window in the direction of the stationary train, but without effect. He then ordered Campbell to proceed on foot and give the driver a verbal message that he was to proceed. Campbell set out to do so, but just before he reached the engine he was struck by a passenger train headed for Ardrossan on the other line. British Rail maintained, not unreasonably, that the man had himself to blame, for, as he well knew, he should not have been walking on that line with his back to oncoming traffic. The people responsible for Legal Aid, upon whose grant we were utterly dependent if we were to reach the courts, took the same view. Indeed I was much inclined to take that view myself.

On reflection, however, I came to think that just as there is a presumption of innocence, so there should be a presumption of commonsense and self-preservation, and that Campbell, being an intelligent and responsible man with lots of experience of the permanent way, must have had some good reason for being where he was—normally he would never have dreamt of walking on that line, especially in fog. That at least seemed to me to be the point from which to begin my enquiries. Which meant that what I was looking for were circumstances that would explain this untypical conduct. I interviewed all the people involved. I wandered around at the scene trying to piece together what might have happened in the fog of that miserable night. Then suddenly one day the penny dropped. The fireman of the stationary goods train, I had learned, had after a little time decided he should walk forward to the signal-box and report the presence of his train, all in terms of the rule book. When still about halfway there, he picked up the message of the green lamp that the signalman was still frantically waving, in spite of the fact that he had despatched Campbell some time before. The fireman hurried back to the engine and told his driver about the green lamp. They gave a whistle and off they set. What they had no reason to know was that Campbell was quite close at hand, approaching on their line. One can imagine Campbell's alarm when he heard the whistle and realised that what had been a dim grey stationary mass was fast coming towards him. Moving bodies can take on terrifying shapes in the fog. What more natural reaction than for him to move quickly over to the other line, unhappily for him right into the path of the oncoming passenger train.

We had recreated the series of events. What was more important, we had identified the element of negligence. For immediately he sent Campbell off on his ill-fated errand, the signalman should have discontinued every other attempt to communicate with the stranded crew. We prepared a new case, Legal Aid accepted it as qualifying for grant, and in due course the Court of Session was so impressed by it as to make an award of, I think, £3000—a considerable sum at that time. And on what a little thing our success had hinged.

My reason for recounting this tale in such detail is not to show myself a frustrated Perry Mason, but to complain that it should be necessary to go to such pains to find a defaulter in the employers' service. I have always thought that this whole business of having to prove negligence is something of a nonsense and that any industry which puts human lives at risk—and there can be few occupations more hazardous than that of a railway surfaceman—the employer should be in the position of an insurer, and unless it can be proved that the victim had himself been the negligent party, and to the point of recklessness, compensation should be paid in the case of death or serious injury following upon an accident. As I suggested earlier there should be a presumption of self-protection which it would be for the employer to rebut. It seems a needlessly cruel addition to an already heavy burden of sorrow, that a mother who has lost husband and breadwinner should have to suffer all the strain and anxiety of a court action (not to mention years of delay) before she can hope to be awarded any kind of compensation—and possibly not even then. A further point is that I was extremely sorry so specifically to have to lay on the shoulders of a young signalman, who had been doing his best under the duress of an emergency situation, the responsibility for the death of his mate. It had never occurred to him that it was thus, and I should have been happy to leave it so. But given the state of the law on the subject, how else could one get for the widow and children what I am sure were their rights. This seems to me to be a department of our law that is in urgent need of being looked at afresh—not by the lawyers, but by the lawmakers.

Another criticism, which from the exalted height of my comparative ignorance of the subject I feel compelled to pass, is on the way in which the very considerable expenses of civil actions which have been appealed through the courts are extorted from one or other of the litigants. It is a subject about which I feel very strongly, the practice appearing to me so manifestly unjust. The whole business of the awarding of legal expenses is interesting. There is a general impression that the loser in a civil action meets the costs for both sides. This, although it represents what generally happens, is an over-simplification, for in fact the principle is that the whole costs of any process of litigation should be borne by the party who needlessly caused it. That, as I say, will normally be the loser, the person who raised or defended an action in which he was unsuccessful, but it need not necessarily be so. Away back in the days when cattle were regularly conveyed by train, a cattle dealer raised an action against the railway company on the ground that neglect of their duties by some of their servants had led to the death of some of his beasts and injury to others. The case was heard in the Sheriff Court and the defenders were exonerated, evidence having been led to show that all proper care had been exercised. The company, however, had withheld permission for the dealer's agent to precognosce their workers, with the result that the only way in which the pursuer could learn whether or not he had adequate grounds for an action was by raising such an action. He recovered his costs from the company whose obstructiveness had made the litigation necessary. This seems eminently reasonable and just. It is a sound principle that anyone who recklessly causes needless litigation should pay for it.

My complaint arises in respect of those cases that are taken by appeal from one court to the next, and not because anyone is reckless, but simply because there are different views held by the most learned judges of what the law requires in a certain situation. In a recent case, for example, the pursuer received a judicial offer of £6000 to settle his claim out of court. He repudiated the offer and went to the Court of Session where the Lord Ordinary made an award in his favour of more than £100,000. The hospital board, who were the defenders, appealed to the Division who replaced the £100,000 with an award of £3000, and, of course, since the award was less than the offer that had been turned down, the pursuer was held to be the person responsible for the needless litigation and had to bear the costs, which far exceeded the £3000 of the award. He was being penalised for having been held right in the lower court. I am not making any comment on the merits of the case (a subject about which I know nothing) but purely on the bill for expenses. However misguided his colleagues may think him to have been, a distinguished Senator of the College of Justice assessed the value of the man's claim at over £100,000—can anyone seriously contend that he, a mere layman, had been reckless or irresponsible in rejecting an offer of £6000 to settle that claim? So why should he be handed an enormous bill for causing unnecessary litigation?

A most terrifying feature of this kind of progression through the courts is that it can all begin in quite innocent fashion. I tremble to think how perilously near I myself came to being caught up in just such a spiral. The Rating Act of 1962 made provision whereby property held for purposes of a charity was to qualify for a mandatory remission of 50 per cent of local rates. It was freely conceded that manses were entitled to enjoy this concession, but the people in Glasgow's rating department maintained that the house which I occupied in virtue of being Presbytery Clerk was not to be regarded as a manse for this purpose, and they served a demand for the full amount of the rates. I was not satisfied they were right—indeed I was quite sure they were wrong—and I felt it would be worthwhile having the Sheriff give his mind to the matter. I would be prepared, win or lose, to abide by his decision. So I made payment of the half which I claimed was the extent of my debt and I came to an understanding with the officials that they would sue me for the balance. In reaching this simple agreement I had no premonition of myself teetering on the brink of a financial precipice. Luckily, from my point of view, I had persuaded the General Trustees to contest the case of a Church Officer's house which the Corporation had also refused to accept as qualifying, and since this was already in process the officials decided to await its outcome before serving the summons on me. The Church Officer's house case ended finally in the House of Lords—in our favour I am glad to say—and the Corporation immediately conceded my claim, although in all honesty I don't think the one case constituted any kind of precedent for the other. It may, of course, have acted as a warning! I found it enormously interesting to sit through the two days of the hearing in the House of Lords. I should not have sat so happily had it been my case with the modest savings of a lifetime balanced precariously on the line.

It not uncommonly happens that just such a case, begun innocently enough in the Sheriff Court, goes on to the Court of Session, being decided in each case, let us say, in favour of the pursuer. The defender, however (and the defender may well be a corporation, a huge industrial concern, or a government department, in each case with unlimited resources at its command) persists to the House of Lords. In the fulness of time Their Lordships' judgment is issued overturning everything that had gone before and finding in favour of the defender. In their judgment they say that the Sheriff had misdirected himself in law, and that the Division had given insufficient weight to some material point in evidence. Having thus generously awarded blame right and left, they go on, no less generously, to hand the bill for the entire performance to the unfortunate pursuer—who up to that moment had thought he was doing fine. I am not for a moment suggesting that the bill should have been divided between the Sheriff and the others on a *per capita* (or even on a *per culpam*) basis, but I do say, and I say in all seriousness, that they had done more to deserve it than had the unhappy recipient.

It is my contention that in this context the whole concept of reckless litigation is a complete irrelevance. For what in fact is happening in cases of this kind is that the law is being hammered out in one of the ways in which law is made in this country, by the decided case, and to this extent it is not needless but very necessary litigation. We have in this country two ways in which the law is principally made—by the passing of statute (in Parliament) and by the deciding of cases (in the courts). It would be hard to imagine what must be the cost to the national exchequer of making statute law—the hours spent by highly-paid specialists in the initial draughtsmanship, and then in the arguing out and the amending and adjusting at the Committee level and in Parliament and then in the Lords. To get a new Act on the statute book must cost a bonnie penny. Is it not reasonable to suggest that the purse which provides so lavishly for all this should also make available the cost of construing the Acts framed at such expense? It appears to me an outrage that it should be met out of the pocket of the private citizen.

They tell a highly disreputable story about two lawyers discussing the will of a very wealthy man whose death had recently occurred. He had disposed of his vast fortune in a highly complicated fashion and had done so in a document of his own devising, what one might call a 'Do It Yourself Testamentary Disposition'. The two friends were teasing out some of the nicer points that would require opinion of counsel and those that would have to be tested in the courts. The conversation ended with one of the pair remarking, 'One can only hope that none of the estate will be frittered away on the beneficiaries'. The fact that it is possible to respond to that story by saying *verb sap* I find extremely sad. I am satisfied it is high time that the question of expenses in actions which involve construing the law at this level was looked at very earnestly with a view to early and radical reform. What truly amazes me is that mine seems to be a fairly lone voice, that mine should be so much a minority report—I should have expected more people to be up in arms about the present state of affairs.

One further complaint and I promise forever to hold my peace. Why must there be such outrageous delays in getting matters dealt with in the courts? That years should elapse before a fairly simple case of reparation can get itself settled in the Court of Session is bad enough in all conscience, for it often means that some poor soul who has a perfectly valid claim is involved in great financial hardship while awaiting settlement. Frequently too it leads to claims being settled out of court for much less than their true worth because the claimant is desperately in need of ready cash. The fact that the damages once awarded will reflect the time that has elapsed between incident and decree is little comfort as you vainly try to meet your bills in the meantime—'Live, horse, and you'll get corn'. One recognises that there are time-wasting complications in cases of this kind—even if these do not account for all the delay. But why should so many months—twelve or more, perhaps —have to elapse before someone charged with some comparatively trivial criminal offence is brought to justice? After all, he may well be innocent. I imagine that for those of us who know something about the courts, who wander in and out of them in happy carefree fashion, it is hard properly to appreciate what it means to someone who has never been involved in any way with the police or in a court of justice to have a criminal charge hanging over his head. The 'ned' (fairly certain to be guilty anyway) couldn't care less—the longer the trial is put off, the longer he'll keep out of jail, but the respectable citizen with a completely clean sheet (who may well be innocent) can be driven nearly out of his (or her) mind in terror of all that may be in store. It is a piece of gratuitous cruelty to keep such people in this state of suspense for months on end.

Some years ago a young lady of my acquaintance was involved in a minor motoring accident at a city crossing, another car and a lorry being the other vehicles concerned. Both cars were slightly damaged, the lorry was unscathed, and no one was hurt. It was the kind of thing which was not really necessary to report to the police. My own impression was that each of the three drivers had contributed an element of carelessness, but undoubtedly my friend's had been the largest contribution and she found herself charged with careless driving. She had been pretty upset by the accident, she became positively ill on receiving the summons. The accident had occurred just before Christmas, but the case did not call until October—nine months in which to get accustomed to the picture of herself in a lonely cell. Came the day appointed and she and her mother (who was a witness, having been in the car at the time) and the two other drivers were shown into a room where they sat, and sat, and sat. Obviously they had been warned of the dangers of careless talk, so they sat in stony silence. The driver of the other car was a doctor whose time, I feel sure, could have been better spent. It would seem that my friend's case was preceded by another where a plea of Guilty had been expected and only very little time would have been involved. The accused had changed his mind, however, and a trial was in progress. Forewarning of the change had been given, but the programme had been left as it was. In the course of the afternoon, someone remembered the four people incarcerated in the witness room. The case in progress was momentarily stopped to allow the accused and witnesses to be brought in and a new date fixed—for February—fourteen months after the incident.

When the day arrived all four gathered once more, the case was heard, and my friend was acquitted—and all inside a couple of hours. Yet it had dragged on for more than a year. I had all along thought the case was a slender one and that the girl had suffered enough—far more than enough—for any carelessness of which she might have been guilty. Surely it did not need all that time to bring it to an issue. And if it was unfair for the girl, what of the witnesses? A doctor, a lorry driver and a housewife losing a day-and-a-half's work over what, in the context of today's traffic maelstrom, was a trifle. Yes, it can be very hard on the witnesses—and they haven't done anything to deserve it.

Only once, I am happy to report, have I been called as a witness. It was in a case involving fraud. I received intimation that I was to present myself at the Sheriff Court on a certain morning at 9 o'clock. From what I knew of the case I was quite clear that they could not possibly get round to having me in the box before lunchtime, so I took a chance and went straight to my office and got a half day's work done. When I got to the court just after lunch I found the room full of witnesses, but nothing at all had happened. I sought out the fiscal who explained that they had not been able to get started because they hadn't a shorthand writer. I told him I was away back to my office and gave him my phone number. He warned me of the awful consequences of such behaviour. 'Look,' I said, 'I'm prepared to give up my time in the interests of the administration of justice, but not to cover up the maladministration of these offices.' I went on to say that I should be happy, if need be, to come down and tell His Lordship just that. We didn't go on to discuss what His Lordship might be happy to tell me by way of reply! I suppose I might have found myself languishing behind bars. It was in fact fully a month later that I was recalled. Witnesses are having to re-organise their affairs to fulfil a public duty; their business (in the case of the doctor, for instance) may be every bit as urgent and important as that of the courts; they should not be put to needless inconvenience.

The inconvenience caused to the witness by these long delays is one thing, the harm done to the value of his testimony is quite another. The human memory is a funny thing and varies enormously in its reliability between one person and another, but in every case it is at its best when the material to be recalled is still fresh. Testifying to an incident shortly after it occurred, the witness will be able not only to supply a fairly full account, but also to answer questions about details not covered in his original statement. As the days pass, it will still be possible for him to reproduce the original account pretty much as before, but the ability to go beyond that may well have left him altogether. When you take a precognition a day or two after the event, you are, as it were, tapping the memory direct; when the witness stands in the box twelve months later, he is replaying a tape which has been stored away in his memory bank; and while that is doubtless honest and accurate enough so far as it goes, it necessarily goes only so far as those aspects of the events that he considered (unconsciously) at the time to be worthy of putting on the tape. 'You have told the court that on the evening of

Tuesday 13th December the weather was fine, visibility was good, and the road was perfectly dry.' 'That is so.' 'You are perfectly clear about that?' 'Yes, I remember it perfectly.' 'Tell me, what were conditions like on Wednesday 14th December?' 'O, I don't remember that.' 'Yet you claim to remember very clearly about the previous night.' The plain fact is that we are here using the word 'remember' in two utterly different senses—what might be called remembering by first intention and remembering by replaying a tape from the memory bank. For the purpose of getting at the truth, the former can be much more valuable than the latter, but because of the delays in bringing cases to court we have always got to make do with the latter —and the poorer.

One interesting thing about the backlog of business at the courts is that they seem always to manage to get through all their business, even if invariably they are doing it many months in arrears—the pile isn't growing any bigger. Which reminds me of an account in a country newspaper of a local sports meeting where it was said that in a certain race, 'From the very start Smith and Brown ran shoulder to shoulder with Smith always that yard in front'. I could perfectly picture the event, even if I couldn't envisage the shoulder! If you substitute 'six months' for 'that yard' you seem to me to have a description of how the criminal courts keep abreast of their business. It would be to the advantage of the accused, of the witnesses, and of the administration of justice, if the gap could be drastically curtailed.

I have never seen cause to regret my short spell of dabbling in the law, even if only because it has let me see that that branch of human activity is, like the Kirk, in need of some reformation!

Chapter 12
In Pursuit of Evangelism

A FRIEND was telling me the other day that, having been away from home at the weekend, he had on Sunday morning gone to worship at the local church. There he spent twenty-five miserable minutes while the preacher assured those present that, unless they had had the conscious experience of being born again, they were one and all condemned to an eternity in hell. I expressed surprise that so long a time could have been occupied saying so little, but I was assured it had been a kind of theme with variations, the latter being mainly repetitive. My friend had spoken to the minister afterwards, venturing to suggest that the mercy of God might be a bigger and more all-embracing thing than his sermon had seemed to indicate. He had gone on to refer to John the Divine's vision of the Eternal City with its twelve gates that face to every airt and close not by night nor by day, and he had hinted that perhaps while the glorious company of the born-again were triumphantly marching through one of these gates, some other of God's sinful but repentant children might, with heads bowed, be filtering through one of the others. The preacher was horrified, he would have none of this heresy —the choice was the simple one he had indicated, and it grieved him to have to tell my friend that he was one of the condemned. By way of comfort he promised to pray for him that he might come to see the light.

And he explained—and to his own satisfaction justified—it all by saying, 'Of course, I am an evangelical preacher'.

My dictionary defines 'evangel' as 'good tidings', a description I find difficult to apply to the news that we are all destined for eternity in hell. It worries me that a small group within the Kirk should claim for themselves a monopoly of this evangel, which to me is as wide and welcoming as they would have it narrow and forbidding. I intensely dislike the use of the phrase 'the evangelical party within the Church'—we must every one of us surely be evangelists, even if we don't all mean precisely the same thing when we use that term, or follow the same course as we seek to practise our calling. To me it has always seemed an unhappy feature of the Disruption that, in what was an honest division of opinion, the one side should have arrogated to itself the name of 'Evangelical Party'.

I suppose that over the years the word 'evangelical' has acquired a specialised significance as the opposite of 'sacramental' when applied to different emphases in the practice of the Christian faith. This is well enough so long as the one is not set against the other as though they were mutually exclusive. The most fervent believer in the power unto salvation which the Gospel supplies must be conscious of how dependent he is for the means of grace upon the sacraments of the Church, while the most exalted high-churchman must perforce turn to the pages of the Gospel if he is to find the origin, the meaning, and the justification of the sacraments by which he sets such store.

From earliest days the faith has been spread by the preaching of the Gospel—the Evangel—and it is natural that the term 'evangelism' should have come to be identified with missionary outreach. An evangelistic campaign is an attempt to win converts to the faith, an evangelist is someone particularly gifted in communicating the Gospel to the unbeliever. However, as she became increasingly successful in her missionary efforts, and more and more converts were won into the fold, it was inevitable that the early Church should come to direct her efforts and shape her message more towards sustaining the Christian life of those who were now within, and less towards winning those who remained outwith. Obviously these must represent two quite different approaches. Hence the complaint once voiced to me by a decent kirk member, 'I've no objection to being converted, but not, please, every single Sunday?' The other side of the picture was sketched rather neatly by a minister who, when he had reached the stage of retirement, remarked a trifle bitterly that he had been commissioned to launch out into the deep and there spread his nets, but he had been kept so busy processing the fish his predecessor had caught, he had never found time to put out to sea, and now it was too late. It was, I think, George MacLeod who drew the distinction between the Fisher of Men and the Keeper of the Aquarium.

That the number of unbelievers is today very high and

growing steadily higher, that many of those within the fold are there more from convention than from conviction, that the number of admissions to Church membership by confession is falling year by year—these are indisputable facts, and they should lead us to ask whether the time is not ripe for us to take a fresh look at our techniques. Is not the condition of the contemporary world presenting a fresh challenge to evangelism today? What have we done, what are we proposing to do, to meet that challenge?

It has been the consistent position of the Church of Scotland to be less than madly enthusiastic about the kind of evangelism represented by the nation-wide campaign involving enormous meetings in this centre and in that, and revolving around some personality of international repute. For it is the long-accepted doctrine of the Kirk that the proper instrument of evangelism is the parish where, given that minister, elders, and members are all united in complete devotion to the task, the faith of the Lord Jesus Christ can, in the most effective way imaginable, be conveyed to all within reach, so that the careless and the unbelieving will be brought within the fold. But, of course, while a most convincing case can be made out in support of this ideal, it is none the less lamentably true that in practice it does not seem to be working out all that well. Evidence for this is to be found not only in the steadily dwindling numbers on the Church's rolls (from 1,292,617 in 1961 to 845,311 in 1986, a drop of almost half-a-million in 25 years) but even more, perhaps, in the half-hearted attitude towards the Kirk and all the Kirk stands for, adopted by those whose names still appear on the communion rolls. Forty-three per cent of them did not attend even one communion service in the year 1987. Judged by results, the parish system is just not working as an effective instrument of evangelism. There are ministers working in what today are generally called 'areas of deprivation', and sometimes 'mission priority parishes', who would go further and say that the straitjacket of the traditional parish pattern cramps their style and restricts their efforts, and that, in fact, it constitutes a formidable obstacle to the work of evangelism in such communities. Unfortunately, though, they have not yet, so far as I know, come up with any alternative structure that has been shown to work.

As a consequence of all this, when a proposal is advanced

to stage some specifically missionary effort of the more spectacular sort, we are in no position to say, 'We are doing very nicely, thank you; our organisation is coping quite adequately'. So, from time to time the Assembly may find themselves in a most difficult situation in relation to, say, a visit to these shores by an evangelist of world renown. By the time the matter reaches us, it has all been arranged—he is coming across in response to an invitation from some independent group of people who do not owe any particular denominational allegiance, but who have co-operated to organise the campaign. The venture has doubtless received considerable advance coverage on the media. The organisers then approach the Kirk to seek her blessing and her backing, and we find ourselves in something of a dilemma. It may be that we are not the least bit enthusiastic, and had we been consulted in advance we should probably have advised against the effort. But to be presented with a *fait-semi-accomplit* is less that fair, for if we decide not to co-operate this will be seen in the worst possible light, while if we decide to throw in our lot and do so in anything less than a whole-hearted fashion, any subsequent failure will be laid at our door.

My own inclination personally has been to welcome these sporadic outbursts of evangelistic fervour so long as we see them clearly for what they are—a way of inspiring people to make a new beginning, of setting their feet on the right road —but emphatically nothing more. They are not of themselves anything like a complete answer to the problem of the churchless. For evangelism is an ongoing process, and it is within that process that the organised Church has perhaps the most significant contribution to make. It is a wonderful thing to be brought to a great moment of decision, still more wonderful to turn completely around in one's tracks; but it is another thing altogether to travel for any distance along a new road. It was a great day when the younger son in the parable 'came to himself', and it was right he should be welcomed home with a grand outburst of rejoicing, but the story doesn't end with the catchline 'and he lived happily ever after'. For he had a long hard road in front of him. The late James Dow of Lochranza made, in typical style, a very telling point in a sermon on the parable of the prodigal. It was the morning after the celebration and the young man had got out of bed rather late and with a very sore head. As he entered the kitchen, he enquired, 'Mother, what's for lunch?' 'Cold veal,' was the uncomforting reply. The celebration is quickly over and the road of recovery is long and rough and steep. St Paul had a long way still to travel after his experience on the Damascus Road. The immediate results of the big campaign I am bound to welcome; but about its persisting contribution to the cause of revival I have my doubts.

The West of Scotland had an experience of a large-scale upsurge of evangelistic fervour as long ago as the mid-eighteenth century. It all happened in what was then the little, neglected parish of Cambuslang, with its poplation of less than a thousand souls, but the repercussions echoed far and wide. In 1731 William M'Culloch was inducted minister of the Parish of Cambuslang. It had been seven years earlier, when the previous minister had died after a protracted illness leaving the place in poor shape, that M'Culloch had been the choice of the parishioners, but the Duke of Hamilton, who as principal heritor had the right of presentation, favoured another and contrived to stall. Because of this the vacancy dragged on month after month for seven weary years, during which the fabric of both church and manse fell into a deplorable state, while the spiritual health of the people' fared even worse. The new minister was essentially a scholar, learned and unostentatious, a cautious, conscientious, and prudent minister, and certainly no firebrand in the pulpit. Scarcely, you might have thought, the *mis-en-scene* for a great revival. Yet in the course of a seemingly so commonplace ministry among so ordinary a people, a massive spiritual awakening was to occur.

It was in the early days of 1742 that a request was made to the minister by the congregation that he hold a weekday service in addition to the Sunday worship, and within a matter of weeks this was extended to become a daily service. Here you find a remarkable feature that, whatever it was ultimately to become, the whole thing began as an uprising from the pew. At the summer communion of that year, over twenty thousand people gathered in the open air at a vast natural amphitheatre close to the dilapidated church, and 'the Cambuslang wark' had begun. It was an outstanding manifestation of what today we should call the charismatic, some speaking in tongues, some beating the breast, some bleeding profusely at the nose, some falling into convulsions. The 'wark' attracted widespread attention and George Whitefield, probably the greatest evangelist of all time, hurried north to lend his support. On the occasion of the August celebration of the sacrament, the number who assembled on what is still called Conversion Brae was said to be in excess of thirty thousand, and it is certain that over three thousand took communion that day. By a strange coincidence, phenomena of a very similar kind, although much less in extent, occurred in Kilsyth around the same time, there being no connection whatever between the two events. The rather sad ending to the Cambuslang story lies in the fact that, writing some years later, M'Culloch is found lamenting how many backsliders there had been, even though he claims there were hundreds who from that day 'had evidently been changed'. A small disturbance, it might be thought, for so massive an explosion.

The closest I myself ever came to this kind of 'wark' was in the famous Billy Graham campaign staged in Glasgow in the early fifties. This was no spontaneous eruption of the spirit, but a fortnight of meetings in Glasgow's Kelvin Hall organised for months in advance down to the last detail. A positive army of counsellors recruited from local congregations had been subjected to most intensive training in their duties, forms had been designed and printed to enable news of all conversions to be conveyed in properly documented fashion to the minister involved, and the resources of the media had been mustered to give the fullest advance publicity. The meetings themselves were arranged with the same professional skill and attention to detail, an atmosphere of intense expectancy was built up, the organ voluntary provided a suitable background of rather sickly sweetness, the praise was chosen with evident care to its emotional appeal. Finally the great man himself appeared, an intensely modest-seeming man in a plain lounge suit, holding a Bible in his hand. He spoke quietly, but with extraordinary power and enormous effect, ending with an appeal to each of his hearers to come forward and make the great act of self-committal. A minute—or maybe two—passed, and then one rose, and then another and went forward until there was quite a trickle, that grew to a flood, of people of both sexes, of all ages, of every description, pouring through the doorways. The sceptics, of whom there were remarkably few, hinted that folk had been planted here and there to get the stream of committal underway. That could be true—but what of it? The one certain thing is that the thousands who nightly made their confession were one and all cases of people whose hearts had been touched in some mysterious way by the experience of being there and of sharing in that service and listening to those soft, gentle, pleading words. I know it to be beyond dispute that some of those who went forward had come to the Kelvin Hall from no more exalted motive than sheer idle curiosity, and no less true that others who quite unashamedly had come to sneer and to enjoy a laugh stayed to pray. You cannot write off what happened to those folk as being due to some kind of mass hysteria. It was all very personal, very real—and very deeply moving.

It was at this point that the counsellors came into action, fulfilling the role their name implies. Among other things, they learned from the person concerned the name of a minister with whom he or she wanted to be put in touch, failing which contact would be made with the minister of their parish of residence. Thus the responsibility for the follow-up fell upon the regular ministry, and the fact that so remarkable an event as was witnessed in the Kelvin during that fortnight had so comp-aratively little lasting effect upon the life of the city, was freely attributed to the hostility, the laziness, the ineffectiveness, the carelessness, or whatever of the parish ministers. I am afraid it is true that the long-term effect of the campaign was a dis-appointment, but to lay the blame for that on the failure of the regular ministry was grossly unfair.

As it happens, I have a modicum of evidence to contribute. I was at the time minister at Houston and was deeply concerned with an event of such significance occurring so near my own door. I thought I should do a bit of testing-out on my own, and so, as soon as the campaign got under way, I made out a list of the people in my parish whose names I might expect to receive in the course of the coming weeks as people who had been brought to the moment of decision under the inspiration of Billy Graham. I had my own good reasons for the selection I made —a parish minister can generally be counted on to know and to understand fairly well not only his members but also his parishioners. As the results came trickling in, it transpired that I was rather better than 80 per cent correct. Quite a few of those concerned I had in my own way brought to a moment of commitment—a decision from which, sadly, they had all, sooner rather than later, fallen away.

I think, for example, of one lassie, a decent, kindly, well-doing girl whose heart, as we say, was in the right place. She had come forward to full Church-membership in the usual way. In the meetings I had with her, I had, I thought, impressed upon her the seriousness of the step she was taking, and also of the ongoing obligations to which she was committing herself. For the next month or two she was unfailingly regular at Church, and then her attendance became more and more erratic. She had become a Sunday School teacher and, once again, I was most emphatic in presenting the importance of the commitment involved, but here too after a grand start her devotion lapsed. She came in the course of time to the manse, bringing her young man, to see me about arranging a wedding. I took the opportunity of telling them both about the need to seek divine guidance and support throughout the new life on which they were embarking and not just on its opening day. Their pew knew them every Sunday—for a time. Then a child came along and the question of baptism brought them to the manse once again. O yes, they had been falling into careless habits, 'but you know how it is, with both of us working and Sunday the only chance we have to get away for a day or to catch up on the arrears of housework. But now with the responsibilities of a family, all that will be different'. Need I go on to say that the pattern exactly repeated itself? Billy Graham awakened them anew and a fresh start was made. I cannot say I felt the great evangelist was due any special credit for having brought that lassie to a stage to which I had already brought her on four separate occasions. Had he been able to reveal to me the answer to the question of how, having persuaded her to put her hand to the plough, she might be enabled to persevere to the end of the furrow, I should have been grateful indeed. That had me beaten I grant you. But don't, please, attribute my failure to carelessness or indifference.

It was inevitable too that I should be concerned with the 'Tell Scotland' Campaign of 1953. This was an experiment in evangelistic outreach of a totally different character in that it was founded on utterly different principles. For one thing it was an evangelistic campaign without an evangelist. It was, essentially, an Assembly-organised effort whose objective, it was claimed, was to do the same job as that covered by the day-to-day work, worship, and witness of the congregations of the Church. It was an attempt not to launch a crusade, but to strengthen the forces already in the field in an ongoing war. Indeed, one of its objectives was to lay a new emphasis on the potential of the parish system, the parish minister, and the congregation as instruments of evangelism. It was not something new and exciting, it was just an old story told with a new intensity. Under the inspired leadership of Ronnie Falconer, to whom the Kirk owes so much for his vision and courage as Director of Religious Broadcasting during the formative years of both radio and television, the BBC co-operated to the fullest extent in the whole affair.

The aim of the exercise, as Horace Walker, Secretary of the Home Board, put it in an address to the Presbytery of Glasgow, was not to create Parish Missions but to create Missionary Parishes. This being so, it was remitted to local people to take the initiative in determining both the kind of campaign that would be best suited to their local needs, and how, with the resources to their hand, they could best secure results. Due to the geographical position of my parish in relation to the south-west corner of Glasgow, I was invited to join as an additional labourer in a special drive being mounted in the Govan area. I was one of a number from as far afield as Greenock, who had been asked to join the local people for ten—I think it was ten—days, in what was designed as a mass assault on a highly industrialised corner of the city. Those of us from outwith the area were to be housed in the Pearce Institute at Govan Cross, and from there we were to radiate out in a variety of ventures. Preparatory work had been done for us by the local ministers in securing entrée to various factories and so on, and our task was supposed to be fairly straightforward, although in the event we had to do quite a bit of extemporising. Jim Lindsay and Hector MacLean, both from Greenock, formed with myself a team of sorts, and we contrived to fill in our time very fully—whether or not very profitably is a question I should find it exceedingly difficult to answer.

We certainly talked plenty, so that by bedtime each night we were all vocally exhausted. We addressed meetings of workers in factory canteens and on the shop-floor, we spoke from the proverbial soapbox at shipyard gates as the workers were skailing, we talked to children in school assemblies and in classrooms, when permission was given we toured workplaces and chatted with individuals, and practically every evening we went pub-crawling in the best tradition of the Salvation Army, albeit without tambourine or collecting box. It was all highly instructive, not to say fascinating, in that it revealed to us facets of life from which, behind the shelter of a dog-collar, we were normally protected; it represented most valuable toughening in the practice of public speaking (for example, the experience of addressing a canteen of men who, as soon as I opened my mouth, one and all ostentatiously turned in their seats so that their backs were towards me and very noisily opened up their papers—at the racing page—was something of an off-putting novelty, for me at least); it gave us something of an insight into the atmosphere in which so many hours of the lives of industrial workers are spent—a rather frightening revelation; it brought us face to face with a section of the people whom we rarely meet in our churches. But I found myself asking quite seriously how far we could be said to be making any useful or meaningful kind of contact, how far we could claim to be advancing the work of the Kingdom. It may well be that in the Providence of God some of the multitude of words spoken fell on good ground and brought forth a hundredfold—but I wouldn't like to count on it.

As I explain in another place, it was my experience as Hospital Chaplain to a small sanatorium, in a day when tuberculosis was still a serious menace involving months and even years in bed, that only after many visits did the patients begin to relax spiritually so that you could get close and be of some help. Maybe it was this that undermined my faith in the value of instant contact.

One incident in particular stands out vividly in my recollection. It was a Friday evening and the three of us were in a pub at the Halfway, a popular howf which at the weekends was packed to the doors. I got chatting to some fellows, others joined in, and I began to feel I was being manoeuvred towards a certain corner. The justification for my suspicion, and the reason for it, became apparent when I found myself confronted with the local apostle of Communism. Clearly, though they had grown a little weary of hearing him preach his gospel unchallenged, the habitues welcomed the prospect of confrontation and debate—what better accompaniment for a pint! Very soon I realised that my opponent had been a most unhappy victim of the depression of the thirties, and that his bitterness then had led to his adoption of Communism as offering the one hope for the future. He chose as his battleground what he claimed had been the desertion by the Church of the working classes during the Industrial Revolution, and he presented his case forcibly and fairly. It was just unlucky for him to have chosen his terrain badly. Normally I'd be pretty helpless in a political fisticuffs, but this was country with which I was keenly familiar, much more so than he was, and I was able—to the vast delight of the considerable audience—completely to overwhelm him in the debate. Something worth doing, you might think. I wonder. As I say, our audience was delighted, but I didn't share their happiness, for I was desperately conscious of the fact that all I had done for my Communist friend was to accentuate his bitterness and increase his hostility. I am sure that in his mind I was the guy who had been having an easy time lolling about a University learning how to be smart, while he had been struggling to maintain an ailing wife and three bairns on the dole. And I certainly had not brought him one solitary step nearer to the Saviour in whose work I was supposed to be engaged. The publican's turnover may well have benefited from our encounter: the same could not, I fear, be said of the work of the Kingdom.

We had one very happy, and what would, I suppose, be described as successful, meeting in Govan Town Hall. But that was a meeting of Kirk folk and we were all adept at preaching to the converted—they don't turn their backs and get on with the racing news. It did cheer us, though, for it reminded us of what can so easily be forgotten, that in every community there is a hard core of decent, dedicated folk, and at the end of the day it is upon them that we have to depend if the work of evangelism is to succeed. Had one of these decent folk proved a 'guid neibour' to my Communist friend in the day of his trouble and need, that I am sure would have commended the Saviour to him in a way that all my smart debating tactics could never equal. Of one thing I am clear beyond a peradventure—you may win people into the Kingdom, but you will never get them there by argument.

My own most vivid memory of the campaign is, strangely

enough, of a visit we paid one forenoon to a factory where they made screw-nails, the employees being almost wholly women. What looked like blunt wire nails of various lengths and thicknesses were emptied by the girls into pans attached to a series of machines and, after the lapse of a few minutes and a great many decibels of excruciating din, they removed the most perfect screw nails from a tray at the other end. A series of mincing machines for metal. The noise I can only describe as indescribable! And never in my life have I met such a company of case-hardened females—they were hard as nails—but then, of course, they couldn't have survived otherwise. How we were expected to commend the Gospel in that atmosphere, not to mention din, I do not know. To this day I never lift a screw-nail without thinking about the cost of its production in human endurance and ear-drum suffering.

The Tell Scotland Campaign was, I think it is fair to say, a more than usually successful affair, and this I attribute in no small measure to the limited objective which it had set itself, and to the highly unspectacular way in which it set about achieving that objective. Thanks, as I indicated earlier, were to a great extent due to Ronnie Falconer for the guidance he gave and for the support which, through his good offices, the movement received from the BBC. I cannot say the same, though, about the efforts which I myself contributed in Govan. I am sure that personally I was much enriched by the experience, but with the best will in the world I cannot believe that the ends of evangelism were noticeably advanced in consequence of my labours. And I can honestly say it wasn't for the want of trying.

It was in 1983 that the General Assembly reached a decision which many saw as the first step towards the inauguration of yet another type of evangelistic policy. I am sure, however, that it would be more accurate—if less romantic—to describe what happened as the sounding of a call to a more intense degree of commitment to a kind of evangelism as old as the Kirk itself, and one utterly integral to her very being. It all began, as I say, at Assembly level, but it could emphatically be said to have sprung from the grassroots, seeing it had its origin in a motion from the floor, a motion that the Mission Committee should be instructed to prepare a coherent, long-term, Presbytery-centred programme for the evangelisation of the whole people of Scotland, and for keeping before the whole Church the priority of evangelistic outreach and mission in its full Biblical sense. What was in mind here was not just a job for the Mission Committee, but a challenge and an urgent call to our whole membership.

I do not know who had been responsible for framing the motion, but he had done so with both vision and skill. What was being asked for was something coherent and long-term, not a series of sporadic outbursts of evangelical fervour, but the production of a strategy which, while essentially national in outlook, would be sufficiently flexible to allow for varieties of working-out as between one area and the next. Then it was to be Presbytery-centred, which is to say that although there was to be a national policy, the responsibility and authority for its implementation would lie squarely at the door of the Presbytery, thus at once providing freedom for local initiatives and allowing no excuse for local *laissez-faire*. Finally, it was to recall the whole Church to a recognition of the fact that it could truly be the Church only in so far as it was an evangelical Church. Does one in this final point detect an echo of the Tell Scotland theme of creating not Parish Missions but Missionary Parishes?

The Committee took up its remit with a degree of enthusiasm not always apparent when the instruction has come from the floor. The result was that the Assembly of 1984 had laid before it a fairly comprehensive report on the whole subject. This began with 'some assessment of the state of the Kirk and its mission in the midst of changing times'. Nor was it a cheering picture which this provided, tracing as it did the drop, in the period since 1945, from 42 to 25 per cent of the population within Church membership, accepting that the ventures of Tell Scotland and the All Scotland Crusade that had seemed so full of promise had produced so little in the way of lasting results, accepting that the annual rate of decline in Sunday School numbers had risen as high as 18 per cent in the years since 1967. A depressing picture if there ever was one—doom and gloom writ large. Loud and clear the message came across that if the Kirk was to survive, let alone to evangelise, there must be a great experience of renewal. What hope was there that folk would be attracted to a Church that was so obviously sick at heart, and, in any case, what would be achieved if they were?

The question that had to be asked was not, 'What kind of members do we need if we are to have effective congregations?' but rather, 'What kind of congregations do we require if we are to have effective members?' And, of course, the yet more urgent question, 'How are we to go about making our congregations conform to such a pattern?'

Pressing on from there, the report went on to note certain 'Pointers on the Way'—the need for a recovery of confidence in the Gospel, the need for the rediscovery of prayer as a central concern of kirk life, the need for a spirit of repentance, the need for a new vision and understanding of the Church, and finally the need for a realisation of the fact that effective mission is an essential expression of the Church's life. Clearly these were not so much pointers in a national programme for evangelism, as elements that would characterise a new Reformation. The whole report, which was entitled 'Towards a National Programme for Evangelism', was warmly received by the Assembly and remitted for study by Presbyteries, which were instructed to forward their comments to the Committee.

By the following year (1985) the matter had been further threshed out, this time with the advantage of the returns from the Presbyteries in regard to the implications of the earlier thinking. The result was the emergence of the concept of the 'Presbytery Development Process', which the report defines as a process flexible enough to embrace the variety of parish situations that exist, a process that would involve action from the whole Church directed to the priority task of evangelism, a process that would involve acceptance of change inspired by the reforming power of the Spirit. The major role in this whole process was to be played by the Presbytery—on the one hand through the exercise of its existing functions, and on the other through taking new initiatives (although unfortunately the report does not enlarge with either specification or clarity upon what that may mean). For my own part, I think that at this point far more emphasis should have been laid upon the responsibility of the congregation within the parish as the place where, in the last resort, the work has got to be done and the initiatives taken. For no matter how faithfully and elaborately the Presbytery may function in the matter of providing tools and furnishing resources, nothing will happen until the tools get into the willing hands of the tradesmen in the parishes. I am sure that this kind of 'providing' is the farthest the Presbytery can properly—indeed possibly—go. Evangelism is something to be effected by minister, elders and people in the context of the life of a parish. I think it is important that we should say so, loudly, clearly, and persistently, rather than convey the impression that evangelisation is primarily a piece of Presbytery business. No matter how complicated the techniques for 'passing the buck' may be, there is always a point at which it stops, and in this case undoubtedly that point is the parish and not the Presbytery.

It was almost inevitable with things moving in the way they were, that the following year should see a proposal for the appointment of a full-time Organiser for Evangelism—thus, it might be added, getting us still one step further away from the congregation. At this stage the report is almost predictable: '"The National Strategy for Evangelism" needs full-time promotion through the Church via the Presbyteries and through the media. The past year has shown that urgent resource material cannot adequately be commissioned, serviced, produced and distributed by part-time conveners and committees already heavily engaged. This has necessitated the appointment of a full-time "Organiser for Evangelism"'. The report goes on to suggest that 'Presbyteries will be able to identify people of leadership gifts who would be willing to serve the cause of evangelism within large Presbyteries or areas of Presbytery'. Such appointments, it is said, would be for varying periods (six months and five years are mentioned), and thought would have to be given to the method of appointment, training, answerability, and connection with the National Organiser—a great deal of thought I should have imagined. The suggestion seems to be that such appointments would be of a full-time, or at least very substantially part-time, character, but no hint is given as to payment—whether, how much, or by whom.

To an old campaigner like myself, it was becoming clear that we were now sailing a fairly familiar course, and I was not taken by surprise when I learned the following year that five ministers were to be taken out of parishes to become full-time Area Organisers for Evangelism working in conjunction with, and under the direction of, the National Organiser. Here are six people, all of them trained and experienced as parish ministers, all of them (presumably) chosen because they have shown themselves particularly gifted in the techniques of evangelism, and they are to be set down in offices recording returns, or sent scurrying round the country exhorting other people to grasp the opportunities offered in a field in which they themselves are gathering no harvest. I think one is entitled to ask whether this represents the best possible use of what we never tire of proclaiming is our very short supply of manpower.

I began as a dedicated supporter of this new effort, for it seemed to me to be emphasising those aspects of revival that can too easily be overlooked: it was paying heed to the provision of the machinery needful for the ongoing work and not confining itself exclusively to the instant conversion of the individual. But I feel we are now in danger of becoming so deeply embroiled in arranging the channels through which the Wind of the Spirit can most effectively blow, as to overlook the fact that the Wind of the Spirit does not seem to be blowing in our airt at the moment and that we haven't any machinery for generating the said wind or for determining its direction.

As I see it, revival when it comes—and pray God it may come soon—will come not at Presbytery level (even if the Assembly have ordained that that is how it has to be), but in some parish, maybe the last you or I would have dreamed of choosing—some parish where, through a faithful ministry supported by a praying people, the strangest things are seen to be happening—and from there the movement will spread and grow and flourish until it covers the whole land. Hasn't this always been the pattern? I seem to remember Luke telling us that it was when Annas and Caiaphas were high priests (the officially appointed National Organisers for Evangelism of their day) that the Word of God came to John in the wilderness. History has a disturbing way of repeating itself.

This is where, it seems to me, we come up against the age-old problem that has beset the Church through its long history, the clash between the rules and forms, the laws and restrictions, in the absence of which no human organisation can properly function, and the freedom—the sheer anarchy if you will—that is of the essence of the movement of the Spirit. We can organise a crusade: we can never organise a revival. The element of organisation which any Church must enshrine can so easily spell death and fossilisation for something that should be alive and growing. The moment you organise and systematise and regularise and legalise, you put behind bars something that can truly exist only in conditions of complete freedom. The Spirit that infuses its distinctive life into religion is a wind that bloweth whither it listeth, and that will not allow itself to be fed into the ducts of our ecclesiastical soul-conditioning system. To institutionalise religion is to pin a butterfly on a card—you preserve something of its outward appearance—but at the expense of its life. It is tragically easy for the Christian Church to become a museum in which the doors are kept tight shut and the windows hermetically sealed lest unhappily the Wind of the Spirit should blow through it and the draught disturb the sanctified cobwebs.

How often in the course of my own lifetime have I seen the attempt to capture what felt like a breath of the Spirit lead to the appointment of a committee, to the devising of some piece of ecclesiastical machinery, to the passing of some Act of Assembly—in short, to the creation of some massive block of establishment that all the gales that ever blew could never disturb. It is a danger against which we have to be constantly on our guard.

For all that so many questions beset me regarding the wisdom of some of our activities today in the field of evangelism, one thing greatly cheers and encourages me, and that is the thought that the day may not be far distant when the word 'evangelism' is going to dominate our thinking and to replace the word 'ecumenism' at the heart of our planning for the Kirk. For far too long we have been infatuated with what to me has always appeared the completely false doctrine that the denominations must unite for the sake of mission. That is to get things the wrong way round, the true order being that when we become sufficiently deeply concerned about the progress of evangelism, we shall find our differences relentlessly dwindling into insignificance. As we discuss these differences in the sterilised atmosphere of the Committee Room, they become steadily more and more meaningful and important and precious: when in the street, the marketplace, the shop-floor we find them obstructing the winning of souls for Christ, we'll get them swept away quickly enough. Do not unite for the sake of evangelism, but evangelise for the sake of evangelism, and union will follow in its own good way.

The Church of Christ must live to evangelise, for evangelism is its life.

Chapter 13
The Minister and the Media

WHEN IN 1981 I retired from the Clerkship of Glasgow Presbytery, a great load of 'blurb' appeared in the press, often to my considerable embarrassment. One item though, which I must confess pleased me a lot, was a full-page spread in the *Evening Times* under the heading 'The Reverend Trouble-shooter', contributed by a young lady, Rosemary Long, whom I have no recollection of ever having met until she came to see me by appointment to collect material for a piece she had been commissioned to write for her paper. Not that I was greatly enamoured of the title, but I did rather appreciate the part where she said, 'Journalists are sulking at the very idea of his daring to retire this July from his post as Presbytery Clerk. For two decades he has told us more than a few home truths about everything from devolution to sex. He never fobbed us off, flannelled us, shot us a line, or led us up the garden path. He spoke the truth as he saw it and never gave a monkey's for what people might think'.

It would be nice to think she was speaking for the reporting world generally when she referred to the cordiality of our relations, for I have always been rather proud of the fact that I have got along remarkably well with the press. I imagine I am very much in a minority when I say I have a very great respect for the press and that my contacts with newspaper reporters have invariably been friendly. I believe the press has a very responsible task to perform in today's society through its role of investigative journalism. The doctrine that the people should know only what their betters consider is good for them can so easily be adopted by people in positions of authority, with a consequent temptation to lay restrictions upon those who would ferret out and publish the whole truth. It is, of course, a doctrine in whose favour a good deal can be said—in a wartime situation it is universally accepted as inevitable (I have always maintained that the first casualty in any war is truth)—but it is a dangerous doctrine for all that, one whose adoption could spell the end of democracy as we have come to know it. What is the sense in giving every man a vote if he is not to know the truth of what he is voting about? A truly free press is our ultimate safeguard against dictatorship. There are times when we find it a nuisance —and that is a kindly term—to have reporters poking about in our private affairs (did not someone once define news as 'what somebody somewhere does not want to have disclosed?'), but it represents part of the price that has to be paid if we are to enjoy the benefits of a truly democratic constitution. It is a big price, you may think; but then things that are worth having don't come cheap.

And, as I say, I have always found reporters a decent bunch of people—I nearly said 'of chaps', but in recent times the ranks are richly interspersed with ladies, and are not only much more interesting but also much the better for it. Invariably I've been willing—indeed happy—to talk to reporters, and while I was Presbytery Clerk they were usually happy to talk to me. If there was a point beyond which I could not go in my disclosures, I told them so frankly. Often to help them to understand a situation better, to see it in its true context, I have, under a vow of secrecy, told them more than I should have done, and I am happy to say that my confidences have never been betrayed. How far this has been attributable to an innate honesty and how far to an intelligent self-interest that told them that one 'scoop' would be a poor reward for the drying up of a valuable well of inform- ation, I just do not know, but I would be prepared to believe that there may have been an element of both! Human motivation is rarely a simple thing.

I am always mildly amused when, as often happens, a man says to me proudly, 'Oho, I can deal with the press all right. I just say "No comment" and slam down the phone'. What does he think he is achieving by such a response? A little imagination and a spot of psychology are all that is called for. Try to visual- ise the scene. An editor has sent out a young reporter to get a story in regard to some incident he thinks likely to be a bit out of the ordinary and therefore worth reporting. Does anyone imagine the young man is going to go back to the office and say to his boss, 'Sorry, I couldn't get anything on it. All the folk I tried just slammed down the phone and said, "No comment."' His career in journalism would be short and sweet. No, the reporter was sent out to get a story and he's not coming back until he's got one. Are you not better trying to co-operate with him in making the kind of story that will not do your cause too much harm? The alternative is to leave him to his own devices in presenting as horrific an account as he can concoct. For mysel, I have always been more than willing to co-operate.

All other considerations apart, the press can usually get the last word. I remember while I was Clerk to the Presbytery of Paisley, we had a 'case' which attracted a deal of public interest. A minister well known in the town was involved, and his reaction to the boys with the shorthand notebooks was not just brusque, it was positively rude. On the night of an important meeting of Presbytery they arrived with a photographer and asked, politely enough, whether they might take a picture. They were told in terms that lacked neither clarity nor precision where to take their camera and what to do with it. The Presbytery met behind closed doors, so in the absence of any real news the need for a picture to fill the vacant space on the front page became all the more urgent. The photographer therefore hung around long after the meeting had concluded and managed to get a shot of the minister as he was leaving by a side door. Realising what was afoot just a moment too late, the victim pulled his coat up over his face. A beautiful picture of this furtive hooded figure slinking out of a back door appeared next day under the caption, 'Dr Blank leaves the Presbytery Meeting'. The press has a terrifying power within its grasp—in the popular modern phrase, it has 'a lot of clout'. It has always seemed wise to me to co-operate with them, or at the very least not to raise their hackles, for if it comes to a fight they are peculiarly well equipped to deliver, and peculiarly adept at delivering, deadly blows under the belt—and there's no referee to stop them.

Newspapers must be having a hard time keeping going these days, partly because their function has so completely changed over the past half-century. It is not wholly clear today what exactly the 'national' ought to be trying to do. Before the emergence of radio they were the sole disseminators of news. Although I was very young at the time, I can remember the days of the First World War when news of all the latest disasters

—and there were plenty of them—came to us through the columns of 'the papers'. I can see, and hear, the newsboy of those days running along the streets with an armful of papers and a newsbill spread across his knees, shouting tidings of the latest ship-sinking or battle-loss, and I can see the people running out to buy a paper and returning with bowed heads as they read about it all. The radio altered all that. In today's world any event of national importance is known to all and sundry long before it can be so much as set up in type, let alone printed. I am mildly surprised that no enterprising newspaper, with a sense of reality as well as a sense of humour, has got around to calling itself 'Fiddler's News'—for of necessity that's what all of them are purveying.

To meet the challenge of this situation, and to secure for themselves a distinctive role in the news business, the press began to provide a commentary on current events, the writing up of background notes, the development of individual human stories centred around the events, and so on. In a word, the newspaper took on something of the character of a magazine. And then, of course, television came along with its boundless capacity for doing this kind of thing so superbly well, so much better than it can ever be done in print. And printing pictures in colour has done nothing to bridge the gap. The result has been that the only papers that seem to be really thriving today are the local journals which do not attempt to cover matters of national importance, but go to great lengths in their coverage of things of interest only to those most directly involved. The winner of the egg-and-spoon race at the Invermuchty Junior School Sports is not likely to feature on the media (unless it transpired that the egg contained a bomb surreptitiously planted there by a middle-eastern terrorist organisation), but it is of interest to parents, relatives and friends over a wide area who subscribe to the paper in the hope that some day, and in some context, the names of their nearest and dearest will appear in print. Yes, the local paper has a function and knows exactly what it is supposed to be doing; the national press is not at all clear about its function and in many cases has taken refuge in sensationalism and sentimentality, or in a mild sexism (sometimes blatant on its page three), or in page after dreary page of full-page advertisements (preferably in colour)—all very far

removed from its true function, and all very much to be regretted—or so it seems to me.

One of my own most bitter complaints against the press
has to do with their insistence that everything should be
'instant'. So far as the straightforward reporting of news items
is concerned, this must obviously be spot up-to-the-minute. But
the same urgency does not apply, or not at least to the same
extent, to commenting upon the news. Here there need be no
desperate rush. People like the Moderator of Assembly can be
particularly vulnerable in this field. His comment on any matter
of national interest is likely to be sought, and often without his
having had the chance to learn the facts of the case, let alone to
ponder its implications. I have said on occasion that the press
tend to equate comment *ex cathedra* with comment *ex cuff*, and
the result is generally to no one's credit.

I was always very much happier in my deliberate contributions to the press, in the occasional things I wrote for
publication. These began almost accidentally. For some reason I
was moved one day, in the summer of 1950, to write a little piece
about an aspect of country life, and being rather pleased with it I
sent it to *The Glasgow Herald* as a possible contribution for their
Weekend Page. To my amazement it was immediately accepted
and I received a cheque for £5 (on reflection it may well have
been for five guineas—that at least would have been more in
keeping with the dignity of the *Herald* of those days). Just about
the same time I was approached by George Adam, who was then
editor of the Paisley and Renfrewshire *Gazette,* to see if I would
be interested in contributing the occasional piece for a casual
column called 'The Easy Chair'. He had a panel of four authors
who among them kept him going. One of his team had retired
and he offered me the vacant place. At a guinea a time it seemed
an opportunity not to be missed, and over the next five years I
must have produced about a hundred pieces, mostly, but not
exclusively, for his Easy Chair. This was a relaxation that I
enormously enjoyed. Writing has never come easy to me as I
always seem to see some better way in which I could have
phrased things and I incline to go on polishing and polishing.
But I get a great deal of satisfaction out of it. I have always
marvelled at people like the late Willie Barclay who could sit
and punch away at his typewriter, then take the material out,

fold it and put in an envelope without even needing to read it over, let alone edit it! An ability I've always greatly admired but never really envied.

In 1959 I had become Convener of the General Assembly's Committee on Publications as it then was, a position I was to occupy for the next nine years. This, naturally, brought me into still closer touch with the world of print and, as it happened, into very intimate contact with the business of managing a newspaper, for it led to my having much to do with the production of *The British Weekly*. It had been in 1957 that our Committee had been offered this publication as a 'gift'. Its eminent editor Shaun Herron (no relation, by the way) had just left for America, and the Trust which managed the paper, which had been running at a considerable loss for some years, was keen to unload its responsibilities. They were responsibilities that we for our part were reluctant to assume. On the other hand we had reason to believe that a very exclusive 'Christian group' were waiting in the wings prepared to take over, and we felt it would be a pity were a journal with the great tradition of *The British Weekly* to fall into the hands of a sect. So, with more misgivings than enthusiasm, we took the plunge. Printing was done at St Alban's, editing and managing in London. For the first few months our manager, Andrew M'Cosh, contrived, no one will ever know how, to keep his own work going in Edinburgh and to travel up to London each weekend to edit the paper. But that obviously couldn't go on.

The appointment of an editor was our all-important priority. Having determined that we must have a layman we drew up a leat of three: two men of professional experience and a minister for good value—and ended up choosing the minister. He was the Revd Denis Duncan and his choice was an inspired one. He had been minister of a charge in Glasgow's Dennistoun area, but he had quite a bit of journalistic experience gained through a most ambitious Church magazine, *Rally*, for which he had had the major responsibility. Before very long we made him managing editor and moved him to premises in Queen Street, Edinburgh—Simpson House, so called because it had been the home of Sir James Young Simpson. In fact, in one of its rooms the discovery of the properties of chloroform had been made. The success of the new venture was quite incredible. Unhappily though, a national newspaper has got to be centred in London. As Scots we may lament the fact to our hearts' content, but we ignore it at our peril. Further, if a paper is to be truly inter-denominational, it cannot remain for ever under the wing of one particular Church. And so, after ten years in Edinburgh, *The British Weekly* returned south and parted company from the Kirk—with goodwill and blessings on both sides. During all that period, and for a long time afterwards, I was a regular contributor to its columns, usually under my own name, but frequently too under a variety of *noms-des-plumes* when writing on highly controversial themes, ecumenical and otherwise. I learned a great deal in the sphere of religious journalism through my connection over these years with my very good friend Denis Duncan.

My next connection with the press was through *The Bush*, Glasgow Presbytery's own monthly newspaper. The credit for the idea that we should publish a paper of our own must go to Bill Black. Bill had been closely associated with Denis Duncan in the Rally project in Dennistoun. Recognising that he was a man of original ideas whose heart was in journalism and emphatically not in his work in the Corporation Rating Department, I had managed to get him on to our staff in the Department of Publication, where he assisted with *Life and Work* in matters of editing, production, and circulation—for all of which he had a positive flair. It was, as I say, at his instigation that a few of us got together to discuss the possibility of having a monthly newspaper that would tell both of what had happened at the recent Presbytery meeting and of what was currently afoot within the bounds. We examined all the possibilities of the situation and found the prospects a bit daunting. But we were all of a mind to have a go.

In the event the little paper instantly caught on and proved surprisingly successful—particularly in view of the fact that everything was done by amateurs on a voluntary basis. Editing was a very demanding job, not least when it came to putting the paper to bed, and we couldn't expect any one man to keep it up for long, so that we had quite a run of editors. As it happened we had two in succession, both men of outstanding skill, but both fired with the same ambition—to see our little paper recognised and quoted by the nationals. They considered that no issue had justified its existence unless a reference to it appeared, preferably on the front page, of the next day's newspaper. For myself I was most unhappy about this, and to this day I feel it marked the first step on our downward path. In my experience the appetite for sensation is an insatiable one, and you are wise not to try to satisfy it. Our objective had been to tell a very simple story about some of the kindly, gracious, generous things that are going on in the world, things too often unrecorded and unrecognised. Telling of the other things we were happy to leave to the tabloids. There was, we believed, news to be told about the way the Kirk was running at the congregational level, news that was worth hearing and that people would enjoy reading. I did not see it as our role to make exclusive disclosures about why Rangers would not sign Roman Catholics, or about the scandalously low fees a Hospital Board was paying an organist for playing at religious services, or other suchlike themes. As we gained headlines we lost readers, and with falling circulation we began to run into difficulty with the income from advertising upon which our solvency was precariously balanced. Once in dire financial straits, we were approached by one of those agencies which arranges for you to achieve an enormous circulation figure by giving away your papers for nothing—so long as you give away enough of them. You no longer have to collect money to pay for it, only distributors to hand it out free in large enough numbers. Having in this way enabled you to hit an exalted circulation mark, the agency collects advertising and the bills are paid. It all sounds wonderful—but it just doesn't work. You cut your losses, and you cut your own throat at the same time.

It is an interesting, if regrettable, fact of life that people insist on valuing things at their shop prices. Give them something for nothing and they accept that as its value. This fact had been borne in upon me early in my time in a country parish. In March of each year we held a Business Meeting followed by a Congregational Social. Year after year for weeks beforehand I pled from the pulpit that my people would attend. They listened attentively and stayed away—that is, all but about thirty regular attenders. It didn't take long to get through the business, then we had a very splendid tea, followed by a musical programme and 'a speaker'—the nearest thing extant to the old-fashioned

Kirk soirée. To meet the outlays we took a 'silver collection', and if you go on the basis that most of the thirty people contributed sixpence, although a few confined themselves to threepence (which was still a silver coin at the time), you will realise that we couldn't bring singers from too far afield if the collection was to cover outlays. However, one day I said to my wife, 'Look, I'm sick and tired of how we run the Annual Meeting. This year for a change we're going to charge for admission at half-a-crown a time, and I want the ladies of your Guild to go round their districts and sell the tickets in advance. The business part of the meeting will, of course, be free, and we won't collect the tickets until we get around to serving the tea'. We organised the affair along the usual lines, except that we catered for 180 instead of 30—and the audience departed saying they had had a great night. They hadn't thought much of the identical thing when they got it for a 'silver collection', but at five times that price they found it more than five times as good.

That was most surely our experience with *The Bush* when we went priceless. We couldn't get the copies collected by the congregations, which in turn reported that they laid the papers out in the vestibule and couldn't persuade people to lift a copy as they passed, not even those who had been our regular readers, not even those who used to appear at the office window demanding to know what was wrong if we were a couple of days late. One congregation which had sold 400 copies with no bother couldn't distribute 100 copies free. All the evidence was pointing to the fact that our paper was finished. My advice to advertisers would be to buy space in a paper which sells at a price, even if the circulation figures are not too high, rather than in one with a massive circulation achieved by giving it away for nothing. In any case, our venture into the field of free issue marked the end of the road so far as *The Bush* was concerned. Personally I was very sorry. Until my retiral I had been responsible for a casual leader-page column under the title 'View from the Centre', and there were months when it proved a bit of a bind, but I think the exercise was supremely worthwhile and I hope the day may come when the Presbytery of Glasgow will again blossom forth monthly into print—something a little bit livelier than the minutes would certainly be appreciated!

I am one of what I fear is a dwindling number of people

who believe in preaching, believe that there is a unique power in the spoken word, given that it is the right word, and that it is spoken with power and conviction. One of the great advantages of radio and television is the way in which they are able to reach out to embrace ever larger congregations for the spoken word. The challenge with which we in the Church are presented is that of shaping our message to conform to the technical possibilities of these two quite distinct media, and this, I fear, we have not so far been able to do in any really significant fashion.

It is rather like trying to picture a different world and a different way of life, but I can remember the day when the ordinary citizen first began to take an interest in 'the wireless', what today we disparagingly refer to as 'steam radio'. I remember when the first messages to Scottish listeners were sent out from a little office-cum-studio near Blythswood Square, to be picked up through headphones by a process of fiddling with a cat's whisker on a crystal, a day when only the élite could rise to a valve set and loud-speaker. Like many other cannie Scots, I was distinctly suspicious of the new medium—I thought it would disrupt our family life and I know not what other fears I entertained, so that it was not until we had been a year or two in my second parish that we equipped ourselves with a 'wireless set'. Needless to say, none of our fears was realised and ere long we were as deeply committed to the miserable affair as were most of our neighbours.

The Church in Scotland was extremely fortunate in having in charge of religious broadcasting in those early days, two men of such real, if diverse, gifts as Melville Dinwiddie and Ronald Falconer. One of the most popular elements in the religious output was the regular Church service, and it was widely accepted as a sign that a man was going places when his people were invited to act as hosts to the BBC. My own kirk at Houston—and I myself—had our first experience of being 'on the air' in June 1950, and as a comparatively obscure country congregation we saw it as something of a distinction to have been so invited and took it all very seriously. Studiously we prepared and rehearsed. The BBC also took these services quite seriously at that time, and on the Thursday evening a team came down to do a kind of rehearsal. It was a lovely summer's evening, and as they took some recordings of the bell being rung the blackbirds were whistling merrily. I understand that some of the tape went into their 'effects' library and was used long afterwards to provide background noises for other programmes. After the service, I received something like eighty letters in the course of the following week—half of them from old Houstonians scattered throughout the country, some from personal friends, some from strangers who had been impressed. I have been involved in many broadcast and television services of one kind and another since that first occasion in 1950, but none has produced anything like a comparable response. Custom may not, as Carlyle claims, make dottards of us all; it assuredly does make us accept as commonplace things that once filled us with wonder and amaze. And I think we are the poorer for it.

As the years passed, I came to be called upon more and more frequently in connection with radio programmes. Over the years, I must have done my share of programmes of the 'Thought for the Day' type, the kind of thing of which you put a series of six or seven 'in the can' at one sitting. These I never found easy to do, much preferring the unscripted discussion type of affair. For me writing has always been a totally different kind of exercise from speaking, and for the simple and rather obvious reason that what can easily be digested by the eye can prove highly indigestible when the intake has to be through the ear. Never, if I can help it, do I write either a sermon or a speech. It may sound laughable, but if I want to get the text of a sermon I arrange for someone to tape-record it during the service and I work backwards from there. Don't misunderstand me. I don't go into a pulpit unprepared (hoping for inspiration and ending in perspiration, as has been said), but I do go without notes and without having memorised the content of a script. Just as the equipment of the reader and of the hearer are different, so the requirements of the writer and of the speaker are different—all that the former needs is pen and paper, whereas the latter needs an audience. And a cold black microphone glowering at you from a table is a poor substitute for an audience. If you were doing a Thought for the Day, you had to write it all down and then try to make it sound convincing and spontaneous. But what a help and encouragement it would have been to have seen some faces and to have been able to gauge how—indeed whether—you were getting a message across.

The absence of a visible audience has its dangers as well as its discouragements, especially if you are performing 'live'. I remember the famous Freddie Grisewood, whom we met on holiday in the Yorkshire Dales (and whose reminiscing made the holiday a memorable one), telling of an occasion in the early days when an eminent English Churchman was conducting a rather important service from the studio. It was to end with a benediction. He had been warned that he must be scrupulously careful about timing, but he had not been warned that after the benediction had been pronounced he must not make a sound until he received a signal from the director. The service went well, but his nationwide audience must have been taken aback when his benediction ended, '... be with you all now and for evermore ... I don't think'. What had happened was that having, as he thought, finished on the air, he remarked to the director sitting opposite him in the studio, 'I don't think I was too long, was I?' An engineer hearing the voice intruding hurriedly 'killed' the microphone, but not quite hurriedly enough. The answer to the preacher's question could well have been, 'Yes, you were three words too long!'

Television has become so much part of our lives that it is hard to remember a time when it wasn't there. And yet it is a very modern phenomenon. It could be said that for all practical purposes its reign has been contemporary with that of our present Queen—something like thirty years. At the time when the late King died, very few people had television, although it had been on the market for some time. I remember in Paisley, on the rather miserable wet day of His Majesty's funeral, seeing groups of people standing outside the windows of the television shops watching events on the screens inside, by modern standards very small screens, and, of course, in black and white. The Coronation which followed in due course, presented 'the telly' with the kind of spectacle with which it can cope so magnificently, and I am sure the event did more than any other single thing to popularise the medium and to bring it into the homes of ordinary folk. Since when it has, in so many cases, taken over these homes.

That television has quite unique potential in the matter of presenting news, that it has boundless resources for the creation of programmes, showing the background to the news, that it can mount nature documentaries of breathtaking excellence, that it can bring sport, music, drama, ballet into our very sitting-rooms in a warm and intimate fashion—all this goes without saying, all these are facts that none would dispute. But it has its insidious dangers.

If I may begin with a small professional grouse. In so many households, the 'telly' has taken over control, and as it is normally to be found in the public room of the house, that room is out of commission for all normal social purposes. Ministers attempting to do parish visiting of an evening can find themselves competing with musicians, comedians, actors, on the box—and usually coming off second best. What can be even more exasperating is when the sound is turned off, but the picture left on. I remember one evening following a programme along the whole length of a street as I moved from one member's house to the next. There is no longer much opportunity for neighbourly chatter among friends—for the television set is not in the background, but in the dead centre of the picture. Where once we sat around the fire talking, we now sit around the box listening, and I don't think it is all gain. My worst experience, though, was in the fairly early days, when it was thought a better picture could be had if you sat in the darkness. I knocked on a door one evening. It was opened by a daughter of the household who welcomed me in a hushed whisper, bade me enter, showed me into a dark room and a seat therein (given a torch and a little apron and she was the perfect usherette). I sat until the programme ended, but as the company sat on into the next programme, I rose and said to my welcomer as I passed, 'Don't bother to show me out. I'll pull the door behind me'. To which she replied, 'Right ho'.

I often wonder how far the brilliant professionalism portrayed on the screen kills rather than encourages the amateur. In a day when millions are glued to screens for hours on end watching tennis at Wimbledon, local tennis courts are deserted as never before. How far does hearing brilliant professional musicians encourage the learner and how far does it have the opposite effect? We talk enthusiastically of what television has done to create a generation of sportsmen. It has done nothing of the kind. It has, certainly, created a generation of sport-watchers. This generation has no time to play games, it is too busy watching other people doing it on the telly.

Another danger seems to me to arise from the fact that if four separate channels are for seven days of each week to be putting out material every hour of the day (and in some cases most of the night), then it is inevitable that the highest quality cannot be maintained throughout. The result is that a great deal of sheer rubbish is purveyed, some of it, I am sure, quite harmful in its effects. When such a charge is levelled—whether by Mrs Whitehouse or anyone else—we are immediately assured that television programmes make very little impact upon human behaviour. From which I can only conclude that a vast number of manufacturers of consumer goods are being cruelly hoodwinked when induced to spend thousands for the privilege of, for a few seconds, parading their merchandise on the box.

One thing which does disturb me very seriously in this field is the growth of what I can only call 'trial by television'. Let it be that there has been an accident on a major scale, the programme that brings us first news of the event goes on quite often to include interviews with all kinds of people closely associated with the incident, people who may well have a criminal responsibility in the matter. A worker, more or less illiterate, is subjected to a gruelling examination by a highly-skilled interviewer on material which may well come to be the subject of an official enquiry and later even of a criminal prosecution. I vividly remember, after the Abervaan disaster when a mountain of sludge enveloped a school, and in the Moorgate disaster when an underground train crashed into a dead-end with heavy loss of life, listening to such interviews and thinking how unfair the whole thing was. It could prove difficult to empanel anywhere in the country a jury that had not already made up its mind on the guilt of the accused. The strictest limitations are imposed on the press in the matter of reporting criminal proceedings, in their interviewing of possible suspects, and so on. Rightly so. It seems to me far more urgently necessary that the same kind of rules should be applied in the case of television reporting.

How many, like me, find highly offensive the kind of close-ups of grief which are so often and so luridly presented to us. A situation from which in normal life decent people would turn away their heads in embarrassment becomes the subject on which cameras zoom in, and tearful comments are wrung from poor souls staggering from the effects of a tragedy they still cannot grasp. With a certain section of the press we are becoming accustomed to this kind of thing—in glorious technicolour. It can be done even more effectively 'on the box'. And for that reason, and to that degree, it is the more offensive. It is the kind of thing against which it is difficult to legislate. We shouldn't need to—good taste should protect us.

What is television doing to advance the cause of religion? The first thing to be said is that it has done a great disservice to the cause of organised religion, by providing counter-attractions to public worship. It would be generally agreed, I think, that the screening of the Forsyte Saga on Sunday evenings some years ago played a major part in killing the Evening Service. That particular diet of worship may have been on its way out in any case—Galsworthy on the small screen most surely hastened its departure.

Leaving that aside, television has made a most significant contribution to the ways in which material can be presented. Services of worship come across especially well, and a skilled technique has been developed in this field, discussion sessions on one subject and another can be well done and convincingly put across, programmes about people and places lend themselves to the medium. It is significant, though, is it not, that few people have operated so successfully on the television screen as the late Willie Barclay, and he did not depend in the very least on any of the 'effects' which the medium can supply—he simply stood and chatted (in a remarkably unmusical voice at that). Yet his appearances were eagerly awaited by thousands who hung on his every word. Forgetting that for the moment, it has to be conceded that we are able to put on the screen with great effect Church services and festivals of hymn singing —both programmes of enormous value to the housebound, both programmes which make a considerable nostalgic appeal to those who have drifted away from the discipline of church-going in which they had been nurtured. We can mount talks, round-table discussions, debates, on a diversity of themes—of varying interest to the committed, but what is done for the uncommitted? Where we seem to me to have failed, and failed lamentably, is in discovering and establishing a technique of Television Evangelism.

Throughout the generations the Gospel has been spread by the preaching of the Word, the conveyance by word of mouth of the good news of salvation: here we have to hand a new and supremely efficient vehicle ready to convey messages to countless thousands, and yet, with the odd notable exception, we are not succeeding in getting our message across. To me it has always seemed remarkable that the maker of a detergent will spend vast sums for a few seconds of television time in which to describe the whiter-than-white-making properties of his product, and yet we, who are in essentially the same business—even if it be the souls of men and not their underwear we want to cleanse—have literally hours put at our disposal free of charge and are unable to take significant advantage of it. We are awaiting an evangelist-cum-broadcaster of genius who will devise a technique for us. How long will we have to wait? Not too long, I hope, for time is not on our side.

I am far from convinced our rulers at Westminster are invariably right in the decisions they reach, but I did think they showed good sense in their firm resolve not to allow the television cameras into the Chamber, and I regret—as I think they may themselves yet come to do—their recent change of heart. One of my reasons for this is that I have never been satisfied that the televising of parts of the General Assembly has proved an unqualified advantage from the Assembly's point of view. That it is good that the public at large should be brought into touch with the supreme court of the Kirk and its business, I readily agree. I am sure too that now that large blocks of Assembly debate are being put on the screen, our people get a great deal of satisfaction—not to say learn quite a bit—from watching. Nor have I any doubt that, judged at the level of sheer debating, we can confidently take our place alongside the party political conference and other similar 'shows' that occupy so much television time. My worry is not with the screens, but with the cameras, with the effect which their presence has on the Assembly itself—the fact that for some it can become something of a performance, that the moving thought should be not what can I contribute to the clarification of this subject, but what kind of show can I put on for the people watching at home. That this may all be completely unconscious is beside the point; the influence is there whether we are conscious of it or not. The most extrovert of us becomes a bit self-conscious when he knows he is being watched. Then there is all the inconvenience of the glaring lights and the terrible heat and the putrid atmosphere which they generate. And there is the unfairness that even when the whole of a debate is put on the screen, there are in the hands of members (but not of the viewers) papers and so on, so that while the two groups are judging the same issue they are doing so on different evidence. I sometimes wonder whether we didn't get through our business better before the cameras intruded on the scene. And I always seem to sense a general air of relief when the lights are turned down and we know we are no longer on the air.

It would be less than fair to blame television for things to which the invention and growing popularity of the video-recorder are subjecting us, but I may be forgiven for saying I am happy to have reached the end of my time as a parish minister before the appearance of this particular device with its attendant problems. Its effect upon the conduct of weddings I find quite disturbing. The whole business of recording weddings for all posterity has always brought its attendant problems. In my early days the guests were left like the proverbial knotless threads while the couple were carried away to a photographer's studio, but not so today. Fairly recently I had occasion to stand in for a few weeks for an absent minister, and during that time the odd marriage occurred, and I found that to conduct the service and to attend the reception up to the point where the speeches were over and the dancing had begun, occupied roughly six hours. During most of that time one was either standing around outside the church while the photographer was arranging groupings, or sitting in a bar in the place of the reception while photographers, still and moving, and video-recording operators, were at work. Apart from the amount of time involved—and six hours makes a big dent in even a minister's working day—I have come to accept the photographs, but it is a different matter when, as in an increasing number of cases, the couple—or more often the parents—want a video-recording of the whole proceedings. I think the minister must have the last word on when video-cameras are to be allowed into the church during a service, but the question can be put in a very awkward way. There is Grannie, lying bedfast in a nursing home breathlessly awaiting having it all brought to her bedside, or there is Auntie Jean, an invalid in far-off California who was so fond of the bride and who would have loved to have been there, and who has sent on the cost of the recording, and to whom it is going to mean so much to be able to see it all on the screen. What harm can there be in that? Are they to be denied their hearts' desire to suit the silly scruples of a stodgy minister?

If it hasn't already arisen in the case of a christening, I am sure it is only a matter of time till it does. And also, of course, of a funeral service. I suppose a video of the funeral service would be less of an insult to the memory of the deceased than some of the headstones I have seen. And more perishable.

There can in my mind be no denying that the presence of cameras intrudes a disturbing and unwelcome element into any service—so easily they can turn it into a performance. This is true of any service of worship, but in the case of the service of public worship it may be accepted because this is one out of many; but in the case of the wedding it is a once-only occasion, and for the couple a mighty solemn one at that. They are entitled to be protected from such intrusion into their spiritual privacy. It is utterly wrong—indeed insufferable—that a bride taking vows should be looking into the lens of a camera. I was conducting a wedding once in Vancouver when, in the course of the proceedings, a man suddenly appeared at my back from I know not where, and to all intents and purposes he rested his whirring cine-camera on my shoulder and proceeded to get the more intimate parts of the service on to film. I swithered whether to stop and chase him, or to go on and ignore him, and in view of the fact that the couple had been through the experience before—in the groom's case once and in the bride's twice—I decided to carry on. But I took good care it didn't happen again.

I think perhaps the time has come for the Assembly to offer some guidance on the question of the tele-recording of services in church, with special reference to wedding services.

I cannot leave the subject of television without recounting one of the most highly entertaining experiences of my life, which came to me through my involvement in a very solemn television programme. It was an STV affair. Someone had come up with the bright idea that it would be something of a novelty to have a pair of programmes, one on a famous character in

Roman Catholic history presented by a Protestant, and vice versa—an ecumenical offering! So it came about that I was invited to do a programme on John Ogilvie the martyr, while the Roman Catholic chaplain at St Andrews took up the tale of Patrick Hamilton. My man was at that time still 'The Blessed John Ogilvie', it being a good many years later that it was discovered that a miracle of healing had been performed on a Glasgow man in consequence of invoking his name and that John was accordingly beatified. I had the job to do from scratch, so I went to work with zest with the fairly scant material on which I could lay my hands and in due course came up with a script. This was duly adapted for filming, and three full days were set aside for this task, almost all of it to be undertaken out of doors.

We began at Glasgow Cross, the scene of Ogilvie's execution. There, standing in London Road with the Mercat Cross for background, I had to say about a hundred words, but the traffic flow was such that there were only a few seconds of comparative quietness in which this could be done. Needless to say, our presence had attracted an interested crowd of bystanders, including a group of youths whose behaviour, surprisingly enough, was impeccable. My piece began, 'From earliest days this has been a busy crossing . . . ,' and the drill was that the producer watched the sequence of traffic lights and gave me the cue when the moment had arrived for the gap in the din. We must have had seven or eight unsuccessful attempts, ruined always by the roar of a motorbike engine, or by some small boy in the crowd leaping up and waving his arms, or by some horn-happy motorist giving us a friendly toot. Just as I was once more waiting for my cue, I was extremely put out to hear at my side a clear voice starting off, 'From earliest days this has been a busy crossing ....' When the prompt takes over from the cast, trouble is bound to follow!

Later that same afternoon we drove up to the Cathedral to take advantage of the sun setting on the great west door. As we were getting out of the cars, we were instantly joined by three small boys who seemed to have been planted there to await our arrival. I was set up against the pillar by the door with a microphone on my lapel and a cable running down inside my trouser leg and across many yards of courtyard to the crew who were setting up their equipment quite a bit away. The small boys contrived once or twice 'accidentally' to trip over the cable. Once they had been safely tucked away just out of the picture, I was asked to run through a bit of my script 'just for voice levels'. This I did and stopped to hear the verdict of the experts. This came from an unexpected quarter as one of the small boys stepped forward and declared in clear tones, 'Ye shud try tae pit a wee bit mair expreshun intae it'.

Standing at the same west door the following morning with the huge brass knocker in my hand, I was completely on my own out there, the crew being all inside, cameras focused from within on the doors, which on my knocking (at a given signal) were to swing open (courtesy of two strong men with ropes) and I would be picked out in silhouette against the daylight. My instructions were to knock really hard, for the oak was thick and solid and it was essential that the noise be picked up on the microphones inside. I was standing there with the knocker poised, ready to send it down with a resounding bang, when from over my shoulder, a voice enquired, 'Are they no' open yet?' I got such a fright I let the knocker drop quite ineffectually. After the doors had been opened to restore communications, I was told that it wasn't nearly loud enough, and in any case I must wait until I got the signal. In all the excitement, I don't know what happened to the would-be visitor.

On one of the afternoons it had been determined that we were to do a shot and engage in some talking somewhere on the fringe of Glasgow Green with, for a backdrop, a wall exhibiting some ripe anti-Popery graffiti. I shouldn't have believed it possible, but it is true that we drove around for quite a while without finding anything to suit the producer's taste, so that we ended up having to buy a stick of chalk and inscribe 'Kick the Pope' in our own fair hand, and in block capitals. Lest there should be any danger of prosecution, I hasten to add that we washed the wall clean once our purpose was accomplished.

These are only some of the entertaining things that happened to us in these three days. In fact, the side-effects were such that I suggested to the producer that a programme could easily be put together on 'Filming a Programme in Glasgow's East End'. This, I felt, would have a far higher entertainment content than much of the contrived material that is put over in the name of humour.

One of my worst experiences in the realm of television centred on a discussion programme regarding a Lambeth Conference (of the sixties) which was due to open within a few days, and, for the only time in my life, I was cast in the role of interviewer. It was a long and completely serious programme, utterly unscripted, and when we reached the end I was happy to think we had done a reasonably good job. As usual we sat around for a minute or two while the technicians assured themselves that all was safely 'in the can'. Imagine my horror when they came into the studio to say that something had gone amiss and that the whole affair would need to be done afresh. Not that I minded the extra time and effort, what did worry me was trying to think, when about to put a question, did I ask that on the previous run or was it just a minute ago on this run? I should never want to have that experience again.

A quite amusing incident followed a programme done with STV in their old studio at the top of Hope Street. I cannot recall what it was all about, but there were three of us involved, the other two being Roman Catholic priests, one of them the prior of the monastery at Fort Augustus. As it happened, the other was on his way to Inverness, so they were both keen to get to Abbotsinch to catch the same plane. Time being short, I offered to run them across and was busy doing so when we found ourselves in the midst of the crowd skailing from a Rangers-Celtic match at Ibrox Park. At times we were positively in a sea of people, all bemuffled and sometimes looking as though they were none too kindly disposed towards dog-collared occupants of cars. My passengers were getting a bit worried. In the event of any trouble, I told them, if they are sporting blue mufflers you two in the back keep very quiet and leave them to me; if they're wearing green, I'll keep my mouth shut and you lads behind can give them a couple of pater nosters and all will be well. Clearly it was a case where we were equipped to make the best of both worlds. Mercifully no difficulty arose and we arrived happily at Abbotsinch in time for the plane.

One last word on television. I always marvel at the quiet efficiency with which the boys (and girls) carry through their work. A crew will arrive on your doorstep and within minutes have all their equipment set up, and your furniture moved around, until you wouldn't recognise your own room, and then in due course everything is restored in perfect order. In my experience, it has always been a great joy to be involved with people who are so completely masters of their craft. Besides that, though, there's no want of goodwill towards the Kirk—all that expertise is there at our disposal if only we can think up the technique that is required to make this wonderful vehicle of communication a medium for the spread of the Gospel. Any bright ideas?

Chapter 14

A Tale of Three Parishes

FOR MANY MINISTERS, considerable satisfaction is to be found in, once in a while, visiting one of his former parishes and occupying his old pulpit. This pleasure, if pleasure it be, is one that is denied me, for each one of the three parishes with which I have been connected has altered out of all recognition, and indeed in two of the cases not even the church building is there any more. My ministry began with an Assistantship in Springburn, then one of Glasgow's most densely populated districts. By the early seventies the houses had almost all been demolished and in due course someone set fire to the church. The Springburn I knew is no more. The first parish I could call my own was Linwood, then a little village with a plain homely kirk at its centre. Quite a time after I had left the parish, the motor industry established itself nearby and the local authority slapped up thousands of houses alongside the village, altering completely the whole character of the community, and leading in 1965 to the erection of a new church and halls far away from the earlier building which was later demolished. Then for close on twenty years I was minister at Houston and Killellan, a very ancient parish of two small Renfrewshire villages and a vast hinterland of farming country. Quite soon after our departure, an estate was taken over for private housing development, and this mushroomed to take in farms all around, so that the population has more than trebled and the quiet quaint little country village is a thing of memories. In this case, I am happy to say, the lovely church still stands secure and I have on more than one occasion been happy to accept an invitation to occupy its pulpit. While it has been pleasant to meet a shrinking number of old friends, I have never been able to feel that I was 'going back to my old parish', for the simple but sufficient reason that the parish I knew and loved is no longer there to go back to.

Come to think of it, this is true of more things than visiting former parishes. It is one of the solemn facts of life, one which, as we grow older, we need constantly to be reminding ourselves, that we cannot go back, for the past is no longer there to go back to. Even the sleepiest rural community changes with the passing years, and we too cease to be the people we had been, so that it is a different place that is being seen, and through different eyes—which cannot but make identification difficult. I knew a man in Liverpool, a native of Auchtermuchty in Fife, who in his old age took a great fancy to revisit the place of his boyhood. This he had left while still a teenager, and in the course of the next fifty years he had never so much as set foot in Scotland. Once retired with time on his hands, he thought it would be really nice to revisit the old place and see all the old haunts. His wife encouraged him and off he set saying he didn't know how long he might stay. He arrived back the following day. Auchtermuchty had turned out to be completely different from what he thought it ought to be, his old school wasn't even there, he didn't see a soul he knew, although after a while he had managed to unearth an old school friend in the local blacksmith and they had a grand crack about auld lang syne. After that he couldn't get away soon enough—the truth was that the Auchtermuchty he wanted to revisit existed not in the Kingdom of Fife but in the recesses of his memory, where he could visit it any time without the aid of British Rail. It was a far nicer place anyway!

I went to Springburn at the beginning of 1933 to be Student Assistant to J Stuart Cameron in the former parish church, known then as Springburn Hill. The Springburn of that day was a mighty populous place, with street after street of tenement buildings wandering up and down its interminable hills. It had seven Church of Scotland congregations with a total membership of some 9000, and Sunday School pupils numbering just short of 3500. Today there is one congregation claiming 824 members and a Sunday School of 78. Our congregation was by far the largest, with a roll at that time of well above the 3000 mark and teeming with young life. It was while I was there that Mr and Mrs Cameron, having snatched the chance of a short break in Argyllshire, stopped on their way home to look in on the little Church of St Oran, that lovely sanctuary erected on Lochaweside by the Campbells of Blythswood. He got talking to the Church Officer who explained that they had normally a minute congregation at their services—'aboot ten or a dizen, mebbe ten shillin's in the plate'. In the summer months, however, what with visitors and tourists, things looked up some-what—'I've seen as mony as forty or even fifty—as much as a couple o' pounds in the plate'. He then went on to enquire where Mr Cameron's parish was and what was the size of *his* congregation. On hearing about the three thousand his instant reaction was, 'Man, what a collection!' 'Yes,' echoed their minister, 'what a collection!'

Of necessity everything was governed by size—it was quite the thing to have three funerals (cremation was little accepted at that time) in one afternoon; on a Glasgow Fair Holiday Friday, between afternoon and evening, sixteen couples might be united in holy wedlock; we had a list of sick, elderly and housebound requiring regular visitation running to over two hundred, as well as a list of what might be called 'occasional' sick at home and in hospital, varying around the fifty mark. During my three years there, I managed to get round the entire congregation on regular visition one and a half times, which I reckoned quite an achievement, for it meant something like twenty-five homes visited every week, as well as my share of the housebound and hospital visits and the funerals. Something that much intrigued me was how few members of the congregation were natives of Glasgow. The work which the locomotive industry had provided less than a generation before had attracted workers from every corner of Scotland. I have a good ear for accent, and I used to boast that within three minutes of entering a house I could place the inhabitants within a county as to their place of origin. That was exaggerating a bit—but not too much.

The parish might have numbers, but it had no claim to antiquity, even if it was technically known as an 'old parish'. The very name 'Springburn' is quite unknown in maps of early eighteenth century Glasgow, when this hilly area to the north of the city was the site of a few big houses and little else. The parish church of Springburn was the last to be built under the 1841 Act for the Erection of Parishes, and it was the last to be planned (and very largely financed) by the Glasgow Church Building Society. The famous Thomas Chalmers, then minister at St John's in the Calton district of the city, one of Europe's worst slums, had in the thirties of the nineteenth century set the whole country on fire for the cause of Church Extension — within seven years £300,000 was raised for this purpose, and 222 new churches were opened throughout Scotland. One of his most devoted supporters was William Collins, founder of the famous publishing house of that name. In 1834 Collins had come up with a proposal that twenty new churches should be erected in Glasgow, and he had then set to work with the aid of some friends to raise the necessary funds. Each church was to have a thousand sittings and it was to cost not more than £2000. Springburn, opened in July 1842, was the last of the twenty. An event of even greater significance for the district had occurred just five months earlier when the railway line joining Glasgow and Edinburgh via Falkirk was opened for passenger traffic. It had taken just three years to build and was as level as a bowling green all the way, except for the last mile down from Cowlairs to the terminus at Queen Street, which by railway standards was very steep indeed; so much so that, until 1908, trains had to be assisted up the hill by a cable pulled by a stationary engine at Cowlairs. It was the railway that was to make Springburn —Springburn and steam trains were to be for ever linked. So it seems only fitting that now, when the steam locomotive has been consigned to the museum, the Springburn that built it has been obliterated from the map.

In its heyday Springburn boasted four great locomotive workshops: there was the Hydepark Locomotive Works of Neilson Reid, the Atlas Works of Sharp Stewart, the Cowlairs Works of the North British Railway Company, and the St Rollox Works of the Caledonian Railway Company. The two latter, although they built the occasional engine, were mainly engaged in the repair and maintenance of their own stock, but the two former made and exported locomotives of every size, shape and description to every corner of the world, as well as adding their contribution to the home market. The journey down to Stobcross Quay on a Sunday morning of these great monsters on the first leg of their journey to faraway places, was quite a spectacle. At Cowlairs too there was an extensive carriage and wagon works. Those people of Springburn who did not work in one or other of these industries were almost all employed in the business of running the railways, as footplatemen attached to

Eastfield and St Rollox sheds, as guards, signalmen, porters, booking clerks, shunters, even the odd station-master. Springburn depended on the railway and the North British Railway at least depended on Springburn. Thus in the early years of the century, Springburn had been a busy and prosperous place constantly expanding, forever drawing in people from distant corners of Scotland. At the turn of the century our church had been extended by the addition of two deep transepts almost doubling its capacity. By my time there, however, the whole nation was deep in the throes of the depression of the thirties, locomotive building was at a complete standstill, not a single order on the books, and there was scarcely a house that did not know the scourge of unemployment. When people today talk about unemployment and compare the present situation with the position then, and even more when they talk about the poverty which it brings, they are discussing things totally different from what their fathers knew half a century ago. During the years I spent among them, I came to admire the courage, the fortitude and the patience, as well as the consistent good humour and hopefulness shown by the men, and the willingness to make-do-and-mend that characterised the women in these dismal days.

Worse was still to come for Springburn as we all know, for the days of steam locomotion were numbered. Today there is not a single works of the heavy industry left on which the entire community once depended. The housing was growing old and done. In the days of controlled rents it had of necessity been completely neglected, and much of it was due, overdue, for demolition. An expressway was to be driven through its centre to take the main traffic from the city to Bishopbriggs and Kirkintilloch, as well as a major road running from east to west. In the course of the long period of knocking down before any proper work of rebuilding could be put in hand, every one of the seven churches came to be destroyed, in almost every case by a fire lit by vandals. It was during my time as Presbytery Clerk that I managed to wring from a reluctant District Council the funds necessary to erect a new building of very modest proportions on the edge of the new shopping area. Anyone who knew Springburn in the days of its greatness would be hard put to recognise a single landmark today. It may be a better place—that's still got to be proved—it is most emphatically not the same place.

When I went there in 1932 it was as Student Assistant, that is to say my time was still officially fully occupied attending University classes and doing the work thereof, and it was only my spare time and Sundays that I could devote to the work of the parish. Since up to that point I had been occupying the said spare time working in *The Glasgow Herald* reading-room, there was no hardship involved—indeed I welcomed the chance to get to bed regularly at a decent hour. For my many and varied labours in the parish, I received the princely sum of £160 per annum (the minimum stipend was £300) and out of this I had to meet my own travelling expenses which, even with the maximum tramfare at twopence, still amounted to a considerable drain. It has to be said that for that same modest sum you could travel from Airdrie Cross to the west end of Paisley, the only snag being that I never had occasion to make that particular journey! In the April of the following year, I finished my University course, and since I was planning to stay on for some time in my assistantship the Presbytery agreed that I should be ordained the following month. This brought me a massive salary increase to £180 per annum. In spite of it all, I contrived (thanks, it must be said, to the help of my mother who had a natural genius for, as well as a lifetime's experience of, economic living) to lay aside a bit of money towards, I hoped, the not too distant prospect of acquiring a wife and having a manse to furnish.

If the financial rewards of these three years were slender, the rewards in every other direction were great. For one thing it was a wonderful place in which to gain experience of every aspect of the work of the parish ministry; for another thing Stuart Cameron was the perfect minister under whom to serve —wise, understanding, patient, himself a superb preacher and a most capable administrator, while Mrs Cameron took me under her wing in the most generous way, treating me as an addition to the family—of whom there were already four. And then, of course, there was the congregation, 'what a collection' as the beadle at St Oran's had said. Visiting them was an enriching experience. You got every kind of welcome, from an invitation into the kitchen ('come awa' ben the hoose') which, it was probably explained, was 'in a guddle', but where life was being lived, to being shown into 'the room' where your hostess would

carefully dust a chair with her apron for her distinguished guest
while she herself either stood or sat awkwardly on the edge of
another (undusted) chair. It could be difficult sometimes to get
across the message that you had come to pay a visit, not to
inflict a visitation! One advantage of the unemployment was
that you rarely got a shut door—either afternoon or evening,
someone was at home passing the idle hours away.

An added bonus had been the actual event of my ordination
service which took place appropriately on the evening of the
Day of Pentecost. Strangely enough it was the first time there
had been an ordination in the congregation and Stuart Cameron
had given the event a fantastic write-up in advance, driving
home to the congregation that it was the duty of everyone to be
there. He had had 1200 copies of the Order of Service printed
and every single copy had been handed out and still folk were
coming in. It was an experience I shall never forget. On Boxing
Day of the following year, Queenie and I were married in the
same Kirk with, once again, the keen interest of the congregation reflected in the numbers who filled the pews. How
could I ever forget the place which had witnessed my ordination
and marriage, the spot where I had stood and made the two
great commitments of my life?

Our congregation included all classes of the community,
from those very much on the breadline in the older and more
derelict tenement properties, through the rather better off
inhabitants of the four-in-a-block-cottage-type local authority
housing of Balornock and other such schemes, to the comfort if
not the wealth of Bishopbriggs. We had quite a few families in
the older parts of Bishopbriggs, then a growing residential
district and now an enormous suburb just beyond the northern
fringe of the city. The district was said, half a century before, to
be inhabited (to the tune of 900 souls) by 'Irish families of the
poorer class', and mining, quarrying and agriculture were reported to be its main industries. The parish is the ancient one of
Cadder, and I do not know where the name Bishopbriggs comes
from or what is its derivation, but I always in my own mind
associate it with a stupid story about an Irish labourer who had
come over to these parts in search of work. A fellow country-
man, already established here, arranged for him to see his boss
about the possibility of a start. He warned his friend that if

asked what he knew about anything at all he should declare himself on very familiar terms—'you'll soon pick it up, the bhoys on the jab'll nat see you stuck'. So, in the course of the interview, the Irish man claimed to know all about earth-moving equipment of every sort, bulldozers, forklift trucks, mechanical shovels—you name it, he could cope with it. 'You seem a likely chap,' said the foreman, 'we can start you on Monday morning. Come straight to the site. Do you know Bishopbriggs?' 'Bishop Briggs,' said his new employee, 'sure I've known him ever since he was a parish priest back home in Connemara.' What can I say?

The residents here were, as I have suggested, better supplied with this world's goods than most of the folk in Springburn, so I got into the habit around tea-time of moving out to Bishopbriggs in the hope of an invitation to tea, as I was planning to work on into the evening. I certainly got plenty of such invitations up the Springburn closes, but I felt that in many cases I was being offered what some other member of the family was far more in need of, and I consistently declined. I had no such conscientious scruples in Bishopbriggs and enjoyed many a very nice 'high tea' which was still the standard evening meal in the Glasgow of those days. One cannot always be lucky, and on occasion I went hungry—or, much more galling, was told by my hostess on the doorstep as I was leaving, 'I might have offered you your tea.' But that didn't happen very often.

I was fortunate to miss the horse-drawn funerals, when hearse and carriages pulled by pairs of big black Belgian horses used to be *de rigeur* for any respectable funeral. It was all very impressive, but it must have been frustratingly time-consuming, especially if the cemetery was at any great distance. Deaths in those days mostly occurred at home, and even when the person died in hospital the body was taken home for the sake of having the funeral service there. One custom that did persist in the Springburn of my day—and one which I utterly detested—was that of waiting until the service was over before nailing down the coffin. In some cases, if you let them, they would have had you conduct the whole service standing around an open coffin. One funeral undertaker in particular had the habit, immediately after I had uttered the word 'Amen', of enquiring in the most unctuous tones, 'Now would anyone care to look upon the deceased for the last time?', while holding the lid half-on-half-off. As sure as fate someone would so care, and before you knew what was afoot you had weeping and wailing and folk throwing hysterics. One of our own elders, a douce, civil little man, was employed as an undertaker. On one occasion he was at a funeral when the minister who was to conduct the service asked for a Bible. This threw the family into confusion as a major search was engaged in. Our little man nudged his neighbour, produced a screwdriver from the pocket of his frock-coat, and remarked, 'I always carry *my* own tools with me!'

I loved every minute of my time in Springburn, the very sound of the name brings back happy memories. But I have accepted the fact that it's not there any more, even if I wanted to go back.

It was the first days of January 1936 that saw me inducted to my own first parish—at Linwood. Queenie and I had been married a fortnight before on Boxing Day and had snatched a few days' holiday in Edinburgh before moving into our first home, which was in fact a very nice house, still lit by coal gas, very spacious and with a large garden. It was unthinkable in those days for a manse to be without a maid, in black dress with white apron and headband, so a suitable young lady was duly engaged, and we found ourselves in business. I have comm-ented elsewhere upon how utterly alone the Moderator of the General Assembly can feel up there on his 'throne': his position is not very much worse than that of the young minister just gone to his first parish, anxiously awaiting the first crisis.

Linwood represented an odd kind of community. It was a village on the Black Cart Water, in the eastern corner of the Parish of Kilbarchan, three miles from Paisley Cross. It housed no fewer than four fairly large public works. First there was a flourishing paper mill, R and W Watson's; then there was a gear-cutting plant, the Reid Gear Company; also a precision-instrument maker, Dent Johnston & Co; and a manufacturer of steel window frames, whose name escapes me. A little way out of the village there was an industry of sorts, a kiln where the wood-shavings from the bobbins, on which were wound the countless miles of linen thread manufactured at Coats' Mill in Paisley, were cooked in some mysterious fashion to produce charcoal, and this went by rail to Ardeer to play its part in the production of explosives. This particular business did not add much to the local economy, but it provided an interest for us at the manse, as at regular intervals the horse-drawn lorries passed with their skips of shavings, and it provided a steady source of income for the local blacksmith. Both horses and lorries needed to be shod with some regularity, as they made the eight or nine mile round trip, I imagine, three times every day. The result of so many industries was that we daily imported a considerable labour force, offset to some extent by the number of girls who left the village on their way to work in the Paisley thread-mills.

The village itself was a quaint affair dating from long before the days of town-planning. The main road from Paisley to Bridge of Weir ran through the middle of the old village, then, taking a sharp left turn, it encountered the new local authority housing, and at the end of that was a fine modern school on one side and a farm called The Green on the other. This main road was crossed early in its course by Napier Street, where a great part of the population was housed in very out-dated accommodation which they maintained in remarkably decent condition. The name 'Napier', incidentally, came from the family of the man who invented (or should it be discovered?) logarithms, and whom many generations of schoolchildren have called blessed (or something else!), for they had a house at Milliken nearby. Blocking Napier Street at one end was the kirk, at the other the Reid Gear works, while along one side was the paper mill.

At one time there had been three coal mines in the parish, and when I say they were called The Redan, Inkermann and Balaclava, it will be apparent they had been sunk during the years of the Crimean War. I gather it had been a fairly poor quality of boiler fuel that was mined. One of my Houston farmers recalled that in his youth he had from time to time to go for a cartload of this fuel, which they burned in the dairyhouse boiler. 'It was hard as rock,' he said, 'ye got a rare heat— breakin' it.' Still, I suppose, nothing that would produce steam could afford to be ignored. The Redan had lain within the compass of the village itself, but all sign of it had been wiped out to make way for a 'tween-the-wars housing scheme. The official title awarded to this area was Hart Street, but to the Linwood native it was still 'The Redan'. Not, incidentally, that street names mattered all that much, as we quickly discovered. As we did our early visiting, we would find ourselves asking some children, 'Where is such and such a street?' They would probably look a little bewildered and respond by asking, 'Who is it ye're lookin' for?' and accurate directions followed without difficulty. About half-a-mile from the village to the north west was all that was left of Balaclava—a single row of what had been rather high-class miners' houses. After the mine was worked out, an oil works was opened under the name of Clippens, which was the name of a farm close by, a name as long-established as the Old Poll-Tax Roll, and that title took over to the exclusion of the Crimean 'Balaclava'. The site of this former settlement is now the centre of the small new town which Linwood has become and it is here that the new Parish Church is to be found.

Inkermann lay fully a mile from the manse on the Paisley side, and in my time it still boasted four rows of single-storey brick houses as well as a nearby school and schoolhouse. The housing conformed to the worst tradition of the miners' row. Between the rows a spiggot to provide the water supply alternated with a dry closet to meet the no less urgent needs of the inhabitants. These closets were emptied three times a week in an open horse-drawn cart. Dogs, cats, hens, not to mention other less reputable four-legged creatures, wandered through the houses and their environs—as did little children. To me it always appeared we had the perfect recipe for a visitation of the plague, although in fact the Inkermann folk in my experience were quite as healthy as any others, and certainly as a community they knew a happiness and a contentment that few of their more hygienically-placed neighbours could equal. I had some wonderful members in Inkermann.

During my time at Linwood I organised and, if I may say so, very successfully ran, a Sunday School at Inkermann. This was held in the school which the Education Authority granted me the use of, on condition that I paid the cleaner half-a-crown for lighting the coal stove on which we depended for heat. The school had had an interesting feature which it no longer enjoyed by the time of my arrival. The rivers Black Cart and Gryffe flow together close by, and not much farther on join the White Cart at Inchinnan to flow into the Clyde near Renfrew at The Pudgeoch

(I feel sure that is not the correct spelling, but I have never seen the name in print and that is certainly how it sounds). The Cart was tidal up almost to the village of Inkermann, with the result that, when heavy rainfall and a high tide happened to coincide, the fields could suddenly be covered in water to a considerable depth. It was not unknown, therefore, for the schoolmaster to have to phone one of the neighbouring farms to send a horse and cart to convey the children home. It never happened in my time, for the dredging of the mouth of the Cart, undertaken to allow for the launching of the Queen Mary from John Brown's yard, had the effect of letting the water away more quickly and preventing the flooding around the school. For all that, we still had our problems. After taking the Linwood Sunday School on Sunday afternoons, one of the teachers and I walked the mile and a half to cope with the class at Inkermann, and it was not unusual throughout the winter months for us to have to resort to gumboots and take to the fields because the road was under water to a considerable depth. The flooding hereabouts was so much a regular feature that a colony of swans made it their winter quarters.

One of our most devoted members at Inkermann was Geordie. He was unemployed, but he was willing and extremely knacky and he used to come about the manse and the kirk doing odd jobs of one sort and another 'juist to put in the time'. His wife was a 'braw wee stoot body' bubbling over with good humour, and when I knew them they had nine of a family, the nicest children you could have met, and all of them were to do well in later life. An addition to the family was due. The doctor proudly announced to the mother that here was another bonnie, healthy wee boy. 'Och, doctor,' she said, 'could ye no' hae made it twins. I was that much lookin' forward to twins, for then I wad hae had a team!' She had only about eighteen months to wait before she got her twins—which gave her a 'reserve' to add to her 'team'. During the war, we used repeatedly to be told that careless talk costs lives: it can also apparently create them. Anyone labouring under the delusion that there is some connection between happiness and wordly possessions should have seen Geordie and his wife and their 'team'.

I have never known better Church attenders than we had in

Linwood. With the exception of the two schoolmasters there wasn't a single professional person on the roll, we had a few of what I suppose could be called white-collar workers, but the bulk of the congregation consisted of simple working-class people—the man who emptied the 'middens' at Inkermann was there with his wife and their little girl with unfailing regularity, his face shining like a new pin. Another member whose presence could be counted on was a dairyman, who not only kept the cows but retailed his milk in Elderslie from a pony and cart, the snoddest turn-out you ever did see. To enable him to get to the Kirk, he started his day on Sunday a little earlier than his normal 5 in the morning, got his round finished by about 11 o'clock, got himself washed and dressed and his dinner hastily devoured, and arrived in nice time for the service which was at mid-day. His seat, unfortunately for him, was in the front row of the gallery ('the breist o' the laft' was its official title) so that he was looking down at, and in full view of, the pulpit. Of course, the sermon had him nodding, and I didn't attribute that altogether to the dullness of my preaching. Manfully he would fight against the drowsiness. Had it not been for the embarrassment it would have caused him, I would have liked to have said, 'Look, Alex, just let yourself go. I can perfectly understand —and so, I'm sure, can God'.

When I said we didn't have a single member who did not belong to the professional class, I was overlooking the fact that we had Willie Galbraith, founder of the grocery chain that bore his name, who lived in a big house in Elderslie and whose name was on our roll. Probably he was not an exception, for he would have claimed—with some vehemence likely, and certainly with some justice—that he very much belonged to the working classes. His story was an interesting one. By my time in the parish he was an old man and not very fit, and I used to visit him from time to time. We would have long blethers which, I believe, gave pleasure to us both. His father, who owned the 'store' in the Linwood of an earlier day, had two sons, John and William. He was a cautious man as was his elder son, but Willie, the younger boy, had adventurous ideas and wanted to put them into practice. Ere long the inevitable happened, there was a row, and Willie packed up and left home. He managed, he never quite knew how, to rent a little shop in Paisley's Well

Street, and to stock it, although when the baker arrived with bread on the morning of his opening day he had to ask for credit, for everything he possessed was already invested in stock. From there he never looked back. He had that indefinable something we call genius and everything to which he turned his hand succeeded as a matter of course. By the time I came to know him, he had over 150 branches, he had his own jam factory, his own pig farm, his own greenhouses and I know not what else. And through it all he remained remarkably unspoilt. All kinds of combines, he assured me, were keen to take him over, but, he said, 'as long as I'm able, I'll keep on running my ain shantie'.

I was preaching one Sunday, pleading the cause of Church Extension, and was urging that we needed new churches in the housing schemes—it wouldn't do to say there was a church half-a-mile down the road. By way of illustration, I remarked that I had been calling on Mr Galbraith a few days before and that he had just returned from a visit to the site of a great new housing development where he had been taking a plot of land on which to build a shop. I expressed surprise at his moving in so quickly, for the scheme had still not a single inhabitant. 'I've got to be there quick,' he said, 'I daurna let my competitors get in afore me.' I drew the obvious moral that we too had our 'competitors' and what made sense for the grocer made every bit as good sense for the Kirk. A couple of days later I got a message that Mr Galbraith would like to see me. Thinking perhaps he had taken ill I hurried off to Elderslie to be greeted with, 'I hear you were giving me quite an advertisement from the pulpit on Sunday'. I tried to explain that this hadn't been altogether my intention. 'Aweel,' he replied, 'intentional or not, advertising costs money; so here's a cheque for your Church Extension scheme.' A man to whom life brought a great measure of success and a great number of disappointments, I had finally the duty of laying him to rest up on the crest of Woodside Cemetery where the great and the wealthy of Paisley lie beneath a unique collection of 'storied urns and animated busts', or at least their equivalent in terms of the Scottish stonemason's craft.

If funerals are the things that stand out in my mind from my years in Springburn, it is weddings that I most vividly remember from Linwood. At that time, being married in church was never even thought of as a possibility in a place like Linwood—any bride with such aspirations would have been guilty of forgetting her station in life, a church wedding being for 'the county' and not for the likes of her. So marriages were celebrated in one of two places, either the hotel or tea-room where the subsequent reception was to be held, or the manse, the latter being the more common. There was an unwritten law that a wedding at the manse involved a 'tip' of a half-crown for the maid—and, believe me, the lassie earned every penny of it considering the confetti that had to be swept up in a day when there might be a vacuum cleaner in every home—but not in ours, for we had no electricity! I remember one bride who arrived in what I think is called a picture hat, a plain enough affair but with an enormous brim. On leaving home she had to descend an outside stair with the neighbours ranged on the landing above pelting her with confetti. The ceremony over, the signing began. I invited the bride to the table, handed her a pen and pointed to the spot where she was to put her name. She took the pen and bent forward to write, when hey presto, the hat discharged its cargo and you could not see the schedule, much less add any writing to it.

Talking of signing marriage schedules reminds me of one of the strangest requests I have ever had at a wedding. The bride asked that, when it came to the point where the witnesses sign the schedule, I would so drape my robe over the paper as to obscure the column showing the age of the bridegroom. I was not given any reason for the request, but I had a pretty shrewd idea. Neither of the high contracting parties was in the first blush of youth, the sister of the bride who was acting as bridesmaid was an inveterate gossip and, I can imagine, having been frustrated in all her efforts to learn the age of her brother-in-law-to-be, thought she knew just how she was going to make the great discovery. The bride was equally determined she was not! I felt that in the circumstances the request was not unreasonable. I had not been so sympathetically disposed to a suggestion advanced at a Springburn wedding, however. On that occasion when I offered a pen to the bridegroom (aged 75), he remarked, 'I'm no' much o' a scholar: the wife'll sign it for me'. Other considerations apart, I felt he was in too much of a hurry to avail himself of the services of his new wife (aged 73).

Linwood manse lay outside the village, for you had to cross the River Cart to get to it, and by that time you were, strictly speaking, in Elderslie. Exactly a mile, as flat as the proverbial pancake, took you to the railway line, and just beyond that to the main Paisley-Johnstone road at Elderslie, and beyond that in turn rose the Gleniffer Braes. Just before the outbreak of war, a great factory was built on one of the fields halfway between us and the railway. It was to be occupied by Beardmores, famous for the forge at Parkhead, and it had some connection with the war effort which was already under way. I remember being fascinated by the fact that the first thing that was done was to enclose the site in a beautiful unscaleable perimeter fence. Talking to one of the boss-men one day, I remarked that I had always imagined you built the fence when you had finished erecting what was to be enclosed. That, he explained, was an unduly simple, unrealistic and old-fashioned view of the position. It could be very difficult indeed to ensure that men employed on a building site were all actually working, but at least it was comforting to know you had them on the site. Before the fence was erected, some had paused merely long enough to sign themselves in before proceeding across the field to a nearby 'bing'. In a little hollow on top they usually spent a pleasant day with a card school before returning to the site to sign off in time to catch the bus for home. Not the healthiest of starts to what unfortunately was never to be a very healthy project.

After the war, the factory was taken over by Pressed Steel which operated for a while without any marked success, and then some time later the Chrysler Car group decided this would be a good place to set up a branch of the motor industry, there being a plentiful labour force on tap. So they built an enormous plant on the fields on the other side of the main road, where the assembling would be done, the bodies being pressed in the older factory with an elaborate bridge carrying the bits and pieces across the highway. A victory of historic moment had been achieved for Scottish industry. The name of Linwood would soon be a household word throughout the land as the home of Scotland's motor industry. The local authority were pressed into making housing available. When they complained they needed time to do some kind of intelligent planning, they were told never to mind the planning but to get on with the housing. And that is exactly what it looks like, this new Linwood that sprang into being on the fringe of the old village. Workers for the new plant were easy to find, for 'the money was good', or so it seemed at the time, but, as was to be expected, it was discovered that while the money might be good enough, it wasn't plentiful enough. The new labour force was soon convinced that it was being shockingly underpaid. Certainly, the dreary repetitive inhuman kind of work on which they were engaged provided no opportunity for job-satisfaction—and that leaves only wage-satisfaction as a possible motivation.

The manager of the cotton mill in my Houston parish was one day showing me around. In the workroom girls stood about, each in charge of a number of spinning devices. When a thread broke, as frequently happened, the girl switched off the affected machine, grabbed the two loose ends, tied them together with great dexterity, then slipped the machine back into gear. I remarked to my guide that, while I could not but admire the skill and speed of the operation, what really amazed me was that a girl could stand there doing that kind of thing hour after hour and day after day and retain her sanity. 'But,' he explained, 'these girls are not really standing there, they're birling around a distant dancefloor in the arms of some handsome screen star.' I suppose he was right and they must have enjoyed some kind of fantasy life to endure the monotony of their real life. The dreamlife of the slaves of the car industry never seemed to take them beyond a vision of standing around a brazier on the picket-line. The plant produced Hillmans, it produced Talbots, it became 'Rootes', but at every turn it was bedevilled by industrial discord. As had been predicted, the name of Linwood became a household word, but in the popular mind it was associated with nothing but strikes and threats of strikes. A few years ago the plant was finally closed down altogether and Linwood, which in my day had been a village with more industry than people to man it, became a small town with a large population and little or nothing for them to do. You see what I mean when I say my Linwood is no longer there for me to go back to.

The manse at Linwood was our first home, and how we loved it. It was there that three children were born to us. Our first child was a boy, a lovely healthy boy, or so it seemed until it was discovered that some part of his colon was solid instead of being tubular, so that while he had been able to feed perfectly, the digestive process could not complete itself. Today I understand a comparatively simple operation can put such a thing to rights, but not so then. It was a great sorrow to us both. The two little girls who followed in due course were models of good health, and indeed still are! For both Queenie and myself our memories of Linwood are happy ones indeed, and we are content to leave it like that.

While the Linwood of my day was a self-contained community, it enjoyed fairly close links with the nearby town of Johnstone which, with adjacent Elderslie, had seven Church of Scotland congregations. To the north-west, on the other hand, lay the ancient parish of Houston and Killellan which to us in Linwood was little more than a name, but with whose minister, George Muir, I had come to be on friendly terms. He had begun his ministry in Bargrennan, that lonely moorland parish that included the Glen of Trool that I knew so well. Towards the close of his ministry he suffered a long illness and I was able to help out occasionally, so it was natural enough that on the day of his funeral the Presbytery appointed me interim moderator in the vacancy. Our villages were four miles apart, but I was a very keen walker in those days, so for me to get there and back represented no more than a pleasant stroll. If the two communities were geographically separated by only four miles, in every other regard they were as far apart as it was possible to be. I am speaking of the summer of 1939, immediately before the outbreak of war. For one thing, Linwood was a comparatively modern growth—a mere excrescence some would have called it—while Houston was a union of two parishes, each of them with roots in the eighth century; Linwood was utterly industrial in both its economy and its thinking, Houston was agricultural in its economy. Indeed, in its thinking, it was a survival of feudalism, with a laird, A A Hagart Speirs Esq of Elderslie, and a 'big house' with stables, gardens, home farm, the lot. Congregation-wise Linwood was embarrassingly alive, Houston was enjoying a peaceful slumber; Linwood had its links with Johnstone and Paisley, Houston stood in glorious isolation—it wouldn't have wanted it otherwise. Yet there was something very charming and attractive about Houston, and the more I came to see of it, and the better I got to know its people, the more I found myself drawn towards it. As a place to work it would have its difficulties, I knew very well—but, after all, that's what makes any job worthwhile. The result was that at the end of the day, and after much diligent heart-searching, I agreed to accept their most enthusiastic and unanimous invitation to be their minister. And so in June 1940 I was inducted to my second (and last) parish, that of Houston and Killellan.

Although the latter half of the name is spelt 'Killellan', it is pronounced 'Kilallan', being a corruption of Cella Fillani, the cell of St Fillan. I believe that over the centuries no fewer than eleven different spellings have been employed. The main advantage of the present spelling is that you could instantly detect the stranger, for he falls into the trap of pronouncing the name as it is spelt. As I have said, both parishes were of eighth century foundation, the original name of Houston having been Kilpeter. It acquired the name of Houston in the thirteenth century, when the lands were given under feudal tenure to one Hugh de Padvinan, vassal of Walter of Biggar, vassal in turn of Walter FitzAllan, High Steward of Scotland, who brought the monks from Much Wenlock in Shropshire to establish the Priory, later to become the Abbey, of Paisley. Hugh built himself a great castle on his new estate. His serfs dwelt in cottages close by—hence 'Hugh's toon'. The church at Killellan was rebuilt in 1635 and one of its ministers had some exciting experiences during the days of the Covenants. Then, in 1760, it was decreed by the Court of Teinds that the parishes should be united on the first occurrence of a vacancy in either, which happened in 1771. The united parish stretched from the outskirts of Kilmacolm in the west, right down on to the level ground where it met the Parish of Inchinnan near the Greenock railway line at what used to be Georgetown Station. Half of the Royal Ordnance Factory at Bishopton lay within the Parish of Houston. Its congregation, as I have said, was not the liveliest within the Presbytery, and the problems facing the new minister were many and varied. But 'stoot hearts were made for stey braes' and it was with high hopes that we moved to our new world.

The very first problem that had to be tackled was that of putting the manse in order, a very splendid house built in 1815 and sitting in the midst of acres of garden—but equipped with neither gas nor electricity. It was true that the electric mains passed close by, but Houston had long inclined to the view that electricity was for the laird, who until shortly before had made his own, and that it was not for ordinary folk. It wasn't installed on the farms—what had been good enough for the fathers should surely suffice for the children. A dairy-farmer a couple of miles away, across whose land the pylons passed, churned butter for the market every day, the power being supplied by a Clydesdale horse walking around a mill rink—exactly as in Old Testament times, only that then it was a donkey or a camel. My predecessor had been happy with oil lamps, and—which was much more important—had been in a position to maintain the necessary domestic staff to keep them filled, their wicks trimmed, and their funnels cleaned. He had also been able to keep a full-time 'man' who lived in and who, with a great deal of help from both the minister and his wife, kept the garden in a very presentable condition. No decorating had been done for many years, so the whole house, all ten rooms of it, was due to be painted and papered after the electricians and fireplace-fitters were done tearing up floors and knocking holes in walls, and joiners and plasterers were finished putting things to rights again. In that connection it was discovered that the doors throughout the house were beautiful six-panelled affairs in Memel pine and it was decided to clean them back to the natural grain and wax-polish them. They were all dismounted and taken outside for the operation when it was discovered that twenty-four coats of paint had to be removed—over the years they had alternated between white enamel and grain-and-varnish, at four coats with each change. With all this work to be done we were able to move in to three apartments (without doors) in August, and it was not until just after Christmas that we got rid of the last of the tradesmen and had the house to ourselves.

I cannot conceive how the congregation managed to survive financially. The total annual income from ordinary collections amounted to just under £100. Considering that the laird who was there most Sundays put in a pound note, the balance worked out at very little per head for the rest of the congregation—lending colour to a story they told of one member who had asked for 'change of a penny for the plate'! And yet they got by—to some extent, I think, on the feudal philosophy that 'the laird'll no' see us stuck'.

The stipend came wholly from teind, and, until only a short time before, the heritors were responsible for maintaining the fabric of both church and manse. The situation here was rather unusual. The church was at least the third to occupy the site. In 1771, when, as already related, the parish of Houston was united with its neighbour of Killellan two miles further up the country, it had been a condition of the union that there was to be erected at Houston a new church adequate to accommodate the united congregation. There is some doubt as to whether this was ever done or whether in fact the walls were heightened and new galleries added. Whatever was done, it lasted for a hundred years. Around 1870, the then laird who had very recently married the Lady Anne Pleydell Bouverie, daughter of the Earl of Radnor, died very suddenly some little time before the birth of his son (our laird). In 1874, his mother, who was now Mrs Ellis of Glengarry, approached the Presbytery for permission to demolish the existing church and to erect a completely new one on the site—this to be a memorial to her son who had died so tragically. This was duly agreed and in 1875 the foundation-stone of a splendid new church was laid. In 1937, extensive dry-rot was discovered in the building and our laird sought per-mission to carry through the necessary repairs, including a number of improvements, to install electric lighting and to provide a pipe-organ—all as a memorial to his mother, the Lady Anne. A very magnificent job was carried through and it was particularly sad that George Muir the minister was by that time too ill to take part in the rededication service. By an odd chance it was I who, on the following Sunday, conducted the first ordinary service in the beautifully refurbished building. So, you see, the upkeep of fabric didn't make big demands on the liberality of the congregation—which was perhaps fortunate.

The parish contained two villages, Houston itself and, about half-a-mile to the south, Crosslee. Houston had enjoyed the distinction of being created a 'new town' as far back as 1780. The then proprietor of the castle and its adjoining lands was an odd character, Captain James Macrae, who ultimately departed from these shores in something of a hurry, having killed a man in a duel, and he decided that the then village, of about a score of houses clustered around his castle walls, was doing nothing for its amenity, and as he planned to build himself a new and very grand mansion on the site, he had a great part of the old stronghold demolished and presented the stone to the villagers to enable them to erect for themselves new houses out of sight of his windows. Not only that, he planned the new village and granted fairly large feus on very generous terms. In consequence there was built a new town of 35 houses in which dwelt 57 families, six of the houses being of two storeys, and a few slated although most stuck to thatch, but, last word in luxury, a few had a separate room for the loom. Although it had been extended quite considerably, this was still substantially the Houston to which I came in 1940. The village of Crosslee, on the other hand, was a product of the Industrial Revolution. As it dropped steadily from the high land above Kilmacolm, the River Gryffe provided a source of power for a great number of cotton mills. One of these was at Crosslee, where the family of Jack were in business for many years. By my time the mill had passed into the control of Imperial Chemical Industries who used it at the time to produce gun cotton. The housing in Crosslee was almost wholly of the four-in-a-block variety so popular with local authorities.

There was a railway station on the old G&SW line from Glasgow to Greenock, but it was two miles distant from the village. A stranger once enquired of a native why they had put the station so far away from the village, to which he received the reply that he supposed it was to have it near the railway. Which goes to show that sometimes you can ask a stupid question and get an intelligent answer. There used to be a horse-bus which connected the village with the trains, and many and hair-raising were the legends that gathered around it, but by my time this had been replaced by a motor-bus, which continued the journey into Johnstone, a mile further away. Since this was scheduled to suit the trains, it ran at the most peculiar times, and not very often at that, which explains why a stranger asking in Johnstone where he might see a timetable for the Houston bus was told—'A time-table? It's a calendar you want for that!'

The nearest thing to a village that the former parish of Killellan could boast was a row of cottages by the roadside about a couple of miles north of Houston—Barochan Row. The kirk itself at Killellan lay in perfect surroundings in a hollow of the hills, a place of glorious peace. It had originally been the site of a cell established by Saint Fillan, who laboured there until his death in 749. The church, which was allowed to fall into decay after the union with Houston in 1771, had been built in 1635, but is quite clearly the extension of a pre-Reformation building. It is now in ruin, but the manse, believed to be the oldest inhabited house in Renfrewshire, was (after my time) restored and improved by Mr Mervyn Noad, a well-known Glasgow architect who lived there with his family for many years. On the evening of the first Sunday of July, an open-air service was held in the graveyard, attended, I'm afraid, by only a handful of local farmers and a few others. These traditional affairs have always held a fascination for me, and I'm happy to say that by diligent 'plugging', by laying on a bus service, and even providing a cup of tea enjoyed in the open air afterwards, I managed to spread some of my enthusiasm so that, in spite of the best efforts of the midges, the event came to be very well attended. It was for me a great satisfaction to be able to conduct the annual service at Killellan as part of my Moderatorial programme in 1971.

Ministers had a habit of staying a long time in Houston—I was only the eighth in the two centuries since the union of the parishes. The incumbent who moved from Killellan to Houston at that time, John Monteath, had gone to the former parish in 1748. He was succeeded by his son, also John, who died while still minister of the parish in 1843—ninety-five years between them. For almost a century, the Kirk Session minutes are signed 'John Monteath—Moderator'. John Monteath the younger was a man of some distinction, but I feel sure that in the latter years of his ministry the life of the congregation must have been at a pretty low ebb, so that, when in the year of his death the Disruption occurred, things were ripe for change. The result was that a very healthy congregation of the Free Church was immediately established in the parish. If not strong numerically, it was very much something to be reckoned with when I went there. On a Saturday night in March 1941, however, the church was completely gutted by fire, only the walls were left standing. Undaunted the congregation set about equipping a little hall and session-house which had been salvaged to act as a church, and there they struggled on until, on the retirement of their minister in 1949, they agreed to unite with us. Thus emerged one of the happiest church unions of which I have any knowledge. Once the immediate post-war building restrictions were beginning to ease, we built, within the walls of the former church, a church hall, a luxury neither congregation had ever enjoyed, a luxury that we soon found to be no luxury but a necessity.

Occasional reference has been made to 'the laird' and to the feudalism of which he was the surviving symbol. One just could not picture, much less begin to understand, the Houston of those days without the laird somewhere in the background. It was not that either he or Mrs Speirs obtruded in any way in the affairs of the community—rather the reverse—it was just that the very fact of their existence exercised an influence. Such is the lingering effect of deeply entrenched attitudes. Alexander Speirs had been one of the group of prosperous tobacco lords of the Glasgow of the mid-eighteenth century, living in a grand mansion, Virginia House in the street of that name, a few yards from Glasgow Cross, then the residential west end of the city. Around 1750 he began an orgy of property buying outside the city. His first purchase consisted of the King's Inch (which was a peninsula rather than an island) on the south bank of the Clyde, near Renfrew. It was here that Walter FitzAllan the High Steward, progenitor of the Stuart kings, had built himself a castle in the thirteenth century. In 1769 Speirs acquired the lands of Elderslie, in 1772 he added vast stretches of ground in the parish of Neilston, in 1777 he bought Blawarthill and Yoker on the north side of the river, and then in 1782 he bought from the last of the Macraes the lands of Houston. Five years before this he had begun the erection of a great mansion house at King's Inch, and this he called Elderslie House. He was followed by an Archibald, then by an Alexander, then by an Archibald Alexander (the one who died young and in whose memory the church was built), then by Alexander Archibald (our laird). The house at Houston was at first looked upon as something of a summer residence, but as the shipyards began to spread down the river, it was extended and improved to become the stately and imposing Scottish baronial residence that we knew.

In the days of Lady Anne, the style appropriate to such a residence was, I understand, very rigidly maintained. The gardener had a staff of eight men looked after in a bothy, the coachman and some ten resident grooms attended to the horses, a butler with a score or more house servants kept up their own style in 'the servants' quarters', a couple of ladies were in charge of the laundry. And all this to maintain a mother and son in the style to which they were accustomed—an admirable illustration of what I am sure is one of Parkinson's laws, that so long as you employ enough workers they will contrive to make enough work to keep themselves short staffed. If any of the servants who slept within the walls wished to be out after 10 in the evening, he (or, an even greater outrage, *she*) had to get from her ladyship a pass for presentation at the lodge—although I imagine a fair amount of wall-scaling must have been indulged in. That was dangerous, though, for the lot of anyone in private service 'dismissed without a reference' was certainly 'not an 'appy one'.

With the passing of the years the whole affair shrank remorselessly, and the call-up to military service on the outbreak of war brought it abruptly to an end. By my time the indoor staff consisted of a butler assisted by a woman who came in some hours a day. One evening I cycled round to the big house to consult the laird about some little thing. After much unsuccessful pulling of the massive front-door bell, I realised it must be the butler's evening off, so I rode back to the manse and phoned to say I was coming and could they let me in? Rather sad, it seemed to me, that two old folk should have to sit in one corner of the library and eat in another corner of it, the whole vast apartment being quite inadequately heated with a peat fire, when they could have been enjoying some comfort in a modern centrally-heated bungalow. On the social plane we were, of course, witnessing the closing scenes in the passing of an era that had had its good points as well as its bad.

Although the population of the parish was small, the area which it embraced was considerable. There was some woodland, but the parish consisted mostly of agricultural land of second-class quality, well suited to dairy farming as well as the growing of oats and potatoes. This type of agriculture was in fact carried on extensively in farms rarely of more than one hundred acres, staffed generally by the farmer and his family. When I went, there was not a single tractor in the parish. The war, and the demand for more and more land to be brought under the plough, brought the first of the mechanisation which has, of course, gone on ever since. I found it interesting that my years in Houston should have seen so great a revolution in the farming industry. On a larger scale we were undergoing the kind of change that Robert Burns had known and that had defeated him in his day. For he lived at a time when the kind of 'croft' to which he had been accustomed had, thanks to the building of walls around fields and the cutting of drains by a new class of landowner interested in 'improvement' (and return on capital investment), become economically unjustifiable, so that the creation of larger units became a necessity (there was scarcely a farm in my Houston which could not be traced on an old map to three or even four separate 'farms' of that earlier day). It was a time when a man with some resources behind him, and a glimmer of vision in his eye, could do very well for himself, but when the small man of conservative ideas was bound to go to the wall. The pattern has been repeated in modern times. In today's economy there is no room for the hundred-acre farm —how can you justify a combine-harvester for that amount of harvest? As the farms in Houston are falling vacant today, they are not being re-let, the new laird-cum-gentleman-farmer is running them all as one single unit. The whole agricultural scene has changed out of all recognition. So, even out in the country areas where you would expect things to stay pretty constant, the Houston I knew is no longer there to go back to.

I was glad the old order survived throughout my time, for I found the farmers and their families wonderful folk. They were cannie and conservative, shrewd and lang-luggit, and they had a wonderful sense of humour, pawky and couthie in the extreme, caustic up to a point, but kindly too in a way. You needn't expect them to enthuse about anything, and the highest word of commendation ever likely to be conceded was that 'it micht hae been waur', or even, to express outstanding excellence of the alpha-plus variety, 'it micht hae been an awfu' lot waur'. Their loyalty wasn't given readily, but once won it was yours for life. The very healthy West Renfrewshire Young Farmers' Club was centred on Bridge of Weir, and with all of its members I was on the friendliest terms. They paid me the distinction of making me their Honorary President, they came as a body every year to our Harvest Thanksgiving Service, and they invited me to judge all kinds of speech-making and other contests. This last was a doubtful kind of honour and a privilege that could have been done without. You need to have a stout heart, a thick skin, and a strong constitution to act as a judge in any agricultural competition. I often wonder how they persuade people to accept the office in cattle shows. Incompetence, blindness and favouritism are among the minor weaknesses freely attributed to judges by the unsuccessful exhibitors. One of my farmers, I remember, had a very fine Clydesdale filly which I knew he had entered for the big show at Ayr and which I later learned had been awarded third prize in a very strong class. Meeting my man some days later, I enquired cheerily how the filly had fared at Ayr. 'O,' he said, 'they judged her first.' 'First?' I said, the surprise no doubt showing in my voice. 'Ay,' he replied, 'they gi'ed the first two tickets to their friends, and then they started to judge them.' If he didn't get the first prize, at least he got the last word!

It was just after going to Houston that I learned to ride a bike. In my youth I had been a keen walker and never thought of any other mode of travel. The distances in Houston, however, were such that my whole time was going to be spent getting from place to place. Besides, the war had started and public transport was badly restricted. I took to the bike like the proverbial duck to water and, within a week of learning how not to fall off, I was using it for the thirty-mile round trip to visit in the Glasgow hospitals. Before long I was covering something like 8000 miles a year, and this I kept up for quite a time (including a three-day cycle down to Kent). I had also bought a bike for my wife who already had some skill at the business. And then we did create a bit of a stir in the parish—and to cause eyebrows to rise in Houston was quite something—when the pair of us appeared on a tandem. We got a great deal of pleasure out of that machine, for at a time when holidays were practically impossible to organise, we were able every now and again to get away for a day on the tandem. The roads at the time were very quiet—it would be a totally different story in today's traffic.

Houston also saw the birth of our other two daughters. 'Poor Mr Herron,' folk were reported to me as saying, 'wi' all thae lassies'. I was grateful for their sympathy, but felt it was utterly undeserved, since both Queenie and I were very happy and contented with our four 'braw lassies'. They were great company for one another, and often they have said how glad they are to have grown up in conditions of such freedom and security as we enjoyed in and around the manse. It was good that they were able to make their own entertainment, for artificial aids to enjoyment in the way of toys were hard to come by. It is perhaps not easy to picture those days when toys were just unobtainable, and the Advent season used to be marked by evenings, after the children had gone to bed, spent in patching up, painting, and so on, such odds and ends of second-hand toys as we had been able to lay hands on. We were fortunate to have a row of outhouses in which they could be concealed while the paint dried. One day around Christmas time I was in Coch-ranes', Paisley's famous drapers of that day, and was speaking to the manager. Suddenly in a conspiratorial whisper, he enquired if I would like a bunny. I could scarcely believe my ears. The question having been purely rhetorical, he took me across to a counter from under which he produced a very splendid woolly model of a rabbit with its white bib and its ears cocked at the ready. He apologised he could not give me any paper to wrap it in, but if I could conceal it 'up my jooks' until I got clear of the shop, it was mine—for the buying! I wrapped it in my waterproof cape and gave it a lift home on the back of the bike. We had been sore troubled that year with the depradations of rabbits in the cabbage patch, so, in recognition of what we owed them (and they owed us), we called our new acquisition 'Savoy'. He was a much loved and respected member of the household for many a day thereafter.

It had been fairly early in my time in Linwood that there began what developed into a very close association with the Peesweep Sanatorium on Gleniffer Braes. The name may seem an odd one. In olden times if you made the steep climb up from the Stanely end of Paisley on to the Gleniffer Braes you doubt-less stopped for a moment to quench your thirst—and to draw your breath—at the 'bonnie wee well on the briest o' the brae, where the hare steals to drink in the gloamin' sae grey'. Travelling onwards for a couple of miles on top of the plateau, you came to a howff where you could get refreshment of a sterner sort, for at the roadside stood a modest cottage with a sign above the door, a painting of a lapwing (a peesweep), and here, according to a writer of 1840, you could get 'a farle of oatcake and a gill of mountain-dew with a commendation to thirsty lips of the water of a spring in the moss as both cold and pure'. This was 'The Peesweep'. It had lost its licence long before my time, and indeed it had lost most of its roof, and the lapwing sign was hanging drunkenly above the gaping door-space when I first saw it on one of my youthful hikes. Today there is not a single thing left to mark the spot. Quite close by, however, is a completely different institution which adopted the same name—reasonably enough, for there are plenty examples of the bird around. This was a convalescent home built by Messrs Coats of the Paisley thread-mills for the benefit of their workers. A crescent-shaped building rising to two storeys in the middle (for administrative and communal purposes) and at both ends (to provide a flat for the matron and the gardener respectively), the space between having nine little rooms on each wing connected with a covered corridor. Its capacity was therefore limited to 18 patients. I do not know exactly when the County Health Authority took over the building from Coats as a sanatorium for cases of tuberculosis, of which there were, sadly, only too many in those days.

What was to be my own very intimate connection with the place came about in an odd way. I learned that a girl I knew had been moved there as a patient, so I set off fairly early one morning, on foot as my custom then was, to pay her a visit. There had been quite a heavy fall of snow the previous day and on top of the Braes it was lying fairly deep—a real Chistmas Card picture. I saw the girl and was about to leave when Matron, whom I came to know as a dedicated and devoted soul if ever there was one, invited me into her room for a cup of tea. In the course of our chat she told me that when she had seen me walking down the drive she had said to Nurse, 'Here's a minister coming; his car must have broken down; he'll be wanting to use the phone'. I am sure she had no intention of being critical, far less insulting, but it seemed to me a sad reflection on us ministers if my appearance approaching the Peesweep could conjure up only a picture of a broken-down motor car. Surely we should be seen coming to give aid, not to look for it. From then on I formed the habit of visiting regularly and spending a bit of time in each of the rooms in turn, trying in the gentlest of ways to get alongside each of the patients—it occupied a whole forenoon, many whole forenoons, but I think it was worth it. I don't believe you can whip around places like that with a spiritual stethoscope, diagnosing the deep unspoken needs of the patients. Just keep going and sooner or later these needs will start coming out. After a little time I was able to organise a fortnightly evening service when some of my choir went up with me—in cars, not on foot. I had, of course, cleared it with the parish minister who was an old man, without transport, and with a manse quite a bit away. So began a connection which lasted until, finally, the whole approach to the treatment of tuberculosis having drastically changed, there was no need for that kind of place any longer and it was closed down. When my stint as chaplain began, surgery was practically unknown in this field and patients were sent to places like Peesweep where they stayed for two years and longer, resting, going for walks, and wearily passing the time away—and invariably they were young people who should have been in the prime of life. Seeing them, as I did, one at a time, week after week, I got very close to them and, I felt, was able to do quite a lot for them. That, certainly, was their testimony. To me it has always seemed that the work I did at Peesweep was possibly the most productive of all my ministry. And it all began because a lady thought I wanted to use her phone!

Throughout the whole of my time in both Linwood and Houston, I had been a most faithful member of the Presbytery of Paisley, this partly as a result of natural inclination, for I found the business quite interesting (even if not always as interesting as the people who took part in it), and partly from a sense of duty; for while I believe that Presbyterianism is a good system of church government, I recognise that it can work satisfactorily only if ministers and elders are prepared to give faithfully of their time and attention. I was particularly fond of the then Clerk, William Runciman, whose son had been in my year at College, and who in a very quiet and unostentatious fashion carried through his duties, which included keeping the Presbytery right at various times. Even at that early stage I felt this was a job I could do and would enjoy doing. I was to have to wait for almost twenty years before the opportunity would come my way. It did come in 1953 when I was appointed part-time Clerk to the Presbytery of Paisley.

Among the many qualities essential for the job, although one I have never seen listed in any job specification, is an ability to extemporise in the emergency situation. I had not been long in office ere the emergency situation arose. When a minister receives a Call from another parish, his own Presbytery has to agree to release him. The various minutes, and so on, are transmitted along with the signed sheets of the Call, the latter all neatly packed in a cylindrical container. Once the translation is agreed to, this Call is handed over to the minister concerned and he is invited to say a word or two by way of a farewell speech. On the occasion in question the papers were all to hand and in order, but the Call itself was to have been brought by special messenger and he had not arrived. In a state of some desperation I managed to lay hands on a couple of copies of *The Glasgow Herald* and a sheet of brown paper and had got together something faintly resembling a Call neatly parcelled in its tube, but demanding very careful handling if it was not to disintegrate and reveal its true identity. As luck would have it we had no chance to warn the recipient, who was by nature a fiery kind of orator, and who in his valedictory address used the makeshift 'Call' much like a conductor, encouraging his players to put everything they had into it! Being a Clerk can bring its anxious moments.

In the chapter on 'Dabbling in the Law' I explain how, first of all, just after the union of the two congregations, we fought off the threat of a new town in 1950, but of how later events caught up on the parish when the estate of Craigends, along with quite a bit of farmland, came to be developed for private housing, so that the whole character of the district has changed out of recognition. From time to time, in recent years, I have been invited to preach at special services of one kind and another at Houston, and while it is always pleasant to be back in the pulpit from which I preached for almost twenty years, it is also a saddening experience to realise how many familiar faces are not there any more. Increasingly I go as a visitor—it couldn't possibly be otherwise. The Houston I knew and loved is just not there. But as a very popular lady on our television screens tells us, 'That's Life'!

Epilogue
By Way of Apology

THE OXFORD ENGLISH DICTIONARY lists three meanings for the word 'apology': regretful acknowledgment of offence; assurance that no offence was intended; vindication. Lest any reader should be looking forward expectantly, and perhaps even justifiably, to an apology of either of the first two kinds, let me hasten to say that it is in the third sense that I use the word here. In these closing pages I propose to offer what to me is a very telling vindication of the minority report, one that might well earn for it a position more exalted than that accorded it in the official evaluation of the General Assembly.

The year was 1974 and the subject was the supremely important one of the place to be accorded by the Church to the Westminster Confession. For quite some time there had been in the Kirk a feeling of disquiet in respect of our relation to the Confession, an idea that the document is the creation of an historical epoch, inadequate, out of touch with contemporary thought, and attempts had been made to formulate a confessional statement that might take its place. These, however, had met with little success—in fact they had failed dismally. This I did not find surprising, for I am convinced that the theological ferment, the doctrinal uncertainties, the utterances of today's ecclesiastical *enfants terribles* are not conducive to the formulation of statements of belief likely to command widespread acceptance. Ours is the generation that asks the questions, not the one that finds the answers, the age that rejects not accepts, the day of the explorer not the cartographer. The day will come when the maps will be drawn—never fear—but it will not be this year, or the year after; the furnace needs time to cool before the crystals form.

There being no sign of any real progress towards a New Statement of the Faith, the Committee concerned turned its mind to a plan simply to jettison the Westminster Confession as the subordinate standard without any comparable document to put in its place. The plan with which they finally came forward was to amend the Articles Declaratory in Matters Spiritual (embraced in the Act of Parliament of 1921) with corresponding adjustments to the Preamble, the Questions, and the Formula used at all ordinations within the Kirk. The second of the Articles was to be amended to read, 'The Church of Scotland acknowledges the Apostles' Creed and the Nicene Creed as Declarations of the Faith of the Universal Church', and to go on to claim that we are 'to be guided by the Scots Confession and the Westminster Confession as historic statements of the faith of the Reformed Church'. This is repeated in the Preamble which goes on to say, 'The Church of Scotland, aware that no confessional statement can be final, affirms its freedom and its responsibility, in dependence on the Holy Spirit, in the light of Holy Scripture, and within the fellowship of the whole Church of God, to formulate such confessions as may from time to time be required, recognising liberty of opinion in points of doctrine which do not enter into the substance of the faith'. The question about the Westminster Confession is replaced by, 'Do you believe the fundamental doctrines of the Christian Faith as affirmed by this Church?', while the Formula in turn is reframed to begin, 'I believe the fundamental doctrines of the Christian Faith affirmed in the Preamble'.

One could have been forgiven for thinking that in its new form the Question was a perfect example of being asked to sign a blank cheque. If the Church was not sufficiently clear in its own mind about what it believed, to be able to frame a statement, how could the ordinand be expected to know what these doctrines were to which he was subscribing. Be that as it may, it was all accepted by the General Assembly of 1972 which agreed to set in motion the procedure appropriate for having it incorporated in the constitution of the Kirk. This is an interesting process—a race with four hurdles. First, the proposals have to be set forth and accepted as an Overture by one General Assembly (the hurdle that had just been cleared); second, it goes down to Presbyteries for consideration and decision and it has to obtain a two-thirds majority there; the results at this stage are duly reported to next Assembly which, third, sends them down afresh to Presbyteries where again a two-thirds majority is demanded; and then the fourth and final hurdle, the Assembly to which this is all reported has itself to approve and pass an Act accordingly.

On the first occasion of this Overture going down to Presbyteries, it was reported that 43 had voted Approve to 18 Disapprove. On the second occasion the majority had increased to 49 against 12—it always interests me in such circumstances to note how many are prepared to switch to what looks like being the winning side.

And so came 1974 when the Assembly was presented with the final report and with a motion that we now agree and proceed to convert the Overture into an Act so that the proposals become law. I was all set to submit a Minority Report. Obviously it was just about as 'minority' as you could wish a report to be—the last count in Presbyteries showed that there was a four-to-one vote in favour, and that out of almost 3000 people who had voted, only 600 had been on my side. As we waited to go into the hall to complete what most commissioners saw as a formality, I remember remarking to the Procurator that, while not a betting man, I was prepared to offer sixty to one against my chance of success. A shrewd man, he offered no comment.

My motion that we do not accept the Overture but resolve to depart from the matter, came as something of a bombshell. I began by saying that while it was no new experience for me to be standing there addressing the General Assembly, I had never done so with a more profound sense of the gravity of the decision I was asking them to take. 'It is with all the honesty that is within me, as well as with all the powers of persuasion I happen to possess, that I urge the Assembly to proceed no farther along this line of changing the Declaratory Articles and the Preamble and Questions.' To change the Articles Declaratory, I urged, was not a step to be taken unless we were utterly convinced that the latter state would be an improvement on the former, that the position towards which we were moving was a better or a stronger or a truer position than the one where we now stood. It was not enough for us to be persuaded that on balance it was probably better, to be inclined to think that if anything it was an improvement. Certainly it was not good enough that, suffering from a feeling of exhaustion after all these years of debating, we should decide we must get the Articles changed somehow and get the whole miserable business out of our system. I concluded by saying, 'I'm all for change—but it's got to be change that will equip us for the future, not merely change that will cut us adrift from the past'.

When the vote came to be taken, my Minority Report prevailed—to my complete astonishment. Looking back on it now, I still think it was good that it should have been so. I am still confident the day will come (although I'll not see it) when they'll be drawing maps, and they will be all the more reliable maps because of the costly, time-consuming exploration that has gone on. In the meantime, let's hold fast to what has served us so well for so long. As the late Archie Craig put it, neatly as well as accurately, 'The old warship may be bruised and battle-scarred, but she's still a warship—don't let's scuttle her and put to sea in a coracle'.

Long live the Minority Report!